Creating Memorials, Building Identities

The Politics of Memory in the Black Atlantic

ALAN RICE

Dedicated to the memory of
Tristan Humphries,
artist and conversationalist
(1962–2000)

First published 2010 by
Liverpool University Press
4 Cambridge Street
Liverpool
L69 7ZU

This paperback edition published 2012

British Library Cataloguing-in-Publication data

A British Library CIP record is available

ISBN 978-1-84631-471-1 cased
978-1-84631-759-0 limp

Arts & Humanities
Research Council

Typeset by Carnegie Book Production, Lancaster
Printed and bound by CPI Group (UK) Ltd, Croydon, CR0 4YY

Contents

Acknowledgements

This project has been nearly a decade in the making and would not have been possible without financial support from the Arts and Humanities Research Council and from the University of Central Lancashire (UCLAN) in Preston. I am especially indebted to colleagues and friends near and far whose faith in it never wavered. Firstly, colleagues in the ever-evolving literature and culture team at UCLAN enabled me to take study leave and also provided crucial intellectual ballast. Over the years, George McKay, Alizon Brunning, Eithne Quinn, John Joughin, Daniel Lamont, Heidi Macpherson, Kay Boardman, Richard Hinchcliffe, Diane Fare, Stephanie Munro, Anne-Marie Evans, Sarah Heaton, Will Kaufman, Michael Parker, Theresa Saxon, Robin Purves, Tom Day, Stuart Hampton-Reeves, Anne Wichmann and Janice Wardle have contributed bonhomie and much more. Elsewhere within the institution, Patrick McGhee, Bernard Quinn, Susan Walsh, Amanda Williamson, Mike Ward, Dave Russell and John Walton have helped in numerous ways. I would also like to thank the many students from UCLAN who have contributed to discussions that have helped my thinking to evolve, and especially those whose work has provided material for the book. Special mention to those such as Charlie Armstrong, Gary Cape and Vicky Bizzell who have gone on to further study in related fields, and to Senam Okudzeto.

Further afield in academia I have had inestimable support from friends in the Collegium for African American Research (CAAR), Multi-Ethnic Studies Association Europe (MESEA), Transatlantic Studies Association (TSA), the British Association for American Studies (BAAS) and from the Society for Caribbean Studies (SCS). Sabine Broeck, Maria Diedrich, Isabel Soto, Mar Gallego and Maria Frias from CAAR have helped me in many ways over the years, especially with close and committed readings and critiques of my work. In MESEA, Dorothea Fischer-Hornung, William Boelhower, Maria Lauret, Heike Raphael-Hernandez, Joke Kardux, Deborah Madsen, Cathy Waegner, Yiorgos Kalogeras and Jopi Nyman provide unstinting support. In the TSA, Alan Dobson and Tony McCulloch have been cheerleaders despite their subject areas being very different to mine.

In BAAS, Susan Castillo, Lisa Merrill, Carol Smith, Jude Davies, Neil Campbell, Patrick Hagopian, Jonathan Munby, Douglas Tallack, Richard Godden, Martin Crawford, Jill Terry and Judie Newman have all at times given useful talking time to this project. In the SCS, Sandra Courtman, David Howard, Diana Paton, Leon Wainwright and Mimi Sheller all deserve thanks for providing brilliant academic and social support, especially through the 'Seminars in the North'.

Other academics who have contributed ideas, critiques and much needed encouragement include some of the brightest and best Americanists in Britain: Fionnghuala Sweeney from Liverpool via Cork, whose work on Douglass is an inspiration to me; Stella Bolaki from Edinburgh; Sarah Meer from Cambridge; Mandy Cooper from Canterbury Christ Church and Jenny Terry from Durham; Dick Ellis, whose madcap dashes to slave sites left me breathless but inspired; and Alison Easton and Lindsey Moore, whose local support has been really appreciated. Thanks too to esteemed professors Gen Doy, Vin Carretta, Stephen Small, Preston King, Neil Wynn, Lynne Pearce, Susan Hogan, Marcus Wood and Peter Kitson for their wisdom. Finally, my old friend Alasdair Pettinger is a solid rock in an academic tempest.

Some of this book is almost ethnographic and I must thank those colleagues who were involved with me in the Slave Trade Arts Memorial Project (STAMP), especially the pioneers: Peter Courtie, Ruth Davies, Sue Ashcroft, Denise Dent, Andy Darby, Gisela Renolds and Sarah Riddle. Thanks go also to all at the Whitworth, especially David Morris, Maria Balshaw, Andrew Vaughan and Dominique Heyse-Moore, and those I worked with later through the *Revealing Histories* project, especially Frankie Mullen and Kuljit Chuhan. Thanks also to Tony Tibbles at Merseyside Maritime Museum and Michelle Cooper at the Lancaster Maritime Museum, and to Melinda Elder, whose encyclopaedic knowledge of Lancaster in the slave trade contributed greatly to any good things in Chapter 2. More recently, Janet Douglass and Simeon Barclay in Leeds have been an inspiration. Throughout the writing of this book I have suffered from chronic fatigue syndrome, so thanks to my acupuncturist Cherith Adams, whose healing powers meant that it did get finished.

Friends outside academia have been supportive in many ways. Will Medd, Katrina Stengel, Doug Purvis and Dave Shooter in Lancaster have given crucial everyday support. Kubi Tchackarov, Ewan Davidson, Paul Baker, Nigel Robson-Smith, Paul Tebble, Sarah Macklin, Judy Pearsall, Helen Chandler, Sue Plummer, Emma Barnard, Trevor Leat, Robert Pigeon, Paul Dunn and Chris Rice contributed in numerous different ways from their different corners of the world.

Artists and writers have been crucial to this book and I would like to thank in particular Lubaina Himid, whose extraordinary works and political commitment have been an inspiration to almost every chapter of this book. Respect to Kevin Dalton-Johnson, whose memorial made dreams a reality; and to SuAndi and Emma Poulter, whom I worked with curating *Trade and Empire*. They truly helped to create an exhibition to be proud of. Writers Dorothea Smartt, Caryl Phillips, Lemn Sissay and Jackie Kay have always been generous to me as I critiqued their works. Althea McNish and her husband John Weiss provided useful information and a wealth of good feeling and experience. Godfried Donkor has always been most generous with his time and in allowing me access to his work. Overall, I would never have the facility to comment on the visual arts without the inspirational friendships of Geoff Quilley and Tristan Humphries. The latter is sadly no longer with us, but would surely quaff a bottle of wine to celebrate a book of mine on the art-form to which he contributed so much.

At Liverpool University Press, I would like to thank Anthony Cond for having faith in this project over several years, and Alison Welsby and Helen Tookey for getting us over the finish line. Closer to home, my PhD student Anne Eichmann has smoothed the process of getting the book ready for press. Finally, I would like to thank Lizzie and my children Amy and Kezia, whose good humour and wholehearted support throughout the long process of writing the book meant I always felt free to do 'just a few more words'.

Portions of this book have appeared in other forms in the journals *Atlantic Studies* (2007), *Patterns of Prejudice* (2007) and *Slavery and Abolition* (2009), in *Black Orpheus: Music in African American Fiction from the Harlem Renaissance to Toni Morrison*, ed. Saadi Simawe (Garland, 2000) and in *Blackening Europe: The African American Presence*, ed. Heike Raphael-Hernandez (Routledge, 2004).

It is more difficult to honour the memory of the anonymous than it is to honour the memory of the famous, the celebrated …

Walter Benjamin

There is no beach that is not also a graveyard.

Les Back

1

Tracing Slavery's Routes
and Looking Inside the Invisible:
The Monumental Landscape
and the African Atlantic

One of the sinister and poignant features of slavery is that it is a phantom industry that leaves scant traces; its capital lies in people, long since dead, not machinery. *A. V. Seaton*[1]

The rupture of the slave trade, then the experience of slavery, introduces between blind belief and clear consciousness a gap that we have never finished filling. The absence of representation, of echo, of any sign, makes this emptiness forever yawn under our feet. *Édouard Glissant*[2]

I think that Afro-Americans, in running away from slavery, which was important to do – it meant rushing out of bondage into freedom – also rushed away from the slaves because it was painful to dwell there, and they may have abandoned some responsibilities in doing so. It was a double-edged sword... There is a necessity for remembering the horror, but of course there's a necessity for remembering it in a manner that can be digested, in a manner in which memory is not destructive. *Toni Morrison*[3]

The problem with memorialising the slave trade adequately, as the three epigraphs above so eloquently show, is that its tentacles spread far and wide and its legacy is often a mere trace that is difficult to comprehend, let alone visualise two hundred years after its official ending in Britain. In this introductory chapter I want to provide case studies of memorials from several locales in the circum-Atlantic that outline the contestations and difficulties of remembering the traumatic history of the slave trade and of slavery. In discussing the slave trade in particular, with over 11 million enslaved Africans transported on European ships, I want to start where many African Americans see the beginnings of what some describe as the 'African holocaust': at the 'Door of No Return', marking the final departure point from Africa. Dionne Brand describes the multiple valences of this actual and imagined location:

> There are no maps to the Door of No Return. The physical door. They are well worn, gone over by cartographer after cartographer, refined from Ptolemy's *Geographia* to orbital photographs and magnetic field imaging satellites. But to the Door of No Return which is illuminated in the consciousness of blacks in the diaspora there are no maps. This door is not mere physicality. It is a spiritual location. It is perhaps a psychic destination. Since leaving was never voluntary, return was, and still may be, an intention, however deeply buried. There is as it says no way in; no return.[4]

The paradoxes of this memorial site are multifarious: because very few African Americans know the actual circumstances of their ancestors' capture, enslavement and deportation, this 'ground zero of African American history'[5] almost always has to be an imagined site of ancestral departure from the homeland. It is, as Brand says, 'not mere physicality' but 'a spiritual location'. As such, African diasporan history seen through this lens is decidedly mythopaeic and hidebound by a curious nostalgia that can undermine a full historical accounting for the paradoxes and complications of the transatlantic slave trade. James Campbell describes the emotions of African Americans visiting Gorée in Senegal and Cape Coast Castle in Ghana as they march from the dark, dank dungeons through the portal:

> The experience, suggestive at once of birth and death, overwhelms many visitors; if the guest books at such sites are any guide, many African Americans feel their kinship with Africans more keenly in that instant than at any moment in their lives. Yet paradoxically, it is also an experience rooted in a distinctly African American rather than African experience. Viewed from the standpoint of the Americas, such places may indeed mark the beginning of the journey, but they would likely not have seemed so to the captives who passed through them. For them, these coastal fortresses were not starting points, but way stations, transit points in journeys that had begun days, even weeks or months before, sometimes hundreds of miles in the interior.[6]

Thus the Door of No Return, so important to the slaves and their descendents, might have been no more than one in a series of markers of displacement, the most important of which was almost certainly when they were first taken from their original home rather than their departure from a continental coastline they did not recognise. The black British writer Caryl Phillips, in his *The Atlantic Sound* (2000), describes the excesses of some sentimentalised appropriations of African locales by African American tourists which, when added to a shallow Afrocentrism, can have, in his acerbic view, far more to do with bogus emotionalism than a proper coming to terms with the past. He comments on one particularly anodyne ceremony at Elmina Castle in Ghana during the Panafest festival, which was undertaken by 'people of the diaspora who expect the continent to solve whatever psychological problems they possess'.[7] Philips's reservations about the appropriation of African memorial space by western-educated black tourists are well put, and are best illustrated by the fact that many local Ghanaians chafed at the festival exhibitions' emphasis on the diaspora to the exclusion of local history. The Ghanaian-British cultural critic Ekow Eshun used testimonies from Ghanaian guides for visiting African Americans to illustrate how the latter's economic advantage creates tensions that undermine pan-African solidarity. A guide relates:

> We took them to the slave fort at Elmina. They all cried when they saw the dungeons. They poured a libation for the souls of their ancestors. But after a while I saw it was all words to them. Each night they stayed in a good hotel. When the food did not come fast they complained. When there was no ice in the water they complained. When the air conditioning broke down they complained. After a while all they did was complain. And they acted so high and proud as if we were their servants and they were the real Africans.[8]

Such cross-cultural misunderstanding clouds relations between Africans in the diaspora. Eshun's subsequent eagle-eyed commentary shows how the dreams of each group are based on unrealistic expectations and are undermined by economic disparity. Eshun comments:

> I looked at the guides in their baseball vests and Nike sneakers. America for them meant Kobe and Shaq and Michael Jordan. Across from them stood the tourists. In their eyes Africa was a land of enduring wisdoms. They were its lost kings and Nubian princesses. Both groups saw in the other a reflection of their own dreams. Africa and America emerged in the car park, each searching the other's eyes for glimpses of jungle or glittering skyscraper.[9]

The Africans desire the modernity encapsulated by African American popular culture, the black tourists their dream vision of an unsullied Africa. Phillips's and Eshun's examples illustrate how tourism in such a contested political landscape brings wealth to hard-pressed economies, but at a significant cost in terms of cross-cultural empathy and understanding. It is echoed in the controversy over the restoration of Cape Coast Castle and its development as a museum space in the early 1990s. African American commentators talked of the restoration as a 'whitewashing of the history associated with the slave trade'.[10] Edward Bruner makes this point most forcefully:

> For many African Americans, the castles are sacred ground not be desecrated. They do not want the castles to be made beautiful or to be whitewashed. They want the original stench to remain in the dungeons. A return to the slave forts for diaspora blacks is a 'necessary act of self-realisation', 'for the spirits of the diaspora are somehow tied to these historic structures'. Some diaspora blacks feel that even though they are not Ghanaians, 'the castles belong to them'.[11]

For many African American tourists, the meaning of the castles is wholly circumscribed by their function as slave forts; however, the locals see the castles as being as much about colonial and post-colonial relations in a complex historical relationship with European traders, where some elite African sometimes had at least limited agency. Hence, the forts can never be just about the victims of the slave trade. These examples illustrate the malleability of meaning for such locales in a black Atlantic replete with varied interest groups. For, in a global economy where the marketing of black memory provides mercantile opportunities for some, there is also ideological payback for those who want to interpret sites like the slave castles through a narrow nationalistic gaze. Those left out in such a marketplace of ideologies are usually the local disenfranchised Africans, who do not have the economic power of the African American tourists. As Ghanain academic Kwame Arhin commented, in response to local chiefs performing a ritual to atone for the complicity of their ancestors in the slave trade at the opening of the 'Crossroads' exhibition at Cape Coast Castle in 1994:

> Why should I apologise for something I didn't do? I find them all [African American tourists] a bit demanding, and if you don't think the way they do, they say you're an Uncle Tom. It's rather harsh … because we're suffering more than they are suffering.[12]

In the context of an Africa starved of financial resources, the colonising mindset is exemplified by the comment of the US historian Edward T. Litenthal, who describes how 'these West African sites are surely an extension of the African American landscape.'[13] The problem with such sentiments is that this emotive attachment from African American tourists, and Anglo-American historians speaking on their behalf, is seen as a colonising gesture by many locals whose economic and political power is far less than that of their western visitors. One example of nationalist excess was in the 1990s, when some tours of Cape Coast Castle given by One Africa Productions, a group of African Americans who have settled locally, included the rubric 'Tour participants who are not of African descent are prohibited from walking through the Door of No Return', because it was not something their ancestors had experienced. The tour continued for those able to exit the door with a ceremonial return to 'Mother Africa'.[14] This classic form of exclusion and insiderism was to generate considerable fee income for the private tour operators, very little of which was 'shared with the (Ghanaian-owned) museum to help it with its operating funds'.[15] Such a crass colonial attitude towards the local economy shows how US cultural imperialism is far from being confined to its citizens of European descent.

As Ellie Lester Roushanzamir and Peggy J. Kreshel warn, '"heritage" can be too easily converted from contested engagements with history to a commodity intentionally fabricated for a consumer audience.'[16] This, of course, is the opposite of the intention of many of those involved in slave heritage tourism, but it is a consequence of a politics that ignores contemporary African realities and instead promotes an essentialist idea of an almost mythic and thoroughly one-dimensional Mother Africa. The slave forts themselves and the colonial ruins that surround them are not always hidebound by such a narrow nationalist gaze, as shown recently by two African diasporan artists, Jamaican-born Mary Evans and Ghanaian Godfried Donkor. Their films, Evans' *Blighty, Guinea, Dixie* (2007) and Donkor's *Jamestown Masquerade* (2006) (Figure 1), refuse a totalising and univocal interpretation of these sites in favour of representations that view them as diasporic sites in conversation with other realms and sites of the African Atlantic. Evans's film, shown as part of the 'Port City' exhibition in Bristol, uses a kaleidoscopic viewfinder to complicate depictions of forts like Cape Coast and Elmina and dialogise them with other African coastal and inland scenes, and locations in Bristol and plantation houses in Williamsburg, Virginia. The kaleidoscopic frame disorientates so that the viewer is forced to juxtapose the locale and is sometimes unable to fully distinguish which of the sites is being viewed. As Jane Connarty describes it:

> The kaleidoscopic viewfinder reflects, dissects, fractures and disperses a patchwork of quietly observed moments; dissolving together icons of the American South – the picket fence, the plantation house, a riverboat in Savannah; mixing scenes of everyday life in Ghana with shots of the ocean viewed from ramparts of Cape Coast Castle and Elmina... and collides contemporary street scenes with architectural facades of Georgian England, reflecting the city's prosperity and power as a trading city in the eighteenth century.[17]

This process emphasises the way that all the sites are linked by their shared history in the transatlantic slave trade, and how their legacies continue to have resonances that are brought to bear in the imagination of the artist.

Godfried Donkor's brief film is, if anything, even more disorientating, though it is filmed with a conventional camera lens. Set in Jamestown, Accra amidst British colonial and Dutch slave merchant buildings from the 1780s in the shadow of the slave fort, his *Masquerade* clothes local people in the dress styles of eighteenth-century dandies and belles as if at a European masked ball. The clothes, however, are African designs, whilst the masques are redolent of nineteenth-century Caribbean carnivals as well as Venetian designs. This potpourri of styles, emphasised by the promenading characters who exaggeratedly bow and curtsey, means the viewer is not given a stable idea of location, but is forced to see Jamestown as a liminal space that contains European relics in African locations that hint at Caribbean and US futures. In Donkor's words, it shows 'conflicting time frames, conflicting ideas people may have [and] conflicting aesthetics ... it's the idea of movement of people and what happens when people move around and how interesting our history has become because of this.'[18] Donkor describes how his work refuses to pin down the Slave Coast locale to a spurious 'home' designation from a roots aesthetic, but shows its thoroughly routed existence, more in keeping with a diasporan aesthetic that tries to come to terms with the multivalency of African Atlantic culture:

> We found this amazing building, where we shot the piece, that was owned by a prominent Dutch family. The whole thing started really with this feeling that I had been somewhere before. So I wanted to do a piece about memory and about forgetfulness or forgetting... In the film the characters wear the Venetian masks and they dress up in masquerade clothes, eighteenth-century English or European fashion, using modern day 2005 printed African fabrics and material and lace. They turn up at this old house with their pristine clothes expecting it to be pristine, and with chandeliers, but in fact the house was derelict so you get this clash of the new and the old, the old and the new. And the music I laid down was music from the Minerva choir which was one of our leading youth choirs, so they're singing classical – it was an African choir singing European music with an African connotation. So that was a whole piece about forgetfulness, darkness, the past, and about memory, light, the present, and then they end up on the beach again where they look towards the west, so they look towards the Caribbean.[19]

Donkor's locations, costumes, music, dance and performance style in *Jamestown Masquerade* cannot be pinned down either geographically or chronologically, and that is the point. His initial sojourn in this district of Jamestown had reminded him of eighteenth-century London and its black presences, as shown by Hogarth and others, and this memory is present in the piece along with the operations of the African slave locale and the New World plantation house. *Jamestown Masquerade* is a memory of slavery and of its aftermath, and shows how its legacies are present still throughout the circum-Atlantic. In creating a wonderful, visually rich collision of styles, Donkor wants us to acknowledge not only the destructive past of slavery and colonisation, but also to revel in the resilience of a people who created vibrant cultures in its wake and despite its horrors. Both he and Evans refuse to interpret the slave forts and the surrounding area through a narrow one-dimensional lens, kaleidoscopically re-imagining them in dialogue with Africans from the diaspora.

This complication in the imaginative interpretation of African slave ports is a welcome sign, and hopefully such works will have purchase in Africa and the US as well as in the UK, showing the way these memorial sites can be dynamically interpreted. This is important because African Americans, as tourists, seek memorial sites in Africa not only because they represent a free 'homeland' precipitating their capture as slaves, but also because there have historically been so few memorial sites in the US. In 1989, the novelist Toni Morrison complained:

> There is no place you or I can go, to think about, or not think about, to summon the presences of, or recollect the absences of slaves; nothing that reminds us of the ones who made the journey and of those who did not make it. There is no suitable memorial or plaque or wreath or wall or park or skyscraper lobby. There's no 300-foot tower. There's no small bench by the road. There is not even a tree scored, an initial I can visit, or you can visit in Charleston or Savannah or New York or Providence, or better still on the banks of the Mississippi.[20]

Although there is still considerable work to be done, Toni Morrison's statement is less true now than it was in the late 1980s. There is now more public acknowledgement of the slave past in the transatlantic world than there was two decades ago, and this has manifested itself in plaques, memorials and events in many sites throughout the circum-Atlantic. These include the annual celebrations of the International Day for the Remembrance of the Slave Trade and its Abolition in Haiti, Liverpool and, more recently, London; national memorials erected in Amsterdam (2002), Paris (2007) and London (2008); and a smattering of local ones, including one dedicated to the *Amistad* rebels in New Haven, Connecticut (1992), one on the quayside in Lancaster (2005) and a plaque finally put up on Sullivan's Island, Charleston to commemorate the slave lives lost in the holding pens there. In terms of museums, there is a new International Slavery Museum in Liverpool, opened in 2007, with memorial space included; and new dedicated exhibition spaces on transatlantic slavery in Bristol, Hull, London, Cape Coast Castle and Detroit, as well as ambitious plans for a memorial and museum on Gorée Island, Senegal. In addition, there was the first placement of Morrison's actual 'benches by the road', sponsored by the Toni Morrison Society and dedicated in 2008 at Sullivan's Island. These all attest to an increased level of public activity over the last two decades.

However, there is not as yet a federal museum or memorial to the slave trade in the US, a shameful omission in a nation where many famous political buildings, including the White House, were erected by slave labour and where, as John Vlach has shown, 'the monumental core' of the city of Washington 'stands on slave ground'.[21] The anomaly of this lack of federal memorialisation is at its starkest in Philadelphia, where recent discoveries by the historians Edward Lawler Jr and Gary Nash outline how the area around Sixth and Market Streets was home not only to the first president, George Washington, but also to his slaves, who lived in 'the first federally subsidised slave quarters' in the country, within earshot of the Liberty Bell.[22] As Nash says, 'Our memory of the past is often managed and manipulated. Here it is being downright murdered.'[23] There are moves afoot to make a memorial here on Liberty Mall to commemorate this ambivalence of the US's founding space of freedom living cheek by jowl with the extremity of chattel slavery. However, as Ingrid Saffron reports, the project is dogged by 'extreme bureaucratic indifference' and is alienating the local African American population.[24]

Such contestation of historical sites that have links to slavery is hardly new, and some of the most iconic signs of the slave locale are the 'everyday' plantation houses that dominate the landscape of ex-slave societies. Tara McPherson articulates well the purchase these historical sites have on the US imagination and the difficulties US citizens have in associating such splendid buildings with the horrors of slavery:

> In many ways, Americans can't seem to get enough of the horrors of slavery, and yet we remain unable to connect this past to the romanticized image of the plantation, unable or unwilling to process the emotional registers still echoing from the eras of slavery and Jim Crow [segregation]. The brutalities of those periods remain dissociated from our representations of material sites of those atrocities, the plantation home.[25]

One example is the Wye plantation house, on Maryland's eastern shore a few miles outside Baltimore (Figure 2). It is, at first sight, a typical site of mythological southern aggrandisement. The long driveway leading to a large eighteenth-century house resplendent with Georgian columns betokens a conventionalised encounter with antebellum myths of southern belles and martial heroism. This particular plantation's historical uniqueness is emphasised by the orangerie, the oldest such building in North America, which is situated a few paces behind the kitchen. Opulence and conspicuous consumption are still foregrounded in the central wing of the house, where

Staffordshire chinaware adorns the Chippendale furniture and European seascapes festoon the walls, showing how this family, like many others in the South, used their fantastic wealth to indulge in luxurious goods imported from Europe. These rooms are preserved in the style of the 1830s, the height of power for the Lloyd family whose descendants still enjoy the luxuries of the plantation. This is no open site, turned over to the garrulous public, however, but still a private home, preserved by the riches attendant on the wealth created by a plantation that at its height had over 500 slaves, working there and on thirteen farms around Chesapeake Bay, containing over 10,000 acres of arable land for the cultivation of the atypical slave crop of wheat.[26]

For the radical cultural historian, such a site of elite myth-making would call forth a demand to look beneath the surface to the materiality that made such wealth possible, and this study will undertake some critiques in this direction. Olu Oguibe reminds us of

> another notable fact of the diaspora experience, namely that the tropes of (African) survival in the Americas are lodged not only in cultural retentions among the descendants of slaves, but also in the master's annals of their violation. Memory finds its anchors in unlikely crevices and interstices of history.[27]

These tropes of survival are littered throughout the archive of Anglo-European history and in the archaeological detritus of plantations, graveyards and even shipwrecks. For 'the ownership of people has generated a culture in which people may become possessed by what we call history, and the plantation itself remains haunted by property.'[28] In this case, of course, the property is people, usually voiceless, marginalised and forgotten in the historical record. Unusually, however, at the Wye Plantation we have a literate, non-elite witness to the realities behind the façade: the imposing figure of that great scion of the black Atlantic, Frederick Douglass, who was born in the shadow of the Wye Plantation in 1818. He was born Frederick Bailey at Tuckahoe Creek, slave of Captain Aaron Anthony, sloop captain and chief overseer at Wye. Douglass soon joined his master on the plantation and he describes the impressive building that confronted him for the first time:

> above all stood the grandest building my young eyes had ever beheld, called by everyone on the plantation the great house ... a large white wooden building with wings on three sides of it. In front, extending the entire length of the building and supported by a long range of columns, was a broad portico, which gave to the colonel's home an air of great dignity and grandeur. It was a treat to my young and gradually opening mind to behold this elaborate exhibition of wealth, power and beauty.[29]

Douglass is in awe of the building, but in his recollection of his first encounter with it he is keen to show his adult awareness of how the Lloyd family are involved in a very public display of their southern white power. This 'elaborate exhibition' is a public avowal of status that he, as a young slave, has access to only as a feast for his eyes. Douglass fills in for us the vast industry around the great house, replete with fields under cultivation, barns, a windmill and numerous slave cabins to house the workers. However, as with most southern plantations, by the twenty-first century all that is left are the big houses themselves, which have become eye candy for the tourists who flock to them to indulge in *Gone With the Wind* myths of an honourable south destroyed by the ravages of the American Civil War (1861–65). As Edward T. Linenthal has discussed, plantations in the south are engaged in 'if not denial, then the transformation into something benign, through a minefield of monumental memory to the "faithful slave" and the "black mammy", the *Gone With the Wind* fiction of slavery'.[30] This is contextualised through tours that concentrate on the fixtures and fittings of the house to the almost total exclusion of the slaves that made the wealth possible, so that on average there are 'thirty-one times as many mentions of furniture at these sites than of slavery or those enslaved'.[31] These sites 'engage in the work of social forgetting' with 'deep wounds and anxieties being confined to oblivion' and, thus, 'meeting the need of whites to create a vision of the nation and themselves as noble and disassociated from racialised atrocities'.[32] The 'symbolic annihilation' of black presence in both public and private museum sites throughout North America has been well documented by Jennifer Eichstedt and Stephen Small.[33]

The Wye plantation is not a museum, but still a family home. However, it is a useful case study, as here almost uniquely we have a written record from a victim to juxtapose with the official history of the house. Moreover, this case study shows how the reactionary tropes associated with plantations were established in the mythology even before Wye became an official tourist site. The symbolic annihilation of black presence is as marked as in the most regressive plantation museum. There are significant memorials to Frederick Douglass in Rochester, New York and in Washington, DC, where the Frederick Douglass House is a national park memorial site. At his birthplace, however, there is no acknowledgement of his fame. In fact, as our party, only the second officially organised tour of the house ever, was escorted around the house, Frederick Douglass was not mentioned once by name. If one of the international group of academics asked about him, the Lloyd descendant escorting us would refer to Douglass as 'he' or 'him'. His fame was an obvious embarrassment to the family, and the tour a necessary trial to be got through in order to appease the National Parks Service, whose financial support they might need in the future. This trial was made even more excruciating for them by the presence in the party of Frederick Douglass IV, who claimed descent from Douglass himself.

Despite the lack of help from our guide in placing the slaves as central to the story of the big house and its surrounds, as Douglass scholars we had the landscape of the plantation from his autobiographies to help us. In a sense, Douglass's autobiography gave us a 'guerrilla memorial'[34] to set against the official amnesia about his presence. Such counter-memories are essential for the fullest interpretation of contested sites like this one. Thus the still-extant smokehouse and plantation bell mentioned in Douglass's *Narrative of the Life of an American Slave Written by Himself* (1845) authenticated the site as redolent with images from Douglass's childhood. However, the most chilling site for Douglass scholars was the Aaron Anthony House (Figure 2), a small cottage tucked in behind the big house where Douglass informs us he entered 'the blood-stained gate, the entrance to the hell of slavery'[35] when he witnessed the brutal whipping of 'Aunt' Hester by Captain Anthony. This is probably one of the most famous scenes in the history of black literature and yet the house is pathetically ordinary. If any house is haunted by the presence of atrocities against slaves this one is, and yet the Lloyd family's plans for it at the time of our visit were illustrated by the builder's sign outside; the house was being modernised to serve as a retirement house for the matriarch of the family.

Pierre Nora has talked about '*lieux de mémoire*, sites of memory… moments of history, torn away from the movement of history.'[36] The Wye Plantation is such a *lieu de mémoire*, where the official family/southern historical frame is contested by a dissident memory which haunts the buildings and transforms them from the idyllic to the horrific. As readers of Douglass look at the glories of the plantation and the bucolic sweetness of the Anthony cottage, the counter-memory of the famous African American cannot help but be imagined:

> Before he commenced whipping Aunt Hester, he took her into the kitchen, and stripped her from neck to waist, leaving her neck, shoulders, and back entirely naked. He then told her to cross her hands, calling her at the same time a d----d b------d. After crossing her hands, he tied them with a strong rope, and led her to a stool under a large hook in the joist, put in for the purpose. He made her get up on the stool, and tied her hands to the hook…. after rolling up his sleeves , he commenced to lay on the heavy cowskin, and soon the warm, red blood … came dripping to the floor. I was so terrified and horror-stricken at the sight, that I hid myself in a closet, and dared not venture out till long after the bloody transaction.[37]

The most chilling aspect of this passage is Douglass's description of a 'hook in the joist, put in for the purpose'. This foregrounds how the plantation is a punishment factory with even kitchen equipment adapted for the torture regime. The meat hook in the kitchen of the Anthony house is transformed into a device to hang live human meat for whipping. It is only with Douglass's memory that the object's evil use in slave punishment can be uncovered; without it, visitors would be unable to fully interpret the interior of the house and the way it inscribes an horrific history. As Peter H. Wood describes, the 'plantation' would be better classified as a 'gulag' because 'beyond the carefully maintained elegance and cultivation of the big house' were 'privately owned slave labour camps, sanctioned by the power of the state that persisted for generations'.[38]

From examples such as this we can see that the plantation and its surrounds are in fact, in Nora's words, a *lieu d'oublier* where the slave presence is elided or, even worse, misrepresented. Even if prepared to include a smattering of African American history, the Wye plantation, like most southern historical sites, is 'not ready to abandon segregated spheres of memorialisation'.[39] This is nowhere more apparent than in the slave burial ground which, according to the segregationist tradition, is separate from the luxurious family plots behind the house with their elaborate tombstones. It is across a corn field and marked by no headstones except a recent general stone placed by the contemporary Lloyd family describing slaves as servants. Often on southern plantations, slaves were designated servants by their masters to obscure their chattel status. Obviously the choice of words here is a deliberate misrepresentation, glorying in a faithful service that elides the forcibly enslaved position of those buried in the gravesite.

The ghostly presences at Wye enable a counter memory to the Lloyd family's attempt at whitewashing history. But even officially sanctioned memorials – the signs that are meant to guide tourists round the district – need to be accorded a sceptical investigation. Douglass is remembered by a plaque in St Michaels, the nearest town to his birth on the Tuckahoe Creek. Erected by town commissioners and the Maryland Historical Society, the marker reads:

> Born on Tuckahoe Creek, Talbot County, raised as a slave in St Michaels area 1833–36. Taught self to read and write, conducted clandestine schools for blacks here. Escaped North. Became noted Abolitionist orator and editor. Returned 1872 as US Marshal for the District of Columbia. Also served as DC Recorder of Deeds, US Minister for Haiti.[40]

This historical marker would seem, at first glance, to be an exemplary brief biographical description of a local hero who gained national and international fame as an abolitionist and leading black political activist after his escape from slavery in the community. However, the neighbourhood of St Michaels was not only the venue for the illicit school for his fellow slaves which Douglass bravely ran during 1835 (under state law in the South, teaching slaves was illegal) but, more pertinently, was the town through which he and his fellow co-conspirators were led in chains after their failed attempt at escape in April 1836. The townspeople shouted that he should 'have the hide taken from [his] back', and 'on reaching St Michaels,' he recalls, 'we underwent a sort of examination at my master's store'.[41] There is no hint on the plaque that St Michaels was the location of such dramatic events, including more than a hint of heavy-handed interrogation, that could have led to Douglass being arraigned and sold away south to an even more pernicious slave regime. Pivotal to his maturation and to his later escape from the institution of slavery, this first attempt is wilfully omitted from the information provided in an attempt to place the town in the best possible light.

Obviously, for the brief notation on a plaque, there has to be a brevity which will leave out the extraneous, but the choice to foreground Douglass's illicit school rather than his radical act of attempting to steal himself away from his master points to a municipal manipulation of facts that, together with the version of history told at the Lloyd plantation, means that the locations of Frederick Douglass's birth, boyhood, youth and young manhood are replete with *lieux de mémoire* which must be dialogised through the information of his autobiographies to yield their full radical meanings.

Official History (here with a capital 'H') – the one presented to tourists – could be characterised as grossly inadequate in its representation of slave experience. Seymour Drescher, in talking about the interface between monuments and history, makes a good point about the limitations of memorials when he says that 'monuments alone will not, in themselves, stimulate a constant rethinking of the past. That remains the task of historians.'[42] However, one cannot help but think that his special pleading for historians minimises the profession's shortcomings which arise, in part at least, from its often obsessional empiricism. The Angolan artist Miguel Petchkovsky highlights the interface between history and memory: 'Memory is an essential attribute of the human psyche and is therefore more personal than historical or material knowledge. History alone cannot enrich memory, because it is systematic and sequential.'[43] Dialogising history with other forms, such as biography, folklore, memorials and artistic representation, helps to fill that contested and empirically dry history with the memories and experiences it needs in order to reflect a more accurate and human face: to 'find an anchor for memory'.[44] The tour of the Wye plantation and environs allowed for such anchoring through a performative counter-narrative, what we might call a 'guerrilla memory', which we tourists sought from our knowledge of slavery and Douglass's autobiography. Pierre Nora has described how 'history is perpetually suspicious of memory and its true mission is to suppress and deny it';[45] at sites like the Wye plantation, there is plenty of evidence to show how dissident memory is denied by the weight of traditional historical narrative. As Jessica Adams discusses, 'the plantation is reduced to a "home" precisely as part of the process that attempts to separate slavery from the meaning of the plantation.'[46] African American guerrilla memory is essential in opposing this wilful amnesia. Hence opening up such buildings and other sites for tourist visitors cannot be undertaken without taking the greatest care to tell their full story, which has at its centre the African slave labour that underpinned the beauty and wealth that becomes ugly and tainted immediately the counter-narrative is introduced. The presence of these counter-memories, of course, accompanies the keepers of these memories, African people in the diaspora, and it is incumbent on heritage sites to include their perspectives when interpreting and memorialising the past.

This hidden history and the need for it to be foregrounded is nowhere more apparent than in London, the city whose port saw the departure of the ships owned by the Royal African Company (founded 1672) and its predecessor company, which had a monopoly on the slave trade in the seventeenth century. Most Londoners are unaware of their city's crucial role in the trade, and only vaguely aware of the later role of its financial houses in underpinning the trade; thus even when London's role as a port became secondary, its financial support ensured that Britain, through the ports of Liverpool, Bristol, Lancaster, Whitehaven and Glasgow, was the dominant slave-trading nation in the eighteenth century. In the wake of the commemorations of the bicentenary of the ending of the slave trade in Britain and its empire in 2007, there was an even keener appreciation of a memorial silence in the heart of London. The artist Lubaina Himid talked to this crucial elision in her satirical performance piece, 'What Are Monuments For? Possible Landmarks on the Urban Map' (2009). In this she altered a glossy 'guide book' to London and Paris and imagined what might have been if the contributions of African peoples to the capitals had been fully taken on board. Onto this 'guide book' she collaged portraits of African cloth designs, African-descended figures, both famous and unknown, and other symbols to denote the way in which the memorial landscape of a city like London could and should be different. Her ironic commentary mimics the tone of a guide book, populating London's history in radical new ways. She writes:

Trafalgar Square, London's main venue for rallies and outdoor public meetings, was conceived by John Nash and was mostly constructed in the 1830s. As part of the drive at that time to end Britain's key role at the centre of the slave trade, a large painted bronze statue was erected of Toussaint L'Ouverture, the leader of the only successful slave revolt in the Caribbean, who had died in 1803 after having defeated the greatest armies of the day, including the forces of the French, the English and the Spanish.[47]

The logic of including L'Ouverture's statue alongside Nelson's column is obvious to the multicultural historian of the early twenty-first century, who would want to tell the full story of the imperial struggle between Britain and France and the ramifications for the slaves, who used the upheaval of war and revolution to revolt throughout the Caribbean and to free themselves in Haiti. However, Himid is aware that even statues of key black British and international figures such as Olaudah Equiano, Ignatius Sancho, Frederick Douglass and Paul Robeson are missing from the memorial landscape, and her astutely nuanced commentary, together with the collaged pages of the guide book (where she puts some of these figures back into the landscape), is designed to make the political point that memorialisation, because of its control by those unconcerned with black contributions, is a deeply troubled arena for Africans throughout the diaspora. The collaged images are sometimes quite crudely drawn or inserted and act as a kind of graffiti, an underground dialogisation that subverts the majority story of triumphant lily-white imperial progress. In this way they are a form of 'guerrilla memorialisation' that works to rewrite the national story from the bottom up. Her praxis is similar to those of memorial artists who work in the realm of the Holocaust, whom James Young has written about so eloquently: in his terms she moves away from

> memory-acts that collapse the distinction between themselves and the past ... [and] proposes acts of remembrance that expose this gulf between what happened in the past and how it now gets remembered. Whether it is national myth and idealisation ... that blurs the distinction between actual past and present memory of it, or whether it is only the muteness of the cityscape that hides its history ... [she] makes as *her* object of memory the distance between then and now, the way that even *her* own act of remembrance cannot but gesture indirectly to what was lost and how we now recall it.[48]

Himid's reworking of the guide book is an exemplary move of such counter-memorialisation (or as I prefer to term it, guerrilla memorialisation) as she enables a complete rewriting of the imperial cityscape that negotiates new meanings out of the interaction between what is there and what is missing, always being aware that what is lost can never be fully recovered. She subverts the imperial national narrative and makes the landscape speak its hidden and diverse history. The city's amnesia and her act of remembrance are counterpoints that create new multiple possibilities in the hitherto monological cityscape. Himid is working against the apolitical notion that the city gives up its meaning without any work on the part of its citizens. This is the reason I term the political work of Himid and others 'guerrilla memorialisation', as it is interventionist and deserves a more engaged vocabulary than that of the counter-memorial. As Susan Stewart asserts, the landscape of the city is a deeply politicised environment wherein the imperial state holds sway:

> To walk in the city is to experience the disjuncture of partial vision/partial consciousness. The narrativity of this walking is belied by a simultaneity we know and yet cannot experience. As we turn a corner, our object disappears around the next corner. The sides of the street conspire against us; each attention suppresses a field of possibilities. The discourse of the city is a syncretic discourse, political in its untranslatability. Hence the language of the state elides it. Unable to speak all the city's languages, unable to speak all at once, the state's language becomes monumental, the silence of headquarters, the silence of the bank. In this transcendent and anonymous silence is the miming of corporate relations.[49]

It is against this 'miming of corporate relations' that Himid's guerrilla memorialisation works toward a new cityscape in London. For example, her guidebook looks at Greenwich, where she envisages a utopian memorialisation of on-ship slave rebellions that revels in black agency and the undermining of the slave power:

> **Greenwich** is best known as the place from which the world's time is measured. It marks the historic eastern approach to London by land and water and is home to the National Maritime Museum. The sea has always played an extremely important role in British history, as a means of both defence and expansion, and the museum magnificently celebrates this sea-faring heritage. There are rooms devoted to trade and empire, but an exterior highlight for visitors is the massive wooden slave ship marooned on the grass. Every weekend and summer weekday, dozens of children take part in chaotic, staged re-enactments of the rescue and repatriation of thousands of soon-to-be enslaved Africans, and the subsequent trial and punishment of their captors.[50]

Of course, during the bicentennial year of 2007 there had been re-enactments involving slave ships, including one in Durham using hundreds of school-children who had, however, lain down passively to re-enact the famous 1787 image of the Liverpool slave ship *Brookes*. Himid envisages a very different and altogether more activist and radical bringing forth of historical ghosts. These re-enactments based on the historical record of at-sea rebellions during the slave trade are obviously utopian, in that very few slavers were prosecuted even during the period of British naval anti-slavery patrols that followed the abolition of the trade in 1807. Himid's point, however, is not historical accuracy; she seeks to imaginatively repossess this site of imperial shame and show how it could be re-imagined as a site of post-colonial rebellion and *jouissance*. Himid's reworking, both here and elsewhere, of the memorial landscape, and her ventriloquising of the language of touristic pleasure, is both a satirical commentary on these markers of empire in a busy slaving nation and a clever signification on the actual absence of markers of black history in London. Her work summons the ghosts of black presence that guidebooks elide, bearing witness to how London and other cities might look, if only we paid attention to these forgotten figures. Her praxis could be explicated by Avery Gordon's idea that we need new imaginative forms of critical theory that pay attention to the operations of such ghosts. As Hershini Bhana Young, in glossing Gordon's ideas, says:

> The dead, the beloved who haunt the … landscape as spectral traces of unresolved social history, of time out of joint, are not mere objects of melancholia as Freud posits (where one excludes that which one cannot forget) nor are they easily locatable whole subjects. Instead they are spectres, 'crucibles for political mediation and historical memory'.[51]

These spectres are summoned by Himid in her work and they act on the landscape of London and Paris to re-imagine them as if they fully took on board their amnesiac history of black presences. Rather than wallowing in the 'melancholia' that forgetting encourages, these spectres are in Himid's work the occasion for the refashioning and re-conceptualisation of European history and of African contributions to it.

Hidden from the glossy guidebooks of Himid's imagination and tucked away near Fenchurch Street station, the City of London Corporation together with Black British Heritage, in a project managed by Futurecity, finally erected its first memorial for the victims of the slave trade – and in honour of those who abolished it – in 2008. A collaboration between the Scottish sculptor Michael Visocchi and the black British poet Lemn Sissay, *Gilt of Cain* (Figure 3) is situated aptly close to the heart of the financial district of the City of London which provided the finance for the British slave trade, and to St Mary Woolnoth church, where the sermons of the reformed slave ship captain John Newton inspired William Wilberforce to take on the cause of abolition. This paradoxical positioning inspires both the sculpture and the poem inscribed on it.

The sculpture is spread over Fen Court with 17 differently sized cylindrical granite columns in front of a granite platform, and these columns take the form of stylised sugar cane stems with segmented growth rings. The number 17 represents the number of years abolitionists lobbied parliament before they were successful in abolishing the trade. The canes represent the way that sugar as commodity and the British taste for it overrode any humanitarian impulses, as the rush to the development of a plantation economy led to the development of the use of African slaves. These columns, in part, represent the commodification of those human beings traded so that sugar could be produced. The repeating form of the canes is spread in front of steps that lead up to a podium or pulpit. The shaping of this platform is deliberately ambiguous so that the composition of columns surrounding it can resemble a congregation listening to a sermon, a group of abolitionists at a meeting or, more disturbingly, the gathering at a slave auction. Visocchi explained the multiple meanings of the structure in an interview with Murdo Macdonald:

> The more research I did on the whole anti-slavery moment – I was slightly intimidated by it to begin with – but the more I looked into it, the more I realised that there was a potential poetic way into the subject matter through the idea of sugar and simply the architectural shapes of sugar cane itself. It is something I remember when I was a child – getting a bit of sugar cane from a relative, I don't know where they got it… I remember being fascinated by this plant that could be crushed and distilled and was incredibly sweet. The idea was that I could somehow use these sugar cane shapes so that they could be read on the site as figures, as anthropomorphic forms – and therefore could they not then surround a pulpit as a congregation? Of course the pulpit or certainly the raised platform has associations with the auctioneer's stance, the parliamentary stand and the courtroom dock as well. These are all linked into the story, so this pulpit form has a multiple meaning. The job was then to stylise these canes so that they read as sugar cane but had a more sculptural feel about them, a more volumetric feel. Sugar cane is like bamboo in a way, slightly convex. I have slightly increased the volume of each segment on these columns, partly for aesthetic reasons but also to reference the idea of sugar barrels, which would have come into the dock near by, so they are very slightly barrel shaped elements; they all sit vertically, one on top of the other.[52]

The complexity of the visual meaning of the canes – agricultural plants, then commodified products to be traded in barrels before being anthropomorphised into various human figures playing different roles in the complex drama of the slave trade – makes this an incredibly rich and dynamic memorial, even before Lemn Sissay's words are added. Sissay's poem, though, makes the memorial speak in ways that enhance its sculptural power; rather like the abolitionist orators it memorialises, it declaims all the possibilities above and more. Words from the poem are cut and pasted onto the columns, while the final section is engraved on the podium. As Macdonald explains, 'a line of text adorns each column as a band or collar, further anthropomorphising the columns and calling to mind the physical restraints placed upon the enslaved.'[53] In a move that adds to the memorial's complicated verisimilitude, the words are engraved using a font common in late eighteenth and early nineteenth century abolitionist pamphlets, referencing the nearby disused printing works where abolitionists met. The multiplicity of the memorial is one of its main strengths; it refuses to be tied down to a unitary vision of the slave trade's meaning for the contemporary visitor. Visocchi talks of his desire to engage those encountering the sculpture as more than passive viewers:

> My main attempt was to allow the sculpture to engage with the flow of the pedestrians and allow people to walk amongst it and to become part of it… It's really important to me and also … the steps on the podium or the pulpit allow the viewer to engage and become part of the story for a short while.[54]

Viewers promenade around the statue or climb the steps to view the canes/columns from a more elevated position, but are always in the midst of the multiple narratives the sculpture brings forth as it encourages us to move away from the notorious binary oppositions of the histories of slavery and abolition. Sissay's poem collaborates in this in weaving a complex multifaceted history, and in part achieves this through his use of the language of the Stock Exchange trading floor and of Old Testament vocabulary and stories. Paradoxes abound here, springing from the title *Gilt of Cain* with its homophonic closeness to 'guilt of cane', indicting a city whose greed for commodities led to the human rights abuse of the slave trade, and present throughout a complex agglomeration of wordplay that holds together the words of god and mammon and shows their disturbing, juxtaposing closeness. The poem begins in the world of the trader:

> Here is the *ask price* on the *closed position,*
> history is no *inherent acquisition*
> for here the *Technical Correction* upon the act
> a *merger* of truth and actual *fact*
> on the *spot*, on the money – *the spread.*[55]

In juxtaposing the abstract nature of the trader taking 'the *ask price*' with the way the slave trade was played out in the world, the poem continues to envisage the consequences of financial dealing. Sissay's positioning of 'history' amongst the financial jargon does not let the traders off the hook, showing that they are responsible for the outcome of their trades. Events do not just happen but are a consequence of their actions; it is 'no *inherent acquisition*'. The second stanza shows these dire outcomes and links them again through the language of the traders with the City of London and its operators.

And great traders *acting* in concert, arms rise
as the *actuals* frought on the sea of *franchise*
thrown overboard into the *exchange* to drown
in distressed *brokers* disconsolate frown.
In *Accounting liquidity* is a mounting morbidity
but raising the arms with such rigid rapidity...
Oh the reaping, the raping rapacious *fluidity*,
the violence, the vicious and vexed *volatility*.[56]

This stanza, linking London's mercantile wealth to the abuse of slaves on the high seas, shows how profits were maximised by jettisoning sick or worthless slaves overboard, having first insured them. The words used here are often multidirectional, embodying many meanings: hence 'frought' invokes 'fought', 'freight', 'fraught' and 'fright' as homophone or constructed past participle of all four. Sissay incorporates all these words to show the slaves were traded as *frightened agents, who travelled on a sea fraught with danger, being used as freight, but who fought back*. Agency is key here to show that the poem's economic logic is always dialogised by a countervailing human logic of revolt against this horror, and this minor key becomes the major key by the end of the poem. At this stage, though, the agency of the slaves is undermined by the power of the capitalist financial market and its tentacles, and they are metaphorically dispatched into the stock exchange where their distress is matched by the insurance brokers who must pay out on this sharp practice. Their human loss is contrasted to the '*distressed* brokers' who make financial losses, showing the heartlessness of financial capital that is only concerned with monetary figures. The second half of the stanza speaks to the enslaved Africans whose deaths are acknowledged in the '*mounting morbidity*' caused by the '*volatility*' of the marketplace, whose '*fluidity*' leads directly to their violent death. The watery language of the stanza conjures up the dire consequences of the monetary exchanges in language: *liquidity* and *fluidity*, much desired attributes at the financial centre, are the cause of death in the waters of the Atlantic. Ian Baucom has discussed the way eighteenth century British capitalism extended 'commodity capitalism into the domain of the human... [causing] the colonisation of human subjectivity by finance capital'.[57]

The poem links the chaos of the trading room floor to the slaves who have been thrown overboard. J. M. W. Turner's famous painting *Slave Ship (Slavers Throwing Overboard the Dead and Dying: Typhoon Coming On)* (1840) portrays the slaves in the water as a series of rigid upturned limbs stretching out of the water, as so much flotsam and jetsam at the mercy of rapacious sea creatures. Sissay's poem feeds off this image, illuminating the chaotic trading floor with traders raising arms to make their deals, mirrored in the chaos of the sea while the terrible language of physical and economic oppression is portrayed through the alliteration of 'reaping the raping rapacious fluidity', as the bodies in the Atlantic waters and colonial economies are used and abused for profits back home. The libidinal and economic gains to be made at the enslaved Africans' expense are emphasised by the images of sexual violence and agricultural increase in 'raping and reaping', and by the alliteration of the final line: 'violence, the vicious and vexed *volatility*', with its hard-edged sounds and conjuring of violent extremity. In discussing Turner's painting, Baucom describes how it is 'less a singular image of things as they are than a representative image of what we do not see (or perhaps a typical image of a global modernity whose most essential, most urgently interesting things are what we don't see)'.[58] Sissay's words, together with the ambiguous visual landscape Visocchi creates, function just as Turner's canvas does. They rip aside the veil that global financial figures and language place over realities to expose the dire consequences of the development of modernity for its victims, the enslaved Africans. This harsh-edged and diabolical vision of finance capital and its development of a slave economy uses the language of finance to envisage the way it creates awful realities in regions thousands of miles away, which comes from its own financial logic of commodifying a human workforce. Or, as Baucom explains, developing capitalism treats slaves:

> not as objects to be exchanged, but as the empty bearer of an abstract, theoretical, but entirely real quantum of value ... as little more than promissory notes, bills of exchange, or some other markers of species value, treats them as suppositional entities whose value is tied, not to their continued, embodied, material existence, but to their speculative, recuperable loss value.[59]

These ghostly figures, 'suppositional entities' who are in fact enslaved Africans, produce both 'gilt' and 'guilt', leaving legacies of riches and horror as the next stanza of Sissay's poem elucidates. It shows how, beneath the veneer of money, human forces fight for space and autonomy both on the ocean waves and in the plantation economy. Sissay's introduction of the biblical story of Cain and Abel here emphasises the moral consequences of the action of the traders in abusing their human brothers through the primal story of fratricide:

> The roaring trade floor rises above crushing waves:
> the traders buy ships, beneath the slaves.
> Sway machete back, sway machete again
> *cut back* the Sugar Rush, Cain.
> The *whipsaw* it's all and the whip saw it all
> The *rising market* and the cargo fall

Who'll enter 'Jerusalem' make the *margin call* for Abel?
Who will kick over the stall and turn the table?[60]

At the centre of this stanza is labour which, created by the actions in the metropole ('the roaring trade floor'), harvests the sugar with the violent action of a cutting machete. Sissay skilfully links this to fratricide through the homophone of Cain/cane and then shows the violence at the heart of slave labour through the dual emphasis on the 'whip' in the fifth line. The *'whipsaw'* also refers to financial instruments as it means to lose on a stock in two ways, foregrounding the risks in dealing in human capital; then in its near neighbour, the personified noun phrase 'the whip saw it all', the panoptical nature of a slave regime which controls labour through the punishment regime of the whip is imagined. Paradoxically, the line emphasises both the ease of violence used to control the slaves and the slippery nature of dealing in a human commodity that is not ultimately commodifiable in the same way as sugar cane. The *'rising market'* is linked inexorably to the 'cargo fall', the destruction of that labour by the harsh regime which in biblical terms is brought about by man's fall from grace. The final couplet questions who might 'buck the market' and demand a humanitarian, revolutionary response that will undermine the fratricide. The *'margin call'* here relates to the idiosyncratic and fringe nature of abolitionism at the height of the slave power in 1780s Britain. The final stanza answers the call:

Cain gathers cane as *gilt–gift* to his land
But whose sword of truth shall not sleep in his hand?
Who shall unlock the *stocks and share*?
Break the *bond* the bind unbound – lay bare
The Truth. *Cash flow* runs deep but spirit deeper
You ask Am I my brother's keeper?
I answer by nature by spirit by rightful laws
My name, my brother, Wilberforce.[61]

The naming of 'Jerusalem' in the previous stanza is picked up here by the echoes to Blake's famous poem ('Nor shall my sword sleep in my hand'), foregrounding the radical opposition to man's oppression of his fellow man that Blake's poetry encapsulated, and the utopian hope for a second coming that would only be possible if sins such as slavery are eliminated. The paradoxical linkage of profit and sin ('gilt' and its homophone 'guilt') are juxtaposed directly with the gathering of sugar cane through unfree labour, which can only be undermined by direct action against the chains so that all can share in the bounties of the earth ('unlock the *stock* and *share*'). Note again here the way that behind the imperative is the existent 'stocks and shares' which commodify the enslaved Africans, reducing them to the same level as the other goods dealt on the trading floor. This paradox is continued, as the '*bond*' which must be broken refers both to the financial deed and to the fetter that holds the slave. The two are dynamically linked, as the former has led directly to the latter. The juxtaposition of '*bond* the bind unbound' highlights the links between the financial bonds and slavery's binds (chains), and the way they can only be disentangled by revealing the links between them and breaking them to 'lay bare / The truth'. The final two couplets exemplify the polemical message of the poet that the money god must be undermined by the human value of brotherhood, encapsulated by the actions of abolitionists like Wilberforce, who are acting in the spirit of the developing Enlightenment and promoting values of human brotherhood.

The poem is interesting enough on the page, but set free in the sculpture, written on the columns and the pedestal, the words take on lives of their own, inviting new interpretations as the viewer catches sight of different juxtapositions. Sightlines bring forth:

THROWN OVERBOARD – HAND, BUT WHOSE? – GIFT TO HIS HAND, MUST CALCULATE – BIND UNBOUND – THE SUGAR RUSH – MONEY – THE SPREAD – EXCHANGE TO DROWN – STOCK AND SHARE – CLOSED POSITION – NEATH THE SLAVES – ACQUISITION – FRANCHISE – WILL KICK OVER – TECHNICAL CORRECTION[62]

The poem is remade in its new form as part of the sculpture where its linear logic is disrupted. It works with the sculptural forms to show its building blocks. Hence, the disrupted, disjunctive story of transatlantic slavery is mirrored by the way the sculpture breaks up Sissay's poem. This in the end is what makes *Gilt of Cain* such a successful memorial, as it not only reflects London's tortured involvement in slavery and the triumph of the abolitionists, but also shows the paradox of trying to express this through slippery verbal and visual languages whose ambivalences never enable the viewer/reader to come to a 'closed position'.

I discussed earlier how Lubaina Himid's satirical performance piece on guidebooks shows the historical inadequacy of London's memorialisation of its historical black population, its influence on black populations in Africa and the Americas, and its complicity in the horrors of the slave trade; here Visocchi and Sissay's magnificent sculpture, at least in part, works against wholesale amnesia. Himid's piece deals also with that other great European world city, Paris (Figure 4). In contradistinction to London, Paris is not a port city and did not functioned as a slaving metropole in the same way as Britain's capital city; however, it did provide the finance for some of the voyages leaving from Bordeaux and Nantes, and the French state through the eighteenth century built up plantations in the Caribbean based on slave labour. The profits from this were fed back to the capital city. Most notably, the hellish sugar island St Dominique needed constant replenishment with new enslaved blacks from continental Africa because conditions there were so terrible. Himid's guidebook remembers these sometimes literally 'thrown away' people:

> The walk along the quays on either side of the **Canal St Martin** is an experience of Paris very different from that of the smarter districts. Here the older surviving landmarks of the neighbourhood, the factories, warehouses, dwellings, taverns and cafes hint at a life in the thriving nineteenth-century industrial working class world. In amongst all this, you can find, nestled near the footbridges, a series of memorial fountains for the lost Africans, thrown overboard by the captains of slave ships on their way to America. On tall columns stand tipping jugs, from which pour continuous supplies of water, pumped up from the canal. Many of the stolen people thrown into the Atlantic were deemed dangerous trouble-makers, but because they were valuable cargo the only justifiable way to get rid of them was to pretend that the ship's water supply could not sustain them for the full length of the journey. The pouring water remembers this lie and the ultimate waste of human life.[63]

Through the description of this imaginary memorial, Himid describes Paris as if it remembered the way its fabulous wealth was built on the backs of enslaved Africans in the colonies. It is interesting that she places the memorial in the working class district where the next wave of profits were made at the expense of a new proletariat, highlighting the rapacious nature of capitalism and its abuse of various forms of labour that has underpinned the wealth of cities such as Paris. The canals of course were used to transport the slave-produced goods from the coast to the capital city, and the placing of the imagined memorial on Canal St Martin emphasises the flow of these tropical goods into European markets. As Hershini Bhana Young contends:

> contextualising slavery situates it within the exploitative networks of global industrial capitalism, showing it not as an anomaly but as part of other forms of involuntary labour. Slavery thus is not an aberration of modernity, as liberal humanists claim, but rather essential to its paradigm.[64]

Civilised Paris, in this conception, is built on the backs of exploited wage and chattel slaves who were essential to its modernisation. The collage in the guidebook shows the tipping jugs precariously perched on tall classical columns, emphasising the evanescent nature of the remembrances of the black people who made the wealth, with the flow of water giving testament to their survival. These memorials are based on visions for a memorial Himid has been pursuing since the 1992-designed *Memorial for Zong*. In her 2003 interview with me, she described how with this and later memorial plans she wanted to make visible the contributions the slaves had made to the wealth of Europe, which the marketplace had made invisible:

> I am trying to talk about the waste, the waste of creativity, the excuses that were used for throwing people overboard – that they were too ill to waste water on. I'm talking about that vast expanse of water between yesterday and tomorrow, Africa and the New World, and I'm trying to talk also about the place where all these people are now in the water. They are the body of the water now, they are it. It's still there and they are still there and they are still contributing. [This is] a moving kind of way of talking of the moving of a people from one place to another, and how those people are the very people who arrived and are still contributing now, that the whole thing is a kind of cycle backwards and forwards. It's a kind of continuum, it's not just an event that happened... All those people are contributing – they're just in a different place, doing it, but all the legacy is still there.[65]

Amidst the satirical critique of Paris for its lack of acknowledgement of black contributions, Himid is making a deadly serious point about the kind of memorials that are needed to fully talk to the contributions made by African diasporan people to European civilisation. Their invisible labour helped to enable the cultural highpoints the guidebook boasts of, as Himid emphasises in her discussion of the importance of slave memorials:

> If the memorial is a memorial to the contribution that black people make to every single aspect of western culture then it's a memorial worth making. I'm sick and tired of living in a culture where that contribution is invisibilised... It's really, really difficult. One is invisibilised, one's friends' and colleagues' work is invisibilised. The memorial is a making visible of the contribution, the way that some of the music we have made, some of the colours and patterns we have made, some of the languages ... all those kind of cultural contributions fit into the fabric of western European life and the memorial's a way of doing that.[66]

Himid's transmutation of the noun 'invisible' to the non-standard verb 'invisibilised' is a conscious decision to foreground the active nature of western civilisation's assault on African Atlantic contributions to European art, music, politics and thought. She is also keen to highlight how in post-slavery societies, racism continues to downgrade the African Atlantic arts, so that the work of Himid and her compatriots are literally 'invisibilised'.

The writer Wilson Harris talked of the need to work against the 'Caribbean complex situation of apparent historylessness' in his essay 'The Root of Epic':

> And furthermore in the Americas as a whole, it would seem to me that the apparent void of history which haunts the black man may never be compensated until an act of imagination opens gateways between civilisations, between racial possessions and dispossessions.[67]

This void of history is not confined to the Americas, and Himid's memorial is 'an act of imagination' that seeks to work against the amnesia about black presence at the heart of Europe's great world cities. In Paris, of course, the 'gateways' had been opened by the presence of brilliant African diasporan writers, dancers, musicians and artists such as Augusta Savage, James Baldwin, Josephine Baker, Romare Bearden, John Coltrane, Aimé Césaire and Leopold Senghor, often lengthy sojourners in the city. However, there is very little trace of their presence there, as Himid's satirical commentary elucidates:

> In the **Latin Quarter,** huge constantly changing, interactive video monuments to African cuisine, jazz music and the black political history of the area are built into the quays along the **Seine** and right into the **Luxembourg Gardens**. The elite students at the Sorbonne and the two prestigious *lycées* compete to name and champion the leading figures of this influential, creative force, seamlessly embedded in Parisian cultural life.[68]

Black presence, rather than being championed by the French elite and celebrated in this important quarter for transatlantic black expression is, as in other areas of Paris, 'invisibilised'. Himid's guidebook cries 'What if...' through its collaged portraits of such figures as Ornette Coleman, but generally Paris is content to marginalise African Atlantic contributions to its cultural as well as its financial economy. However, in the Luxembourg Gardens there is a compensatory gesture, a new national memorial commemorating abolition unveiled by President Jacques Chirac in May 2007. Unlike the UK, where there is still no national memorial, in France, in the heart of the capital city, a memorial has been constructed; the important political statement made in commissioning such a work and having it unveiled by the head of state should not be underestimated. However, despite having the imprimatur of the French state and its financial and cultural resources, the memorial is deeply disappointing in many ways. The memorial is quite small and placed amidst a welter of other statuary, including a copy of the Statue of Liberty, a memorial to theatrical performers and a commemoration of the student radicals of 1968; so it is not only hard to find, but seems already abandoned in sculpture-park hell with few people knowing of its existence. France officially remembers, but without a memorial that makes an impact.

The sculpture by Fabrice Hyber, *Le Cri, L'Écrit* (Figure 5),[69] is a 3.7m-high polychrome bronze consisting of three chain-like ovals, one rising out of the ground linked upwards to a full chain and then from that to a broken chain symbolising the moment of abolition. This broken form also symbolises the open mouth that utters *le cri* of the title. This 'shout' relates to the cry in an African language, or no language, that emerged from the bowels of the slave ship and resonates forward to the cry that will set off maroon uprisings. One side is bronze and grim, whilst the other is brightly coloured in green and red patterns, emphasising the joy and colour of liberation. The abstract memorial's bronze side is covered with engraved words talking to slavery and abolition, such as *'inhumain'*, *'commerce'*, *'économique'*, *'fraternité'* and *'liberté'*. To this viewer at least, it is insubstantial and uninspiring without the dynamic dialogisations caused by the interplay of words and sculptural form contained in Visocchi and Sissay's *Gilt of Cain*. The UK lacks a national memorial, but its city memorial has a dynamism that Hyber's piece distinctly lacks.

The Dutch memorial in Amsterdam is more successful than the French; shaped like a ship, Soviet-like and triumphalistic and around 30m long in bronze, it depicts an enchained slave coffle walking through an arch and striding forth into freedom, characterised as a female figure shaping the ship's prow (Figure 6). Designed by the Surinamese sculptor Erwin de Vries, it again presents a rather linear view of liberal progress from unfreedom to freedom. The figures in the coffle are realistically drawn, emaciated and in pain, and serve as an effective representation of the horrors of the trade, whilst the female figure emerging from this horror, as De Vries states, 'underlines the predominant drive for freedom and a better future'.[70] In the end the memorial seems rather commonplace and unremarkable without the complexity in terms of composition or underlying philosophy that might have given it more gravitas. The ceremony to inaugurate the memorial in July 2002 made an entirely understandable political statement in asking Queen Beatrix to lead the ceremony. However, the security felt necessary in the wake of the post 9/11 terrorism threat and the number of dignitaries drawn because of her presence meant that many local people of African descent, the very descendants of slaves whom the memorial was meant to be about, were denied entry to the Ostpark. In reflecting the need for national atonement, the Dutch failed adequately to represent local black aspirations and needs. As the first national memorial to victims of the slave trade in Europe, the Dutch monument is an important marker and is already a memorial site; when I visited in November 2002 and again in August 2006 it was festooned in floral tributes, reflecting how it has become a place where people come to remember their enslaved ancestors. As such it is an effective memorial, one used by local people to remember the horrors of the past. On these days, with its colourful flowers, it transcends its everyday form and is made more meaningful, showing how the owning of a memorial by an important constituency can invigorate it and make it effective.

It is ironic that of these three twenty-first century memorials concerning slavery and abolition in European cities, the one not sanctioned or commissioned by a national government, *Gilt of Cain*, is by far the most effective. Its effectiveness is, though, crucially compromised by its position in Fen Court, a quiet, obscure square away from London's major landmarks. Himid's imaginary guidebook creatively envisions a different memorial landscape where slavery and black presence is at the centre of the city's story about itself. As she says at the conclusion of her performance piece:

> I often wonder how powerful and dignified London and Paris would be now, if their citizens, the landowners and the politicians *had really* sanctioned, then paid for, such dynamically visible, beautifully located, commemorations, memorials and monuments to the people of the Black Diaspora.[71]

However, in reality we are far from this utopian moment in Paris, London, Amsterdam or indeed in just about any other location in the world. The next chapter will discuss a much smaller city and its attempts to lay its slavery ghosts to rest: the minor slave port of Lancaster.

Notes

1. A. Seaton, 'Sources of slavery – destinations of slavery: the silences and disclosures of slavery heritage in the UK and US', in G. Dann and A. Seaton (eds), *Slavery, Contested Heritage and Thanotourism* (London: Haworth Press, 2001), pp. 107–129 (117).
2. É. Glissant, *Caribbean Discourse: Selected Essays*, trans. J. Michael Dash (Charlottesville, VA: University of Virginia Press, 1989), p. 201.
3. Quoted in L. Eckstein, *Re-Membering the Black Atlantic: On the Poetics and Politics of Literary Memory* (Amsterdam: Rodopi, 2006), pp. 227–228.
4. D. Brand, *A Map to the Door of No Return: Notes to Belonging* (Toronto: Doubleday Canada, 2001), p. 1.
5. J. T. Campbell, *Middle Passages: African American Journeys to Africa 1787–2005* (Penguin: London, 2006), p. 427.
6. Campbell, *Middle Passages*, p. 429.
7. C. Phillips, *The Atlantic Sound* (London: Faber, 2000), p. 173.

8. E. Eshun, *Black Gold of the Sun: Searching for Home in African and Beyond* (New York, NY: Random House, 2005), p. 40.

9. Eshun, *Black Gold of the Sun*, p. 41.

10. T. Singleton, 'The slave trade remembered on the former gold and slave coasts', in S. Frey and B. Wood (eds), *From Slavery to Emancipation in the Atlantic World* (London: Frank Cass, 1999), pp. 150–169 (156).

11. E. Bruner, 'Tourism in Ghana: the representation of slavery and the return of the black diaspora', *American Anthropologist* 98, 2 (1996), pp. 290–304 (291).

12. C. M. Kreamer, 'Shared heritage, contested terrain: cultural negotiation and Ghana's Cape Coast Castle exhibition "Crossroads of People, Crossroads of Trade"', in Ivan Karp et al. (eds), *Museum Frictions: Public Cultures/Global Transformations* (Durham, NC: Duke University Press, 2006), pp. 435–468 (457).

13. E. T. Linenthal, 'Epilogue: reflections', in J. O. and L. E. Horton (eds), *Slavery and Public History: The Tough Stuff of American History* (New York, NY: The New Press, 2006), pp. 213–224 (218).

14. Kreamer, 'Shared heritage', p. 467.

15. Kreamer, 'Shared heritage', p. 467.

16. E. L. Roushanzamir and P. J. Kreshel, 'Gloria and Anthony visit a plantation: history into heritage at Laura, a Creole plantation', in G. Dann and A. Seaton (eds), *Slavery, Contested Heritage and Thanotourism* (London: Haworth Press, 2001), pp. 169–189 (183).

17. J. Connarty, 'Mary Evans', in *Port City: On Mobility and Exchange*, ed. Tom Trevor et al. (Arnolfini, Bristol, 2007), pp. 92–99 (92–93).

18. A. Rice, interview with Godfried Donkor, http://www.uclan.ac.uk/ahss/journalism_media_communication/literature_culture/abolition/godfried_donkor.php [accessed 27 July 2009].

19. Rice, interview with Godfried Donkor.

20. T. Morrison, 'A bench by the road', *The World* 3, 1 (1989), pp. 4–5 & 37–41 (4).

21. J. M. Vlach, 'The last great taboo subject: exhibiting slavery at the Library of Congress', in J. O. and L. E. Horton (eds), *Slavery and Public History: The Tough Stuff of American History* (New York, NY: The New Press, 2006), pp. 57–74 (69).

22. I. Saffron, 'Changing skyline: slave memorial could let city stand out, but design risks sending wrong message', *Philadelphia Inquirer*, 14 February 2003, at http://www.ushistory.org/presidentshouse/news/inq021403.htm [accessed 18 February 2005]. Thankfully an alliance of community activists and concerned historians have enabled the slave presence to be included in the exhibition. President Obama inaugurates the new exhibit in 2010. See http://avengingtheancestors.com [accessed 31 August 2010].

23. G. B. Nash, 'For whom will the Liberty Bell toll? From controversy to cooperation', in J. O. and L. E. Horton (eds), *Slavery and Public History: The Tough Stuff of American History* (New York, NY: The New Press, 2006), pp. 75–102 (82).

24. Saffron, 'Changing skyline'.

25. T. McPherson, *Reconstructing Dixie: Race, Gender and Nostalgia in the Imagined South* (Durham, NC: Duke University Press, 2003), p. 3.

26. W. S. McFeely, *Frederick Douglass* (New York, NY: WW Norton, 1991), p. 14.

27. O. Oguibe, 'Slavery and the diaspora imagination', in G. Oostindie (ed.), *Facing Up to the Past: Perspectives on the Commemoration of Slavery from Africa, the Americas and Europe* (Kingston, Jamaica: Ian Randle Publishers, 2001) pp. 95–101 (99).

28. J. Adams, *Wounds of Returning: Race, Memory and Property on the Postslavery Plantation* (Chapel Hill, NC: University of North Carolina Press, 2007), p. 11.

29. F. Douglass, 'The life and times of Frederick Douglass' (1881), in H. L. Gates Jr (ed.), *Autobiographies* (New York, NY: Library of America, 1994), pp. 453–1045 (488).

30. Linenthal, 'Epilogue', p. 214.

31. J. L. Eichstedt and S. Small, *Representations of Slavery: Race and Ideology in Southern Plantation Museums* (Washington, DC: Smithsonian Books, 2002), p. 109.

32. Eichstedt and Small, *Representations of Slavery*, p. 15.

33. Eichstedt and Small, *Representations of Slavery*, p. 10.

34. My use of this term here and elsewhere in this study is to describe the way memorialising sometimes takes on an overtly political character in order to challenge dominating historical narratives. I prefer the term to the idea developed in Germany around Holocaust monuments of 'counter-memorials', because it is a more active and performative expression and seems to more accurately describe the processes and creative works I describe. See my discussion on pp. 13–14.

35. F. Douglass, 'Narrative of the life of an American slave, written by himself' (1845), in H. L. Gates Jr (ed.), *Autobiographies* (New York, NY: Library of America, 1994), pp. 1–102 (18).

36. P. Nora, 'Between memory and history: *les lieux de memoire*', in G. Fabre and R. O'Meally (eds), *History and Memory in African American Culture* (Oxford: Oxford University Press, 1994), pp. 284–300 (289).

37. Douglass, 'Narrative of the life', p. 19.

38. Linenthal, 'Epilogue', p. 219.

39. M. Tyler-Mcgraw, 'Southern comfort levels: race, heritage tourism and the Civil War in Richmond', in J. O. and L. E. Horton (eds), *Slavery and Public History: The Tough Stuff of American History* (New York, NY: The New Press, 2006), pp. 151–168 (158).

40. Maryland Historical Society plaque in St Michaels, MD, visited September 1999.

41. F. Douglass, 'My bondage and my freedom' (1855), in H. L. Gates Jr (ed.), *Autobiographies* (New York: Library of America, 1994), pp. 103–452 (320–321).

42. S. Drescher, 'Commemorating slavery and abolition in the United States of America', in G. Oostindie (ed.), *Facing Up to the Past: Perspectives on the Commemoration of Slavery from Africa, the Americas and Europe* (Kingston, Jamaica: Ian Randle Publishers, 2001) pp. 109–112 (112).

43. M. Petchkovsky, quoted in G. Oostindie (ed.), *Facing Up to the Past: Perspectives on the Commemoration of Slavery from Africa, the Americas and Europe* (Kingston, Jamaica: Ian Randle Publishers, 2001), p.xxxvi.

44. Oguibe, 'Slavery and the diaspora imagination', p. 100.

45. Nora, 'Between memory and history', p. 285.

46. Adams, *Wounds of Returning*, p. 17.

47. L. Himid, 'What are monuments for? Art of the Black Diaspora: possible landmarks on the urban map', presentation given at the Collegium for African American Research Conference, Bremen, 26 March 2009. In May 2010, Yinka Shonibare's work *Nelson's Ship in a Bottle* was unveiled on the fourth plinth in Trafalgar Square, providing a Black Atlantic counterweight to the square's imperial narrative. I discuss this fully in a forthcoming *Atlantic Studies* article.

48. J. Young, *At Memory's Edge: After-Images of the Holocaust in Contemporary Art and Architecture* (New Haven, CT: Yale University Press, 2000), pp. 66–67.

49. S. Stewart, *On Longing: Narratives of the Miniature, the Gigantic, the Souvenir, the Collection* (Durham, NC: Duke University Press, 1993), p. 2.

50. Himid, 'What are monuments for?'.

51. H. B. Young, *Haunting Capital: Memory, Text and the Black Diasporic Body* (Lebanon, NH: Dartmouth College Press, 2006), p. 33.

52. M. Macdonald, 'The uneasiness inherent in culture: a note on Michael Visocchi's memorial to the abolition of the transatlantic slave trade', *International Journal of Scottish Literature* 4 (2008), p. 3, http://www.ijsl.stir.ac.uk/issue4/macdonaldOP.htm [accessed 10 June 2009].

53. Macdonald, 'The uneasiness inherent in culture', p. 3.

54. M. Visocchi, email correspondence, June 25 2009.

55. L. Sissay, *The Gilt of Cain* (2007), http://www.cityoflondon.gov.uk/NR/rdonlyres/94CC1E18-C97F-4475-B082-C9E92316E5CE/0/MC_cain.pdf [accessed 27 July 2009].

56. Sissay, *Gilt of Cain*.

57. I. Baucom, *Specters of the Atlantic: Finance Capital, Slavery and the Philosophy of History* (Durham, NC: Duke University Press, 2005), p. 139.

58. Baucom, *Specters of the Atlantic*, p. 275. See also my discussion of Turner's painting in *Radical Narratives of the Black Atlantic*.

59. Baucom, *Specters of the Atlantic*, p. 139.

60. Sissay, *Gilt of Cain*.

61. Sissay, *Gilt of Cain*.

62. L. Sissay and M. Visocchi, *The Gilt of Cain*, Fen Court, London (2008).

63. Himid, 'What are monuments for?'.

64. Young, *Haunting Capital*, p. 11.

65. A. Rice, 'Exploring inside the invisible: an interview with Lubaina Himid', *Wasafiri* 40 (2003), pp. 21–26 (24).

66. Rice, 'Exploring inside the invisible', p. 24.

67. W. Harris, 'History, fable and myth in the Caribbean and Guianas', in A. Bundy (ed.), *Selected Essays of Wilson Harris: The Unfinished Genius of the Imagination* (London: Routledge, 1999), pp. 152–166 (166).

68. Himid, 'Monument talk', talk given at the Dukes Theatre, Lancaster, 15 November 2003.

69. F. Hyber, *Le Cri, L'Écrit*, Luxembourg Gardens, Paris, 2007.

70. E. De Vries quoted in Oostindie, *Facing Up to the Past*, p. xix.

71. Himid, 'What are monuments for?' (emphasis in original).

2

Discovering Traces of Slavery in a City Fraught with Amnesia: Creating Memorials and Building New Identities in Lancaster

[Memory can] be tapped, unleashed and mobilised through oral and public history to stand as an alternative to imposed orthodoxy and officially sanctioned versions of historical reality; it is a route to a broadly distributed authority for making new sense of the past in the present. *Max Frisch*[1]

Once the history of empire becomes a source of discomfort, shame and perplexity, its complications and ambiguities were readily set aside. Rather than work through those feelings, that unsettling history was diminished, denied and then if possible actively forgotten. The resulting silence feeds an additional catastrophe: the error of imagining that post-colonial people are only unwanted alien intruders without any substantive historical, political or cultural connections to the collective life of their fellow subjects. *Paul Gilroy*[2]

Paul Gilroy's discussion of the legacy of empire, which makes of black British people little more than 'alien intruders' in a British polity that eschews such 'unsettling history', has resonances in locations throughout the UK, but nowhere more so than in the ports that were central hubs of imperial trade, some of which now apparently show remarkably few legacies of this glorious and sordid past. For instance, there is virtually no maritime commercial activity any more on the quayside at Lancaster. The once bustling port is now home to upmarket flats and strolling tourists navigating between the old Custom House building and the maritime-themed pubs. The source of Lancaster's wealth in direct trade with the West Indies and in the transatlantic slave trade have traditionally been detailed in the rather outdated exhibits in the Maritime Museum,[3] which is housed in the Custom House, designed by the furniture manufacturer Robert Gillow in 1764; however, the city had always buried this history away in the background of its tale of civic pride through mercantile endeavour. In fact, the local oral history of Lancaster slave traders is often about how Lancaster merchants coming from the fourth largest slave port were mere gentleman amateurs in comparison to the professionals down the coast in Liverpool. However, as Melinda Elder describes in her history of the Lancaster slave trade and in subsequent research, Lancaster traders were involved in frantic and murderous slave raids on the African coast,[4] and indeed were engaged in joint ventures with Liverpool merchants, so that some voyages counted in the statistics as belonging to the larger port had such significant input from Lancaster merchants that many think they should be counted as Lancaster voyages.[5]

With very few black British residents and the large majority of these being of Asian origin rather than Caribbean or African, there has historically been little impetus in Lancaster to foreground this aspect of its past. In contradistinction to Bristol and Liverpool, with their large African-Caribbean communities, Lancaster had never experienced a sustained political demand to atone for its history of slave trading. However, many Lancastrians felt there was a political imperative for white people to remember the trade and their ancestors' exploitation of Africans for profit, and that the best way to do this was for them to be reminded, as they went about their daily life in the city, of the centrality of the slave trade to its history.

As long as the story of slavery in the city was mainly confined to the museum, it was readily ignored. Black presence, as well as contributions to the wealth of the city derived from the slave trade, had historically been completely silenced. For instance, the many black slaves/servants in the city were usually ignored in the discussion of the city's fine Georgian terraces. This was compounded by the absence of civic memorials to victims of the trade. For, as James Young has asserted, the right kind of memorial shows us 'not literally what was lost, but that loss itself is part of this neighbourhood's history, an invisible, yet essential feature of its landscape'.[6] This interesting idea that memorials are not just about remembering tangible, already well chronicled history but about witnessing the invisible and intangible as well is crucial to a city like Lancaster, where civic memorialising already bears more than sufficient witness to the achievements of its merchant class. As Marianne Hirsch and Valerie Smith remind us, 'what a culture remembers and what it chooses to forget are intricately bound up with issues of power and hegemony'.[7] Hirsch and Smith describe how this affects gender issues; however, their illuminating remarks have relevance for issues of class and race also, and it is the latter that is most important in challenging the hegemony of Lancaster's lily-white public image of itself. This challenge comes about through a new form of engagement with the past, which is determined to look beyond the traditional historical and museum archive. One Francophone historian, Catherine Reinhardt, in her seminal study

Claims to Memory (2008), articulates a post-historical analytical methodology that this study also essays. She describes how she foregrounds:

> the dialogue between fact and fiction, between past and present that sheds light on obscured, silenced, forgotten and even erased fragments of the slave past. It is at the interstices of these documents that memory can be found.[8]

The 'erased fragments of the slave past' must crucially be reconstructed by memory work in order for the full history of Lancaster to be told. This work is best undertaken through interdisciplinary case studies that move beyond the merely documentary and historical and into the performative and contemporary realm, where the full implications of Lancaster's involvement in the slave trade can be teased out, in contradistinction to the way the traditional historical record obscures the city's involvement.

For despite the amnesia around the black presence in, and contribution to, Lancaster, local people have sought ways to memorialise these important historical figures, in particular at the remarkable and, I would contend, virtually unique gravesite of an African boy, 'Sambo' (died 1736) at Sunderland Point at the head of the Lune Estuary, which leads into the port of Lancaster. Here painted stones, flowers and funerary ephemera surround a memorial plaque first laid in 1796 (Figure 7). This plaque was replaced in the early 1990s after an act of vandalism, and an injunction on the new brass plate exhorts visitors to 'Respect this Lonely Grave', which broadly seems to be adhered to. I have discussed this gravesite before; however, it is such a dynamic site of memory and there has been so much new activity related to it in the last decade that it provides a compelling case study in memorialisation and merits further consideration here.

According to the *Lonsdale Magazine* of 1822, Sambo arrived around 1736 from the West Indies in the capacity of a servant to the captain of a ship (to this day unnamed):

> After she had discharged her cargo, he was placed at the inn... with the intention of remaining there on board wages till the vessel was ready to sail; but supposing himself to be deserted by the master, without being able, probably from his ignorance of the language, to ascertain the cause, he fell into a complete state of stupefaction, even to such a degree that he secreted himself in the loft on the brewhouses and stretching himself out at full length on the bare boards refused all sustenance. He continued in this state only a few days, when death terminated the sufferings of poor Samboo. As soon as Samboo's exit was known to the sailors who happened to be there, they excavated him in a grave in a lonely dell in a rabbit warren behind the village, within twenty yards of the sea shore, whither they

conveyed his remains without either coffin or bier, being covered only with the clothes in which he died.[9]

Sambo was buried in such a lonely grave because he was not baptised and had to be laid in unconsecrated ground. Like most Africans arriving in Britain as 'servants' (usually slaves), he appeared to suffer a profound sense of culture shock, being landed amongst strangers with whom he could not communicate. There has been much speculation about the cause of his death, ranging from the pragmatic (pneumonia) to the sentimental (profound homesickness). The latter provided the grist for anti-slavery panegyrics such as the Reverend James Watson's 1796 elegy, which was eventually appended to a brass plate on a freestone slab at the site itself. James Watson's interest in the slave grave is not without irony, however, as his brother William Watson was a leading light in the Lancaster slave trade. William Watson was 'one of the most committed investors in Lancaster slavers [whose] tenacity was no doubt instrumental in keeping the slave trade alive at Lancaster'.[10] The tone of the memorial is sentimental in the extreme, praising Sambo as a 'faithful Negro' who had died because of his 'service' to his master. The poem consists of seventeen verses including the epitaph of the final three verses which appears on the grave. It reads:

> Full sixty years the angry winter wave
> Has thundering dash'd this bleak and barren shore,
> Since Sambo's head, laid in this lonely grave,
> Lies still, and ne'er will hear their turmoil more.
>
> Full many a sand-bird chirps upon the sod,
> And many a moon-flight Elfin round him trips;
> Full many a Summer's sunbeam warms the clod,
> And many a teeming cloud upon him drips.
>
> But still he sleeps, till the awak'ning sounds
> Of the Archangel's Trump new life impart;
> Then the great Judge his approbation founds,
> Not on man's colour, but his worth of heart.[11]

Such a clarion call for the humanity of the slave reflects the late eighteenth century construction of an anti-slavery sentiment that simultaneously elided Africans as actors in their own struggles at the exact time of the Santo Domingo uprising (1791–1803), which exemplified a revolutionary African diasporan tradition. African agency is downplayed by such a discourse, and a character like Sambo is saved from obliquity by the workings of English sentiment long after it does him any practical good. This feeling that Sambo's actual biography is misinterpreted by the poem is exacerbated by the

Christian sentimentality of the final lines, which allow him life after death despite his heathenism. The later addition of a wooden cross to the grave only serves to emphasise the mismatch between the slave refused a Christian burial and subsequent Christian sentimentalists trying to reinstate him and atone for his earlier dismissal.

Watson collected the money for the memorial from visitors to Sunderland Point. These visitors would follow the trail along the terrace of houses to the footpath which starts at the inn and leads across the headland to the rabbit warren where Sambo is buried. In retracing Sambo's steps they and subsequent visitors would be able to see the upstairs room where he had died and his body had been laid out, then follow the passage of Sambo's coffin down the path. Today the trail is unaltered and the inn, now renamed Upsteps Cottage, still stands. The repeated pilgrimage over two hundred years is in itself a memorial event that works to remember not only this boy's life and death but also the larger issue of slavery. Paul Ricoeur, in his discussion of the sepulchre, notes the importance of such repeated acts of remembrance of death to the development of memorialisation:

> Sepulchre, indeed, is not only a place set apart in our cities, the place we call a cemetery and in which we depose the remains of the living who return to dust. It is an act, the act of burying. This gesture is not punctual; it is not limited to the moment of burial. The sepulchre remains because the gesture of burying remains; its path is the very path of mourning that transforms the physical absence of the lost object into an inner presence. The sepulchre as the material place thus becomes the enduring mark of mourning, the memory aid of the act of the sepulchre.
> It is this act of sepulchre that historiography turns into writing.[12]

In 'transforming the physical absence of the lost object into an inner presence', visitors to the site take on the task of inserting the boy into a historical record that would traditionally have reduced him to mere chattel. Ricoeur's formulation privileges the historian as transformative; Sambo's grave and memorialisation show how the actions of ordinary citizens can be just as important to effective historical retrieval. A traditional way to mark a pilgrimage to a gravesite is to bring a stone, and Sambo's grave has been replete with such markers. From at least the 1970s schoolchildren have been encouraged to bring stones painted with scenes and panegyrics to Sambo's memory, to enable them to empathise with a boy of around their own age whose life was cruelly foreshortened by the operation of a transatlantic slave trade originated in Lancaster. These stones, with their scenes of seafaring and lost African landscapes, add to the colourful and poignant scene that creates in Pierre Nora's words a *lieu de mémoire*, a site of memory, that is deeply affecting.[13] The loneliness of the grave, created by the fact of his burial in unconsecrated ground set off from other plots, adds to this sense of a desolation which visitors seek to make more palatable through inhabiting the grave with objects. In keeping with the gravesite of a child, visitors have also brought small toys, and recently young girls have been tying hair bobbles to the cross at the site, showing their intimate attachment to the story and its importance to them. These mementoes bring the grave alive in ways that help to transform Sambo's status from solitary human chattel to socialised human being, if only in death.

The most recent memorial at the site, erected in 2009, is placed several feet from the grave as if in acknowledgement of that already crowded space. It is a group of around thirty small memorial stones with personal messages from the children at Alston School, Cumbria. These are attached on top of bamboo canes, forming a circle of memory like a bunch of flowers or a group of toadstools. These organic forms have poignant personal messages in white paint from the schoolchildren (Figure 8).

Many might see in this memorial and in the other memorialisation gestures outlined above a sentimentalisation not that far removed from James Watson's poem; however, I prefer to think of it as important memory work that makes sure that Sambo's story is continually brought back into local discourses about slavery, emphasising the human story that the cityscape can so readily elide. In Michel de Certeau's words, this memory work could be said to 'exorcise death by inserting it into discourse'.[14] Hilda Kean, in discussing the memorialisation around the grave, describes how it is 'both a site of public history and one which has been created through the personal and unofficial acts of people operating outside the constructs of academic history'.[15] Such guerrilla memorialisation by a variety of recent visitors ensures the grave is not wholly constrained by limiting ideas of public remembrance and reduced to a part of that dry historical record which we might label 'heritage'.

Sambo has also been memorialised in folk song through Alan Bell's 'Sambo's Song', written in the 1970s, which tells the story of the lonely grave, the boy abandoned and his burial by 'kindly seamen' in its chorus and first two verses. The final verse speaks of him witnessing activities around the grave that continue today:

Now children walk the grassy shore
To place sweet flowers upon your grave,
You'll never want for more.
And traveller, if you e'er pass that way,
Pause and think of Sambo,
And man's old dreary ways.[16]

Similarly to Watson's poem, the song makes moral capital out of Sambo's abandonment and death, though in keeping with the more secular late twentieth century, the moral is more concerned with universal human rights than with Christianity. The song itself created controversy in left-wing folk forums in the 1970s because of Sambo's name. A senior Labour politician insisted that singing about a boy named 'Sambo' was 'offensive',[17] yet offered no alternative name. The London-born, Bajan-descended poet Dorothea Smartt responds to the problematic of Sambo's historically-freighted, racist name in her marvellously elliptical '99 Names of the Samboo'. In the title, she follows the spelling of the name on the 1796 brass grave plate, before embarking on a tour through African and European naming practices at the time of the slave trade and their legacies for good and ill. She starts with Sambo's imagined original name and then contrasts this with his slave status:

Bilal
ibn
beloved
son
brother
husband
father
grandfather
elder
ancestor

sold
livestock
cargo
chattel
property
guinea-bird
savage
enslaved
captive
servant
worker[18]

The poem illuminates the way Africans are dehumanised through the process of enslavement and reduced to ciphers for European concepts of otherness. The sparse vocabulary of the poem emphasises the reductive nature of such a stereotyping discourse:

heathen
cannibal
beast

blackamoor
darkie
nigger
uncivilised
wog
fuzzy-wuzzy
coon
negro

tamed
eunuch
pet
uncle tom
minstrel
golliwog
survivor
mirror
mask
chameleon
creole[19]

The poem is not hidebound by this limiting discourse, and shows how, by using such techniques of masking, Africans fight back to make their own space in language. The poem circles back to Bilal, Sambo's imagined African name, which emerges triumphant despite the power of the institution of slavery and the racist discourse it promulgated. This work, and Smartt's earlier poem sequence 'Lancaster Keys', specially commissioned for the 2003 Lancaster Litfest, writes back directly to Watson's elegy and provides at the same time a commentary on the city's wilful forgetting of the trade that made it rich. Litfest's decision to print 24,950 copies of the poem, 'each representing a person shipped into slavery by Lancaster slave traders between 1750 and 1800', and deliver them to all secondary school pupils in the district attempted to make a dramatic gesture of rememory in the cultural life of the city. This public acknowledgement of the dissident memories that Sambo's history ignites outlines a politics which seeks to intervene in the traditional amnesia of the city about its slave past and reinvigorate the narrative, not as sentimentalised panegyric, but rather as radical counter-memory; it is in keeping with Richard Price's impassioned call for diasporic memorials to run beyond building materials:

> memorials [should] run less to bricks and mortars than to knowledge and its diffusion. What if we tried to make sure that every schoolchild in Europe, the Americas and Africa is exposed as fully as possible to the history of slavery and its legacies?[20]

Smartt's poem is reproduced alongside information on Lancaster's involvement in the trade, with quotations about the importance of memory. Such a pamphlet has the kind of memorial function that Price demands. It focuses not only on the direct slave trade, which indicates the interweaving of Lancaster with the slave economy, but also on the city's trade in slave-produced and harvested goods such as rice, cotton, sugar and particularly mahogany, which made the fortune of the Gillows furniture company in the eighteenth century. Smartt's poem seeks to redress the city's amnesia about the slave trade, and the opening of the section 'The brewery room' reflects on how the routes that Sambo took to get to Sunderland Point were smoothed by the commercial networks established by Lancaster merchants:

> Keys to the city awarded
> to entrepreneurs in the new world trade.
> Adventurers of high finance.
> Slavery a key to England's glory days,
> civic largesse and the city's architecture,
> of streets and the high seas
> glistening with gold.[21]

As the poem indicates, many of those involved in the trade were prominent members of the elite that ran the city, including mayors such as Dodshon Foster. Moreover, the poem delineates how the raw materials exchanged for slaves in the West Indies came back to Lancaster too, helping to create distinctive, prestigious industries at home that belied the trade in human bodies that made them possible. As detailed above, the most famous such factory in Lancaster was Gillows, where mahogany from the Caribbean was fashioned into high class furniture. Smartt's poem shows the interrelatedness of this industry and the slave economy, positing Sambo and his fellow slaves as the labourers on whose backs large profits were made:

> The Plantation Estate, brewery source,
> furnished salon of mahogany. Gillows crafted
> wood, the Sambo farmed and forested.
> Torn from root system to harden and die.
> To be shaped into something new
> and of use to Lancaster Town.
> A primrose path of mahogany furniture.
> Fallen nature, hardness of heart,
> shameless dishonesty, blood courses,
> evil courses, water courses.[22]

Just as the mahogany has been 'farmed and forested', so the Africans have been uprooted to furnish labour for the plantation, becoming a human commodity which hardens and dies just like the wood to which it contributes labour value. In this way Sambo's death in Lancaster is a function of his use as a commodity and the denial of his humanity by those who benefit from the trade in all its three corners. The economy of language here, so that Sambo is both the subject and object of the verbs 'farmed and forested', points to the duality of the slaves' position, crucial to harvesting the mahogany, but also harvested themselves in Africa to provide the labour power that makes possible the operation of the colonial economy. Both labourer and commodity, Sambo is tremendously over-determined in his meanings within the British slave-owning empire. This is true too when mercantilism is superseded by sentiment in the late eighteenth century, and Smartt speaks to this in reinterpreting Sambo's perceived pining for his master, which, according to such self-serving views, led to his death.

This Sambo
pines for his master, mythical, imagined,
key and the centre-piece of his room.
But the room is but many,
in one house, in one compound, in one
village, in one district, in one country, in one
empire, in one continent spanning continents.

The 'Ship's Inn',
I the Sambo pour out of this Brewery Room
into my fermenting home brew spilling
kicked from its calabash pot.[23]

The meaning of Sambo here as sentimentalised torch-bearer for his beloved master is transformed to Sambo as avenger, whose legacy has the power to leap out of the confines of white guilt-ridden sentimentality and reinvigorate debates around slave history from the village of Sunderland Point, through cities like Lancaster to the UK and across the seas to the intertwining nexus of slave-owning empires. In this reading Sambo's fertile tale cannot be confined to its historical trace but erupts like the 'fermenting home brew' of the brewing room he is confined to by illness. Sambo's revenge is in his re-imagining by later generations which, as Smartt shows, relate how Anglo-American cultures kept 'for themselves the harvest' yet in doing so 'ferment a bitter brew'.

The Manchester-based poet SuAndi's poem about Sambo's grave envisages a similar resurrection of the boy, but this time he returns to Africa, going back through the Door of No Return in contradistinction to its historical and mythical narrative of permanent exile:

Sometimes when the moon is full
He pushes the earth aside
Scattering the gifts, toys, tokens
And stands on the highest point
Tip-toed to extend his boyish frame
And he looks out to sea
For now he can see beyond water and land
Right to the coast of Elmina
Through the Door of No Return
And into his village and his mother's arms
And he smiles once again[24]

In pushing away the freight of keepsakes left for him, the boy rejects his status as sentimental victim of white guilt and returns to an African homeland without conflict in a fantasy projection that replaces sentimentalised white projections with a return to homespace. Hortense Spillers has talked about how 'African persons in the middle passage are literally suspended in the Oceanic',[25] and Sambo is a prime example who complicates SuAndi's wished for return. His known life was conducted almost exclusively shipboard, and in Smartt and SuAndi's imaginations his after-life legacy permeates the transatlantic world where his memory, despite all attempts, cannot be repressed or neutralised. Suspension, a negative in Spillers's theorisation, is dialogised by Smartt and SuAndi's lyrical interventions. As Aldon Nielsen succinctly describes in talking of such black Atlantic texts, 'a different kind of scholarship may be called for here, a study that listens to seas and is owned by their terrible poetry.'[26] If nothing else, Smartt's brewery room lyric and SuAndi's fantasy projection need this kind of transnational, oceanic scholarship to fully interpret their black Atlantic resonances. Their guerrilla memorialisation interprets the gravesite anew, articulating an African presence that is in contrast to sentimentalised and objectified representations.

As Smartt details in her poems on the gravesite, there are occasional reactions, such as the vandalism of the grave, which are at the least problematic and sometimes deeply disturbing. For instance, in August 2008, I visited the gravesite where a visitor had placed a small golliwog amidst the flotsam and jetsam dispersed over the grave. This example of racist memorabilia was the equivalent of graffiti, undermining the joyous cacophony of objects that spoke to a more appropriate memorialisation. It shows that guerrilla memorialisation is not necessarily always positive and that our memorial sites cannot be left entirely to those whose knowledge of the appropriate gesture might be grossly out of kilter with the site's historical resonances. But despite such potential problems, enslaved Africans dispersed throughout the Atlantic triangle are, I believe, most effectively remembered at such local sites that conjure up their thoroughly routed existence. Remembering slavery from nearby is an urgent task in all parts of the circum-Atlantic and beyond, as Livio Sansone reminds us:

> Transatlantic slavery was by definition a transnational phenomenon, which has created a universe of suffering, dehumanisation and racialisation, spanning across many regions of what we now know, after Paul Gilroy, as the black Atlantic – a region that reaches to the tropical lowlands of the Pacific coast of Central and Latin America. Yet the way in which it is remembered as well as the legacy felt within today's life and race relations, show that the memory of slavery is often a surprisingly 'local', relational and contingent construction.[27]

The imaginative leaps that Smartt and SuAndi make from this lonely gravesite to reinvigorate lives lost in the black Atlantic are exemplary moves in the light of Sansone's comments, creating poems that use the local site to make links across geographies and chronologies. They are of course memorial gestures in themselves, guerrilla memorialisations. The poem contributed to a feeling in Lancaster that the city should build an effective memorial, one used by local people to remember the horrors of the past. Lubaina Himid talked about the possibilities of building such a memorial at the launch event of the Slave Trade Arts Memorial Project (STAMP) in November 2003:

> The monument could be for the people of a city and its visitors to be able to learn to accept and give forgiveness. In which case it could relate to today, to the past, to the future and could work visually on several levels. There could be texts, there could be water, there could be structure, there could be movement, colour, and even growing, living things.
>
> A monument needs to move, to move on, to help the people who engage with it to move on, it needs to be able to change with the weather, the seasons, the political climate and the visual debates of the day.[28]

Any successful memorial would need to be a *lieu de mémoire* that would adequately represent generations to come as well as the past and the present: a memorial that conserves memory without being conservative. That is, so that it truly helps 'the people who engage with it to move on', so that it becomes associated not with stasis but with dynamism. Such a task was daunting and humbling, but it was felt that our collective amnesia must be overcome by local gestures of remembrance (however small) which raise the collective consciousness of slavery's ghostly presence that still haunts our shared circum-Atlantic space. Such memorialisation is born out of the struggle with conservative forces that prefer to bury difficult histories, and played out through a guerrilla memorialisation that refuses to accept the status quo.

In the absence of such a memorial in Lancaster, STAMP worked with a number of artists, schools and community groups to increase public awareness of the slave trade and developed a series of commemorative exhibitions and performances from 2003–2006, culminating in a permanent memorial to the Africans who were transported on board Lancaster ships, unveiled in October 2005. The committee had been formed in September 2002 at a training day for teachers around issues raised by the slave trade held at the Maritime Museum. Their frustration that there was not a focus in the city for remembering victims of the slave trade that they could share with their pupils galvanised the small group of curators, educators, local NGO representatives and community workers into forming a campaign. As an academic in the field, I became STAMP's academic advisor. Throughout the project, our committee were aware of the tortured history of British imperialism and the city's own contribution to some of its excesses, made worse by a wilful historical amnesia. Barnor Hesse outlines this problematic and the way to overcome it with a welcome articulacy:

> Part of the difficulty with the dominant cultural form of Britain is the inability or reluctance of its institutions to accept that European racism was and is a constitutive feature of British nationalism. While this remains unexamined, resistant to decolonisation in the post-colonial period, it continues to generate a myriad of resistances and challenges to its historical formations. These dislocate the narration of Britain as a serialised essence, articulating the storylines of a nation that is diversely politicised and culturally unsettled. Residual multicultural disruptions are constituted as forms of disturbance and intrusiveness by those resurgences of meaning, arising from the imperial past. They continually put into question, particularly in unexposed places and at unforeseen times, matters deemed in hegemonic discourses to be settled, buried and apparently beyond dispute.[29]

I quote Hesse in full because his intervention speaks to the legacy of UK cities like Lancaster and the possibilities of overcoming the straitjacket imposed by amnesia and indifference. For the committee there was much unfinished business: a colonial legacy that still informed relations and ideas in the city, and which was highlighted by its involvement in the transatlantic slave trade. However, because it had never been properly debated there was a vacuum which we felt needed to be filled so that the link between current racism and the historic chattel slavery which had helped form the very bricks and mortar of the city could be foregrounded and exposed. Our aim was to use the memorial and other project activities as 'residual multicultural disruptions' in the city to help undermine what we might call, following Paul Gilroy's adoption of Patrick Wright's phrase, 'the morbidity of heritage'.[30] We wanted to make a vibrant living response to the historical legacy of slavery and imperialism that would reawaken debate and not allow a complacent settling of the debate in favour of a monoglot UK nationalism that had historically marginalised a critical stance on this contested issue. As Lessie Jo Frazier, in discussing counter-memory in Chile, contends:

> The memories of state violence incommensurable with national-state memory took the form of aberrations or flaws in what was presented as an otherwise whole cloth of national memory in a functioning political system… It is possible to read the rhetorically whole cloth of national histories, not only against the grain, but in its very weave.[31]

We wanted to highlight such 'aberrations or flaws' in the history of slavery (Britain's state violence) as essential to a complete national memory with a full accounting of the historical record, and to bring back to view the full story, the 'very weave' of it, through our monument. In this, we were part of a wider movement of localism that disdained a monoglot national narrative that refused to give up nostalgia for the imperial past, and were aware too of the importance of a transnational approach to a memorial that would be truly post-imperial. As Jay Winter commented, in discussing the importance of shifting focus away from the national sphere (replete with its hubristic and often chauvinistic monuments) to smaller-scale local memorials, the most effective sites of memory are often 'created not just by nations but primarily by small groups of men and women who do the work of remembrance'.[32] Paul Ricoeur had asserted that 'the nation remains the major reference of historical memory';[33] however, for a complex black Atlantic history such as this, the local and the transnational should surely trump it. As Paul Gilroy says, anyone involved in such needful political work would best situate themselves:

> close to the centre of Britain's vernacular dissidence, lending energy to an ordinary, demotic multiculturalism that is not the outcome of government drift and institutional indifference but of concrete oppositional work: political, aesthetic, cultural, scholarly.[34]

With its committee of academics, local community activists and creative workers, and with support from radical local folk, STAMP mobilised exactly the kind of vernacular dissidence that enabled the action required to build the memorial. Perhaps our agenda is best discussed in the light of the unveiling ceremony in October 2005, which was attended by around 200 people, most of them local, but which also included an African ceremony: the launching of a burning wicker boat festooned with plants used on that continent for ceremonial burials. Although the mayor of Lancaster and civic dignitaries were present, their presence did not dominate the agenda of the ceremony, which reflected the roots of the project in the local community and its links to communities from the black Atlantic and its history. Nowhere was this more evident than in the local schoolchildren playing percussion after intensive workshops with African drummers.[35]And our international speaker, the distinguished African American political scientist and civil rights activist Preston King, had been a resident of Lancaster for over a decade whilst in political exile in the UK. The project was interested in embedding memorialisation about slavery in the city, and intent on leaving a legacy so that the memorial was not felt to be imposed from above by an elite, and so that the city and its residents had ownership of the process and finally of the monument itself. However, it was felt that this ownership should be in the context of a critical take on local, national and international histories that did not allow them to remain 'settled, buried and apparently beyond dispute', as Hesse had warned in his prescient commentary. Lubaina Himid, at the public meeting which launched STAMP, articulated the need we all felt to honour the African dead and abused who had been loaded onto ships fitted out on Lancaster's quayside, and the profits from whose sale had helped build the wealth of the city:

> If you are going to honour the dead who have been ignored, suppressed or denied when in peril in the past, you must do it because as a city you want to show that you would do differently now, that you would be able to defend those people now. You will first have to acknowledge that your city would not be the city it is, without the sacrifice of those who were sold by or used by the city in the past. This city can only aspire to being truly great if it can I suppose in some way seek forgiveness. Could it be that a monument is a tangible seeking of forgiveness?[36]

The very notion of 'forgiveness' in the context of a historical wrong from two centuries ago was bound to provoke uneasiness in some sections of the populace, and a number of local residents vented their fury, particularly when the proposal originally planned to site the modern monument directly in front of the eighteenth century Custom House on the quayside[37]. Probably the most splenetic response came after the memorial design was published in the local paper, the *Lancaster Guardian*, in December 2004. James Mackie's letter left no doubt about his disgust:

> to find that a green light has been given to the erection of this nonsense is just upsetting. The quay is one of the few near-perfect parts of Lancaster that still remain and the old Customs House is one of the most beautiful and interesting landmarks in the county. Who in their right minds

thinks that the area will be improved by a mosaic-encrusted plinth and a vessel in the grass verge containing 20 cast iron enslaved figures? The artist's impression that you printed with the article was not very large or detailed but is quite enough to show that the proposed artwork is simply repulsive.[38]

Mackie was not alone in his opposition, and the erroneous belief that the city council was funding the monument added to the venom. *Lancaster Guardian* reader Betty Norton wrote that a monument 'depicting misery and shame is no enhancement to the city, it will turn visitors away'.[39] However, at no point did the opposition to the monument gain any political leverage on the council, nor attract support from any councillors in the ruling Labour group or their opponents. In fact the council leader Ian Barker sprang to the defence of the STAMP committee in response to Mackie's letter, crafting an informed and elegant response:

> History is more than the sanitised version sometimes served up by the heritage industry. We are privileged to live in a historic town. An understanding of its history can teach our children and us a lot. But it won't do so if we deceive ourselves by ignoring the painful and repellent aspects of that history.
>   I have no doubt that some of Lancaster's prosperous slavers were outstanding men in the local community, kind and considerate to their family and neighbours and yet simultaneously capable of inflicting barbarous treatment on unknown Africans. If the Slave Trade Arts Memorial Project (STAMP) helps us reflect on that contradiction and how it could happen, it will be worthwhile.[40]

Barker's articulate support makes the point that citizens like Mackie who worry about the disruption to the 'near-perfect' quay by the visual complications of a memorial to the victims of the slave trade are merely supporters of a sanitised history that the city has been complicit in for too long. Opposition voices continued, but they never gained any coherent body of support. Maybe the fact that the council fully endorsed STAMP but did not provide any of the core funding meant that opposition was neutralised. Most of the money for the project came from the North-West Arts Council and the Millennium Commission, with the council providing vital logistical and technical support. There were no specific council grants for opponents to identify and build opposition around. Another key factor in neutralising opposition was the way the STAMP project used the money from the Arts Council to engage with local schools and community groups, running workshops that enabled thousands of locals to be engaged with the project well before the final monument was unveiled, providing a legacy with ramifications for citizens from many different backgrounds.

Allied to this community work was an awareness in the committee of the need for a different kind of engagement with the past than would normally happen in the cityscape. The committee had decided early on that they should make the encounter with this past an everyday occurrence rather than a pilgrimage or part of an educational tour. This was key to moving slavery and its important lessons about human rights and injustice from the periphery to the centre of consciousness. As Lubaina Himid articulates, this is done not by the grand gesture, or by shock tactics, but by everyday encounter:

> If the person pushing their buggy past the memorial isn't thinking, 'Oh dear what a pity all those people died', but is thinking or just catches a glimpse of fabric out of the corner of their eye or a sparkle of water then there's a kind of flowing imprint, visible, physical, the sound of the water or the flash of the colour that flows into their life as they go past. There's no point even in trying to place something like that in people's lives. But memory is not about that, it's about tiny moments, little flickers of recognition. I'd want people to meet at the memorial; a place where you feel there's a kind of continuum, where there's a going on, a tomorrow. It would be there to enter into the fabric of the day.[41]

The everyday nature of the encounter with the public work of art is key to its quiet effectiveness, and Himid's future-focused intervention informed Kevin Dalton-Johnson, our commissioned sculptor, as he completed the designs for his *Captured Africans* memorial (Figure 9). The final design of the memorial uses a variety of materials including stone, steel and acrylic to create a multi-textured take on Lancaster's slave trade history. The plinth is a circular stone with an inlaid mosaic of the Atlantic triangle, with lines showing the movement of ships between the continents of Europe, Africa and the Americas. Above it are a series of acrylic blocks named for the goods traded – cotton, sugar, mahogany and tobacco – with wealth named at the top because it is the prime motivation, and slaves named at the bottom because they are the goods upon which the whole trade depends. Inlaid in the acrylic are icons of the goods, so that for wealth there are coins and notes, whilst for the slaves there is a diagram based on the famous depiction of the slave ship *Brookes*. Just beneath this bottom block are small bronze casts of black slave figures which Dalton-Johnson developed with young people at risk in Lancaster. He felt it was very important that at least one part of the sculpture should be created by local people who do not consider themselves artists in any professional sense. The acrylic blocks are hung by poles between a steel panel and a carved piece of local Peakamoor stone, both of which image the shapes of a ship.[42] In an interview with Dalton-Johnson, I discussed how the sculpture as commissioned fits into its location so that it can become part of the everyday life of the citizens of the town. Dalton-Johnson agreed, and describes how:

> as the public come down and round the bend, just at the top of Damside, you're looking straight at the side of the sculpture, so you're looking through the spaces in between the acrylic blocks to the water on the other side, and that's picked up again by the blue of the mosaic, because it's predominantly blue, so that works really well. And the stone which is going round the outside, that once again fits with the new buildings on either side. It operates on very different levels in as much as it suits the context of a ship in the triangle, going down the slipway, off it goes after it's just dropped its cargo off. It also fits very well with aesthetic context where it's positioned, the colours of the apartments and the buildings that are built either side, and it works perfectly with the slipway going straight into the river. Having seen it erected, I'm quite confident that it'll work on different levels, both in terms of subject matter and also aesthetically in terms of the environment in which it's been placed.[43]

What the memorial successfully does is arrest the attention of passers-by when they first encounter it. For instance, a woman who did not know about the town's slave past told me how she caught out of the corner of her eye the words *Captured Africans* on the metal side of the sculpture, and was compelled to move towards it to find out more. What Dalton-Johnson wanted to do was to make the slave trade and its history central to the stories the city told about itself, so that they could never be elided again. Exhibiting the slave trade in a public space[44] away from its usual relegation to an often tired museum gallery enables its full historical and contemporary implications to be teased out. Sue Ashworth, from Lancashire County Museum Service and a founder member of the STAMP committee, discussed how important it is to move beyond the walls of the museum and how Dalton-Johnson's sculpture had achieved this:

> We've always acknowledged the slave trade ever since the Maritime Museum first opened 20 years ago. But it was always dealt with in a very dry way that just focused on the facts, the tonnage and the products involved. We saw an opportunity to let people actually contemplate what had happened rather than just be bombarded with figures. There doesn't have to be a disparity between something that's informative but also appeals to your senses.[45]

Ashworth underlines the importance of the memorial doing different memory work that foregrounds the emotions as well as the intellect. The contemplative aspect of the sculpture, however, is combined with serious political goals, as Dalton-Johnson has a strong message for contemporary race relations from his engagement with the history of slavery.

> Well, it's just a fact that black people could be treated like that, and if it could happen then, it can happen again now. The reason why we need to have a memorial is so it isn't repeated – it operates on that level. There's also the other political level, in that I'm not trying to get my own back, but I'm turning the tables, as if to say, you're getting a taste of how that feels. Putting the slave trade almost on trial, on exhibition, in the way that it's actually being presented, and the fact that it's a black artist doing that, re-emphasises the political statement.[46]

His desire to put the slave trade on trial is because of its implications for race relations in the here and now. As Dalton-Johnson himself says, the pedagogical aspect of the memorial is very important and is 'the reason why the ships' names are there, and the actual numbers of slaves that were on those ships. They're very clear, and they're not abstracted in the way that other parts have been.'[47] Additionally, the names of the ships' captains are listed in chronological order. Many of them are traditional Lancashire surnames which might well be shared by their viewers. The sculpture does not resist such uncomfortable realities; in fact it foregrounds them to make them part of the public memory so that white Lancastrians have to acknowledge these atrocities and hopefully learn from them. At the moment, slave traders are primarily remembered as citizens of note and many were prominent in the eighteenth century polity, such as Thomas Hinde, who became mayor of the city in 1769 and has a significant plaque in his honour in the city's Priory church. Through naming these slave traders, Dalton-Johnson's statue is a guerrilla memorialisation that works against traditional historiography. Such guerrilla memorialisation confronts Lancaster's citizens with their past in ways that work against a traditional memorial praxis which has tended toward unifying viewers principally around sympathy with the victims. Dalton-Johnson does this, but also acknowledges that the perpetrators of the historical atrocity should be remembered and marked lest Lancaster's citizens forget their ancestors' role in the trade. James E. Young has talked about the importance of such reminiscence in comments about Holocaust memorials which can be related to *Captured Africans*:

> [the] aim is not to reassure or console, but to haunt visitors with the unpleasant – uncanny – sensation of calling into consciousness that which has been previously – even happily – repressed.[48]

The repression of uncomfortable historical facts has been key to white British responses to slavery and colonialism, and Dalton-Johnson's 'haunting' of visitors to his memorial through the uncannily familiar names is a device he uses to counteract complacency about the historic responsibility of white Lancastrians for the trade that helped to make the city's wealth. As Dalton-Johnson explains, the memorial has different resonances for black people, himself included: 'I don't feel I have to do the sculpture in order to remember, because I won't forget'. He continues:

> So myself, and many other black people, do not necessarily need something physical in order to remember, because we live it every day, and the way that we're treated brings it all back, what our ancestors went through, even though it's not the same degree. Outside of the black perspective, inside the white community, it's very easy to forget, and I think there are many people that would like to forget; there's a combination, a mixture there, and for that reason I think this is very important, just to remember the atrocity that happened to the slave because that's got to be core.[49]

Thus the memorial is designed not simply to honour the memory of the slaves carried on the ships, but to engage with the complexities of that history, to name the perpetrators and highlight the centrality of slavery to the fiscal and cultural economy of the city as a means to move forward. As Paul Ricoeur says of such kinds of memory work, 'it is justice that turns memory into a project, and it is this same project of justice that gives the form of the future and of the imperative to the duty of memory.'[50] Memorials at their most effective speak to their future contexts as much as to the past they commemorate, to a future-orientated responsibility, rather than a guilt-charged retrieval of a static past.

Ricoeur's statement is particularly pertinent in the wake of the nearby Morecambe Bay tragedy of February 2004, where 23 ethnic Chinese cockle pickers died due to Victorian working conditions and a bonded labour regime that must to them have seemed akin to slavery.[51] Hence, the memorial now has local contemporary resonances and can speak to modern forms of bonded labour too, showing how the local community in Lancaster has to respond not only to the human rights struggles of the past but also to the corrupt practices of global capitalism that continue to throw up bodies on our beaches over 200 years after the end of Lancaster's involvement in the slave trade.

Notes

1. Quoted in H. Kean, 'Personal and public histories: issues in the presentation of the past', in B. Graham and P. Howard (eds), *The Ashgate Research Companion to Heritage and Identity* (Aldershot: Ashgate, 2008), pp. 55–69 (62).
2. P. Gilroy, *After Empire: Melancholia or Convivial Culture?* (London: Routledge 2004), p. 98.

3. I discuss in detail in Chapter 3 the way Lancaster used the 2007 bicentenary commemorations to inaugurate new exhibits. These temporary installations have now been removed and the Maritime Museum now has a small and much improved permanent display about Lancaster's involvement in the slave trade.

4. As Melinda Elder states, 'Lancastrians over the years gained a something of a reputation for operating outside the accepted practices of the trade.' M. Elder, *Lancaster and the African Slave Trade* (Lancaster: Lancaster City Museums, 1994), p. 15.

5. M. Elder, *The Slave Trade and the Economic Development of 18th Century Lancaster* (Keele: Ryburn Press 1992). Elder's subsequent research has been communicated to me and my students in slave site tours of Lancaster, which I have organised with her on a regular basis, and has been confirmed by curators at the Maritime Museum in Lancaster. It awaits a fully referenced article or the commissioning of a new edition of what is the most comprehensive book on the Lancaster slave trade.

6. Young, *At Memory's Edge*, p. 73.

7. Quoted in Whitehead, *Memory*, p. 13.

8. C. A. Reinhardt, *Claims to Memory: Beyond Slavery and Emancipation in the French Caribbean* (Oxford: Berghahn Books, 2008), p. 15.

9. J. T., 'Samboo's Grave', *Lonsdale Magazine and Kendal Repository* III, xxix, 31 May 1822, pp. 188–192 (190).

10. Elder, *The Slave Trade*, p. 144.

11. Quoted in J. T., 'Samboo's Grave', pp. 191–192.

12. P. Ricoeur, *Memory, History, Forgetting*, trans. K. Bramley and D. Pellauer (Chicago: University of Chicago Press, 2004), p. 366.

13. Nora, 'Between memory and history', p. 289.

14. Quoted in Ricoeur, *Memory, History and Forgetting*, p. 367.

15. Kean, 'Personal and public histories', p. 58.

16. A. A. Bell, 'Sambo's Song' (Fleetwood: Tamlyn Music, 1973).

17. Correspondence with A. A. Bell, 13 June 2008.

18. D. Smartt, *Ship-Shape* (Leeds: Peepal Tree Press, 2008), p. 29.

19. Smartt, *Ship-Shape*, pp. 29–30.

20. R. Price, 'Monuments and silent screamings: a view from Martinique', in G. Oostinde (ed.), *Facing Up: Perspectives on the Commemoration of Slavery from Africa, the Americas and Europe* (Kingston, Jamaica: Ian Randle, 2001), pp. 58–62 (61)

21. D. Smartt, *Lancaster Keys* (Lancaster: Slave Trade Arts Memorial Project, 2003), n.p.

22. Smartt, *Lancaster Keys*, n.p.

23. Smartt, *Lancaster Keys*, n.p.

24. SuAndi, 'Untitled Poem', 2006, unpublished ms.

25. H. Spillers, 'Mama's Baby, Papa's Maybe: an American grammar', in A. Mitchell (ed.), *Within the Circle: An Anthology of African American Literary Criticism from the Harlem Renaissance to the Present* (Durham, NC: Duke University Press, 1994), pp. 454–481 (466).

26. A. L. Nielsen, *Writing Between the Lines: Race and Intertextuality* (Athens, GA: University of Georgia Press, 1994), p. 104.

27. L. Sansone, 'Remembering slavery from nearby: heritage, Brazilian style,' in G. Oostinde (ed.), *Facing Up: Perspectives on the Commemoration of Slavery from*

Africa, the Americas and Europe (Kingston, Jamaica: Ian Randle, 2001), pp. 83–89 (89).

28. Himid, 'Monument talk'.

29. B. Hesse, *Unsettled Multiculturalisms: Diasporas, Entanglements, Transruptions* (Zed Books: London, 2000), p. 18.

30. Gilroy, *After Empire*, p. 109.

31. L. J. Frazier, 'Subverted memories: countermourning as political action in Chile', in M. Bal, J. Crewe and L. Spitzer (eds), *Acts of Memory: Cultural Recall in the Present* (Hanover: Dartmouth College Press, 1998), pp. 105–119 (115).

32. J. Winter, *Remembering War: The Great War Between History and Memory in the Twentieth Century* (New Haven, CT: Yale University Press, 2006), p. 136.

33. Ricoeur, *Memory, History, Forgetting*, p. 397.

34. Gilroy, *After Empire*, p. 108.

35. The involvement of schoolchildren was vital to the legacy of the project, and in the aftermath of the unveiling of the memorial, the organisation Global Link together with the Friends of the Lancaster Maritime Museum commissioned the artist Sue Flowers and the historian Melinda Elder to work with children from Dallas Road Primary School to devise a thoroughly researched Lancaster Slave Trade Town Trail, which is available for tourists and residents for walking tours of the city. It can be downloaded at http://www.globallink.org.uk/slavery/. On the site there is also a radio programme made by children at Bowerham Primary School about slavery and inequality: http://www.globallink.org.uk/r4c/bowerham_cp_school/index.htm

36. Himid, 'Monument talk'.

37. The monument was eventually placed above Damside slipway at the opposite end of the quay from the Custom House, due to plans for new flood defences that would have complicated its erection on the original site.

38. J. Mackie, 'Why be slaves to our past?', letter to *Lancaster Guardian*, 7 January 2005, p. 6.

39. P. Collins, 'Lancaster faces up to its shameful past', *Lancaster Guardian*, 28 October 2005, p. 2.

40. Councillor I. Barker, 'Slavery is part of what we are', letter to *Lancaster Guardian*, 14 January 2005, p. 6.

41. Rice, 'Exploring inside the invisible', p. 24.

42. Images of the sculpture and an explanation of the STAMP project can be found at http://www.uclan.ac.uk/abolition [accessed 27 July 2009].

43. A. Rice, interview with Kevin Dalton-Johnson, August 2005 and February 2006, available at http://www.uclan.ac.uk/abolition [accessed 27 July 2009].

44. The public space where the memorial has been placed is on a main thoroughfare into the town right on the quayside. The committee and the artist felt it important that the memorial be close to the water that enabled the trade, rather than in the town centre where it would have been dwarfed by buildings and, in part at least, decontextualised.

45. Quoted in Collins, 'Lancaster faces up', p. 2. Later in 2007, the city's museums used the impetus from the STAMP project to commission new installations; see Chapter 3.

46. Rice, interview with Kevin Dalton-Johnson.

47. Rice, interview with Kevin Dalton-Johnson.

48. J. E. Young, 'Daniel Libeskind's Jewish Museum in Berlin: the uncanny arts of memorial architecture', in B. Zelizer (ed.), *Visual Culture and the Holocaust* (Athlone: London, 2001), pp. 179–197 (194).
49. Rice, interview with Kevin Dalton-Johnson.
50. Ricoeur, *Memory, History, Forgetting*, p. 88.
51. Nick Broomfield's film *Ghost* (London: Beyond Films, 2006) brilliantly highlights these aspects of the tragedy.

3

Revealing Histories, Dialogising Collections and Promoting Guerrilla Memorialisation: Museums and Galleries in North-West England Commemorating the Abolition of the Slave Trade

The British cultural memory of slavery is … not an innocent thing, and the 1807 abolition moment must in part be remembered as a device cleverly constructed to police a particularly ghastly part of national memory. We must consequently look at everything that is put on display around this bicentenary with open, curious and even suspicious eyes.'
Marcus Wood[1]

As John Oldfield relates in his excellent book *Chords of Freedom: Commemoration, Ritual and British Transatlantic Slavery*, the commemorations of the centenary of the abolition of the British slave trade in 1907 'passed with barely a murmur',[2] as government and its agencies as well as extant anti-slavery groups such as the British and Foreign Anti-Slavery Society (BFASS) virtually ignored the marker date of March 25. At the height of Britain's imperial power, there seemed little incentive to mark a date that celebrated a landmark social reform which, in the conception of many influential commentators, impacted on few current British citizens. What a difference in the multicultural Britain of 2007 where, as James Walvin – reviewing Oldfield's book and detailing a host of local and national initiatives – comments: 'even for those working in the field and involved in some of these activities, the volume and ubiquity of the commemorations have been staggering.'[3] Of course, the commemorations have not been unproblematic, with many questioning the almost universal veneration of the parliamentary white man's role, while black British contributions have often been marginalised. This vision of white philanthropy and black subservience was highlighted in the film *Amazing Grace* (2007), where black contributions to abolition are sidelined and an opportunity to tell a more nuanced narrative of inter-racial radicalism is spurned.[4] Moreover, the commemoration of the passing of the Act of Abolition, whether in 1907 or 2007, should never be seen as wiping the stain clean, for as Marcus Wood says:

> this act could not and never can ... wash the traumatic inheritance of slavery from our collective national memory. A national moral failing of such incalculable proportions cannot disappear with the passing of an act, and so it will continue to burrow away into the cultural fat of our collective repression, and to reappear in various metamorphosed forms, some attractive, some terribly ugly.[5]

As it burrows away, this moral failing and the memory of slavery that accompanies it becomes responsible for traumatic hangovers that are with us to this day, and which the best of the memorial exhibitions sought to ameliorate.

One of the few publications to mark the anniversary in 1907 was the *Manchester Guardian*, which in an editorial on the legacy of Wilberforce named him as the 'apostle and evangelist of abolition'.[6] In 2007, and indeed in the run up to the commemorations during 2006, print and broadcast media (with the contemporary *Guardian* and the BBC taking a leading role) served up a bumper crop of articles, dramas and documentaries about the anniversary, debates about reparations and links to the struggle against contemporary forms of slavery, which still affect millions of people in cocoa plantations, domestic service, the sex trade and textile manufacture in all corners of the world. Notably, contemporary campaign groups such as Anti-Slavery International have been able to proselytise in a favourable context, as the subject is at the forefront of the UK public's consciousness. People-trafficking was highlighted most effectively in an advertising campaign which riffed on the famous image of the slave ship *Brookes*. The 1789 image of a Liverpool slaver with serried ranks of enslaved Africans packed into the hold of the ship was brilliantly juxtaposed onto a diagrammatic image of a modern passenger jet, showing how the exploitation of human labour for profit continues into the twenty-first century. If nothing else, the commemorations of 2007 thankfully did not allow us to view slavery as a purely historical issue; its contemporary face has, thanks to campaigners for fair trade and against modern slavery, been very much pitched to the foreground.

The opening of the Museum of International Slavery in Liverpool and the exhibition 'The British Slave Trade: Abolition, Parliament and People' at Westminster Hall, London inevitably garnered much of the national and international attention in the bicentenary year. Other events, such as the excellent exhibition 'Equiano: An Exhibition of an Extraordinary Life' at Birmingham Museum and Art Gallery, the remodelling of the slave exhibitions in Hull at the Wilberforce Museum, the new 'Atlantic Worlds' gallery in Greenwich at the National Maritime Museum, and the exhibition 'Breaking the Chains' at the Empire and Commonwealth Museum in Bristol attracted quite substantial interest, which of course is in part related to their generous funding. This attention reached its zenith when the new slavery exhibitions at Bristol and Liverpool were shortlisted for the Art Fund prize for museums in early 2008. However, there was also much activity in a range of sometimes surprising locations that did not have the funding available to the showpiece venues. I want to concentrate on exhibitions in Manchester and Lancaster that ultimately enabled these cities to make valuable contributions to the commemorations of the bicentenary.

In this chapter I want to use my experience of curating and advising during the commemoration year to discuss the way memorialisation was undertaken away from London and the most significant slave ports, Liverpool and Bristol. In doing this I want to use Tony Bennett's astute observations on developments in museology. Describing the importance of using Bakhtin's theoretical legacy to discuss new radical forms of curating, he discusses how

> the perspective of dialogism stresses the need to dismantle the position of a controlling centre of and for discourse, paying attention instead to the multi-accentuality of meaning that arises out of the dialogic to-and-fro, the discursive give-and-take, that characterises processes of cultural exchange.[7]

Such radical museological praxis was central to the exhibitions with which I was involved in Manchester and Lancaster, which used dialogism to make dynamic exhibits during 2007. These exhibitions promoted new perspectives and engaged with audiences in innovative ways by foregrounding permanent collections as jumping-off points for the juxtaposition of artworks that investigated the legacies of transatlantic slavery. This was in marked contrast to most other 2007 exhibits, which attempted a comprehensive and often essentially curatorially conservative historical overview. As one of four guest curators at the exhibition 'Trade and Empire: Remembering Slavery' at the Whitworth Art Gallery, Manchester, and as an advisor to Lancashire Museums' 'Abolished' project, my comments come from an insider's position, but I hope that this increases rather than diminishes their worth.

At the Whitworth Gallery, the different perspectives of the co-curators (Kevin Dalton-Johnson, Emma Poulter, Alan Rice and SuAndi) meant that the exhibit eschewed a univocal approach in order to tell a tale of the local and the global and their interaction; of the wealth created for Manchester and its savage consequences for enslaved Africans. Malachy Postlethwayt in 1746 contended that 'the Negro Trade and the natural consequences from it may be justly esteemed an inexhaustible fund of Wealth and Naval Power to this Nation,'[8] and this wealth continued beyond the abolition of the trade in 1807 as Manchester, along with other cities of the empire, established its riches at least in part on the basis of slave-produced goods.

The commemorations in 2007 gave the Whitworth's co-curators the opportunity to tell the historical story of Manchester's involvement in slavery and abolition in a new spirit of openness and scholarly vigour. Our brief as guest curators (for all of us it was our first major curating commission) was to scour the lists of objects researched by the Whitworth curators to find ones that could reveal narratives that would tell the complex story of trade and empire and help us fully to remember the slave past.

Selection for such a chronologically and geographically wide-ranging exhibition was difficult, a trial and error process that led to some interesting objects being jettisoned. It is important here to discuss these judgements, because important objects left out of the exhibition, mainly because of space or aesthetic taste, meant that certain narratives remained in the storeroom.

For example, Richard Cosway's engraving *Mr and Mrs Cosway* (1784), a wonderfully decadent Italianate garden scene with an ornately dressed black servant, would have enabled us to tell the amazing story of that servant, John Stuart, otherwise known as Quobna Ottobah Cugoano. Having been kept as a slave in Grenada, he eventually came to London where he served the court painter Richard Cosway, whose depiction of him here indicates the exotic nature of the luxury and wealth that flowed into Britain from the system of chattel slavery. The conspicuous consumption that enabled the employing (or owning) of a black servant and the dressing of him in finery is a familiar trope, and one that has often been commented upon by academics and displayed by curators in recent exhibitions of black presence. Probably it was the familiarity of the image that meant that none of the curators were inclined to use it; the depiction is almost too familiar and has, in the context of black representation, become commonplace. However, with the development of SuAndi's installation the *Door of No Return*, this image could have come into its own. Her installation, constructed under the staircase of the gallery, consisted of a door into a small dungeon-like room where a video showed an African drummer playing a lament for those taken from Africa, with a poem spoken over it urging visitors to remember. After leaving the room, visitors were asked to take a rope and tie it outside along with others to remember an important person in their lives who had died. In mourning for our lost ones, we can remember those lost in the Atlantic too. This created a notably non-essentialist remembrance, in contrast to the worst excesses of the nationalist African American tours of the slave castles discussed in Chapter 1.

A survivor of the Middle Passage, Cugoano was much more than a manservant, being one of the most important London-based African opponents of the slave trade in the 1780s. In fact his autobiography, *Thoughts and Sentiments*, preceded Olaudah Equiano's more famous 1789 *Narrative* by two years, and contains one of the most graphic and verifiable African eyewitness accounts of the process of enslavement on the West African coast. A Fante born in around 1757 in the village of Ajumako, Cugoano was kidnapped aged around thirteen before being sold off from the coast. He was kept for three days in the dungeons at Cape Coast castle, a mercifully short stay in those hellish rooms. He describes how he

> heard the groans and cries of many and saw some of my fellow-captives. But when a vessel arrived to conduct us away to the ship, it was a most horrible scene; there was nothing to be heard but the rattling of chains, smacking of whips, and groans and cries of fellow men. Some would not stir from the ground, when they were lashed and beat in the most horrible manner. I have forgot the name of this horrible fort; but we were taken in the ship that came for us, to another that was ready to sail from Cape Coast.[9]

The historian William St Clair notes that Cosway's picture 'of splendid civilised living ... contains the only representation that is known of a person who passed through the dungeons of Cape Coast Castle'.[10] As such, it has tremendous historical value in documenting an individual African's journey from slave dungeon to manservant, a job he used as a stepping stone to a significant role in opposing the very trade that had transported him around two sides of the Atlantic triangle. The very image we rejected because of its seeming familiarity within the discourse of images of the African 'other' in fact contains a backstory that not only complicates our understanding of slavery, but also throws light into the darkest of sites of memory that inhabit the circum-Atlantic, the dungeons of the African coast slave forts. Juxtaposed with the Door of No Return, it becomes an important historical document of survival against all the odds of historical forgetting. To have had it facing the viewer as they passed from SuAndi's *The Door of No Return* would have told a story of survival and would have helped to establish Cugoana's presence despite the layers of amnesia about his past, and that of black Britons, that Cosway's depiction of him as servant in an aristocratic tableau promotes.

Another interesting object that none of the curators took up was an arresting portrait of an aristocratic black figure depicted as a sporting Renaissance man. Identified as le Chevalier de Saint Georges (c.1740–1799), he could have provided for the exhibition a positive image of black achievement against great odds. Maybe he was a little too exotic and continental to tell the particularised Manchester stories we wanted to tell. His real name was Joseph de Bologne, and he was an international composer, violinist and reputedly one of the best fencers in Europe. As discussed by Phillip Herbert in a recent biographical sketch, he was born in Guadeloupe, the son of the wealthy plantation owner George de Bologne and an African slave, Nanon. From 1753 he received a gentlemen's education in France at the Royal Academy of Arms, a prestigious fencing academy run by La Boëssière. His musical prowess was prodigious, and he became leader of the Concerts des Amateurs orchestra in 1769, but was prevented by racial discrimination from becoming a director of the Paris Opera in the late 1770s. He gave fencing exhibitions to the Prince of Wales, and between 1790 and 1793 was involved in the French Revolution as a member of the National Guard. Such a larger-than-life biography would have provided an interesting counterpoint to the performative life of Henry Box Brown, and would have enabled us to contextualise the wallhanging *Le Trait des Negres*[11] with an actual French/African/Caribbean man, born to a slave mother but becoming a gifted equestrian, musician and fencer, an aristocrat and latterly a revolutionary.[12]

I hope this description of two extremely interesting objects we declined to use in the exhibition exemplifies the wealth of materials that a gallery like the Whitworth possesses that could have potentially illustrated the nuances of the legacies of the slave trade in dynamic and informative displays. These sins of omission were dictated by constraints of space, but these images and their potentiality can also be reflected on. They show that sometimes what is left out is not marginal to the central narrative of the exhibition; rather its nuances are only latterly fully understood by hard-pressed and sometimes monocular curators. Only when these objects were sidelined did their nagging images work on my conscience. Their back-stories deserve to be told as much as those of the works we chose to exhibit. Our selection meant that some narratives were privileged, or perhaps canonised, thus blanking out other important objects. Sometimes what is left out or forgotten can be as illuminating as what is exhibited. Museums have a memorial function; however, the selection process itself should always be seen as a crucial and potentially restrictive aspect of it.

Some of the objects we chose for the exhibition were already quite familiar to regular visitors to the gallery. Watercolour views of St Kitts and Montserrat by Thomas Hearne (1744–76) were given a new focus by the show's determination to contextualise these seemingly innocent views by juxtaposing them with realities they occlude. These are two of eight surviving watercolours from a set of twenty commissioned by Sir Ralph Payne, Governor-General and Captain-General of the Leeward Islands. The impression that Hearne intended to convey for his patron in *View of St. Christopher's* was that the island was a well-defended, well-planned and stable British colony.[13] At the same time, the image effaced the inhuman misery of slavery that underpinned the economic and social system. This work, and *The Island of Montserrat*, were rather like contemporary company annual reports, celebrating economic success and power.[14] The seven windmills visible on estates around the island were for processing sugar cane. Sugar production had developed by the 1770s into a process that closely resembled the modern assembly line, so that such bucolic scenes only served to hide the realities of labour and daily life on the islands. Plantations throughout the Americas fed the European (and particularly British) desire for sugar. Such tropical commodities were crucial trade goods in the development of the modern world. As David Brion Davis notes:

> slave-grown commodities were the precursors to the endless number of products, many of them still produced by poverty-stricken, low-paid workers in the developing world, that we now purchase in the shopping malls of modern high-income societies, in the expectation that they will satisfy non-subsistence or psychological needs.[15]

These watercolours, then, were (and are) key pointers to the development of modern economies despite their depiction of a rural idyll. Not content with Hearne's romantic view of slave contentment in a benevolent British empire, we determined to give voice to a black witness to life on these two adjacent islands. The veracity of the African passages of Olaudah Equiano have come into dispute since the publication of Vincent Carretta's contentious *Slavery and Abolition* article;[16] however, there is no dispute about Equiano's sojourns in Montserrat and its neighbouring islands, firstly as a slave owned by the Quaker Robert King and subsequently as a free man. In the exhibition, his eyewitness accounts of the cruelty of conditions for the black slaves on the island are movingly read by a local actor. The level of everyday abuse throughout the Americas in the slave system makes a mockery of Hearne's bucolic scenes. Eyewitness accounts are sprinkled through the autobiography, attesting to the everyday nature of the abuse of slaves in the plantation economy. Equiano writes:

> While I was in Montserrat, I knew a negro man named Emanuel Sankey who endeavoured to escape from his miserable bondage, by concealing himself on board of a London ship: but fate did not favour the poor oppressed man; for being discovered when the vessel was under sail, he was delivered up again to his master. This Christian master immediately pinned the wretch down to the ground at each wrist and ankle, and then took some sticks of sealing-wax, and lighted them, and dropped it all over his back. There was another master who was noted for his cruelty, and I believe he had not a slave but what had been cut, and had pieces fairly taken out of the flesh: and after they had been punished thus, he used to take them get them into a long wooden box or case he had for that

purpose, in which he shut them up during pleasure. It was just about the height and breadth of a man and the poor wretches had no room when in the case to move.[17]

Equiano's testimony is supported by James Ramsey, who used his nineteen-year sojourn on St Kitts to produce his attack on the iniquities and cruelties of the plantation system, *An Essay on the Treatment and Conversion of African Slaves in the British Sugar Colonies* (1784). Resident on the sugar islands contemporaneously with the African who brought himself out of slavery there in 1766, Ramsey's account attests to a similar catalogue of horrors. He describes how he

> once saw an instance of a negro on suspicion of having stolen some poultry hung up about eight or ten feet from the ground, the weight of his body being supported by his hands tied behind his back with a rope passed over a beam. He was kept suspended in great agony for many hours, but no discovery was made.[18]

Equiano's fame has grown greatly over the last twenty years, culminating in his image adorning a Royal Mail stamp in 2007 to commemorate the bicentenary of abolition, and indeed his starring role in the Birmingham exhibition mentioned above. The portrait used on the stamp comes from the frontispiece of his book, published in 1789, which exemplifies the incredible journey he made from his status as chattel slave in Montserrat to a self-made literate gentleman in London. Much to the chagrin of his pro-slavery opponents, he married a white woman, Susan Cullen, and had two daughters. When he died in 1797 he left £950 to his surviving daughter Joanna in his will (Equiano was one of the very few Africans-descended Britons to write a will in the eighteenth century). Such a vast sum (around £80,000 in today's currency) shows Equiano as an extremely successful author and marketer of his work, enabling him to become 'the first successful professional writer of African descent in the English-speaking world'.[19] Showcasing a figure like Equiano enables us to tell a much more nuanced story than the Hearne watercolours alone could tell. He not only provides an insider commentary on the scenes they depict, showing their partiality and occlusion, but also illuminates the way that some slaves, despite the horrific oppression in the plantation colonies of the Americas, managed to escape and construct lives that exemplified their courage and resourcefulness in the face of seemingly overwhelming odds. It helps us to fully memorialise those whom the workings of the imperial cultural economy would have us forget.

Henry Box Brown's incredible escape from bondage in Virginia in 1849 was another courageous example of slave resilience that needed to be memorialised. After his family were sold to a man in North Carolina, Henry

Brown decided to flee to freedom. His method was to have himself posted in a box from the slave-controlled South to the relatively free North. Aided by a free black American, James Caesar Anthony Smith, he was posted from Richmond, Virginia to the city of Philadelphia. Marked 'This side up with care', the box (3ft long, 2.5ft deep and 2ft wide) was mailed to James Johnson at 131 Arch Street. On one part of the journey Brown's box 'was surrounded by a number of passengers; some of whom stood by and often sat on the box. All was quiet and if he had attempted to turn he would have been heard.'[20] Despite his sign the box was actually upended on two occasions. The 350-mile journey took 27 hours to complete. In Philadelphia the box was opened and the phlegmatic Brown declared, 'Good morning, gentlemen!' as if he had travelled as a passenger. The engraving of his resurrection from the box has become an iconic abolitionist image, and Brown himself was an overnight sensation, changing his name to Henry Box Brown to commemorate his unique method of escape. The irony of Brown choosing to incarcerate himself in a confined space (much like the cramped coffin-like conditions on the notorious slave ships, or indeed the boxed punishment described by Equiano above) to facilitate his emancipation gave his story particular resonances for our 'Trade and Empire' theme.

However, our display of materials about Brown was not only to allow us to make such needful if general connections, for Brown can be linked to Manchester and indeed the wider north of England through his visit as an abolitionist speaker and performer just after his escape, and later by his residence in the area. He arrived at Liverpool in 1850 in order to relay his story and help internationalise the cause, in common with other black abolitionists. He brought with him a remarkable diorama, *The Mirror of Slavery*, and toured throughout Britain with it. In the north-west of England he displayed it at many venues in Manchester, as well as in Darwen, Blackburn, Bolton, Preston, Atherton, Leigh, Carlisle and Leeds. The Leeds appearance, in May 1851, exemplified his showmanship, as he had himself posted from Bradford to Leeds; 'he was packed up in the box at Bradford' and forwarded to Leeds on the 6pm train. 'On arriving at the Wellington station, the box was placed in a coach and, preceded by a band of music and banners, representing the stars and stripes of America, paraded through the principal streets of the town… The procession was attended by an immense concourse of spectators.' James C. A. Smith, who had packaged Brown for his original escape, 'rode with the box and afterwards opened it at the musical hall'. In all, Brown was in the box for two-and-three-quarter hours, a mere bagatelle in comparison with the occasion of his amazing escape. The carnivalesque atmosphere of such events upset many of the more po-faced abolitionists, but was undoubtedly extremely important in publicising the abolitionist cause to the widest possible audience, the non-literate as well as the literate. Tickets for the show in Leeds cost from one to two shillings, and Brown's transmogrification from abolitionist orator to performing showman was sealed by his successful *coup de théâtre*.[21] Soon after this amazing performance, Brown broke with his collaborator Smith in an argument over money; their split was made public in the *Manchester Guardian* of 9 August 1851, where a joint advertisement advised that their partnership had been 'dissolved by mutual consent'.[22]

The re-enactment at Leeds is an example of a kinetic or guerrilla memorialisation that brought home to a population thousands of miles from the US plantation economy the horrors of a system that would force a man to risk death by suffocation in order to escape it. The box and Brown's escape symbolise more, however: in the box he was a commodified package, but on leaping from it and delivering his speech and diorama, he was transformed into a radical transatlantic figure transcending his degraded slave status and becoming a free agent able to influence the world around him.

In the exhibition we showed this through understatement, in a small display case with a rare sighting of the second edition of the narrative of his escape. For it was in Manchester that Brown made the contacts that enabled him to publish the second, definitive, edition of his book, *Narrative of the Life of Henry Box Brown* (Figure 10), which was published in 1851 by Thomas G. Lee, Minister of the New Windsor Chapel in Salford.[23] The successful publication of this work in Manchester attested to the widespread support for abolition in the city and the surrounding cotton towns. Brown, like many other abolitionist visitors, tapped into this nascent transatlantic radicalism. Over the next twenty years Brown flits in and out of view, but continued his career as a performer; his box and new diorama remained essential props as his range increased to include mesmerism and magic as well as abolitionist discourse. A recently uncovered playbill from Shrewsbury (Figure 11) attests to the multivarious nature of Brown's performance. In performances during December 1859 at the music hall in the town, Brown showed his 'Grand Moving Mirror of Africa and America! Followed by the Diorama of the Holy Land!' Central to the former was his escape in the box, which also provides the only major visual image on the bill. The playbill, held in the Shropshire archives, is a significant *lieu de mémoire* of Brown's life in Britain. It was uncovered too late to exhibit at the Whitworth Gallery, but it shows how there are still new discoveries to be made about pivotal figures in transatlantic abolitionism.[24]

One such discovery was displayed in public for the first time in this exhibition: intriguingly, new census evidence from 1871 (uncovered as recently as 2005) has Brown living at 87 Moreton Street, Cheetham, Manchester, with his Cornish wife Jane, two daughters and a son. He was by now doing well enough in his chosen profession of public lecturer to have a servant.

Jane had given birth to Agnes in Stockport in 1861, and Annie in 1870 in Manchester.[25] Later handbills to accompany his lectures in Worcester, Massachusetts in 1878 showed him still trading on the notoriety of his box and his marvellous feat of escapology, but now elevated to Professor H. B. Brown. He was director of a range of entertainments, including a 'Wonderful Sack Feat by Miss Annie Brown, such as was never before performed by any child' and 'The Wonderful Mysterious Second Sight Performance ... by Madame Brown'.[26] After 1878 Brown slips from view, but his radical transatlantic performativity was aptly celebrated in Manchester, which provided him with a new family life and with abolitionist and artistic career trajectories. Like Frederick Douglass before him, Brown found his trip to Britain a truly liberating sojourn[27] that changed not only his own life but helped to form a more radical consciousness in Britain, particularly in the north-west of England.

Manchester's radicalism had been a byword in British political life from the late eighteenth century, and it played a significant role in the fight against the slave trade. In December 1787 the city organised a petition of 10,000 signatures, the largest of the 1787–1788 campaign. It represented around 'two-thirds of the town's adult males'. As Seymour Drescher contends:

> Manchester's contribution was particularly valuable to the London Committee. It undercut the traditional morality/policy dualism in British culture that had discouraged or undermined earlier appeals against the Anglo-Atlantic slave system. Manchester was the epitome of a booming hard-nosed manufacturing town.[28]

The town also made a significant contribution to the successful campaign of 1806–1807, when in response to a pro-slavery petition of 430 signatures from Sir Robert Peel and other cotton manufacturers, around 2,400 anti-slavery signatures were gathered in very short order.[29] Many of the signatories to both these famous petitions owed their livelihood to slave-produced goods such as cotton, yet for some the moral case against slavery outshone their seeming economic interest. An 1843 pamphlet by an anonymous Mancunian shows how this perception continued into the campaign against slavery after the ending of the slave trade. Although the author's call for a boycott of slave-produced cotton did not sway the captains of industry in the city, he or she argued:

> If you buy stolen goods, you become a 'participator in the crime'... If we purchase American cotton, knowing that wretched system under which it is produced, we become aiders and abettors of the American slaveholder and participators with him in the criminality of the system of American Slavery.[30]

The American Civil War of 1861–1865 brought to a climax the paradox of Manchester's slave-produced wealth and its humanitarian radicalism, and this was foregrounded in the Whitworth exhibition by Emma Poulter's brilliant juxtaposition of J. M. W. Turner's English landscapes[31] (Figure 12) with a daguerreotype from Bolton Museum[32] of the black labour that ultimately enabled their purchase. The Turner landscapes, purchased by cotton merchants in the city and eventually donated to the Whitworth, illustrate the way cultural investments are often sullied by the origin of the wealth that purchased them. The McConnel and Broadhurst families, who donated the paintings, made some of their money on the backs of slaves through the cotton trade. Poulter makes this point by placing these pictures on the daguerreotype of African Americans picking cotton in the American South. The juxtaposition led to much debate amongst staff at the gallery, who would have preferred to see Turner displayed and glorified on plain white walls rather than dialogised in a polemical collage. However, Poulter's dialogisation is an exemplary juxtaposition that makes its point and does not allow the Turners to be canonised and abstracted away from the commodification that implicates them in Manchester's support of cotton-rich plantation economies. The trading system seeks to elide the origins of the money in slave labour, but here those origins are revealed and critiqued in an exemplary curatorial guerrilla memorialisation that helps to remake the narrative of Manchester and its involvement in the horrors of chattel slavery abroad and wage slavery at home.

There is of course more to the enslaved Africans and their emancipated yet still exploited descendents in the late nineteenth and early twentieth centuries than the sum of their labour, however, and we decided to show this through the wonderful blues songs which were created in the very regions of the American South that produced the cotton for Manchester. These songs, played next to the Turners in a tape loop, exemplify the triumph of the human spirit despite poverty and degradation. The paradoxical fatalism and radical naysaying of the blues is an apt response to the alienation caused by exploitative plantation and post-plantation labour regimes. These work songs make repetitive work more palatable, and protest the oppression of single-crop cultures and the debilitating economic systems they encourage. For instance, 'Boll Weevil' by Willie Williams highlights the degradation caused by the insect to cotton workers tied to the production of this single crop:

Boll weevil here, Boll weevil everywhere,
Boll weevil here, Boll weevil everywhere,
Looked in my meal barrel, and boll weevil,
He was there.

Boll weevil flew up, he took a circle 'round the moon,
Boll weevil flew up, he took a circle 'round the moon,
Said, 'Good-bye farmers, I'll see you another year.'[33]

In the exhibition, these blues songs were juxtaposed with contemporary versions of Manchester weavers' songs that spoke to the harsh conditions in the factories that made finished goods from the raw cotton. For instance, in the ballad 'What Shocking Hard Times', class war is adduced as the only solution to the worker's oppression:

The Cotton Lords of Lancashire, they think it is no more;
They say, bedad, the trade is bad, and they must have short time;
They eat their beef and mutton, aye and sport about on Monday,
But they do not care a button if you eat a brick on Sunday.[34]

These ballads are, of course, synthesised with African American forms, a significant contributor to the blues that developed in late nineteenth century black American culture. But our point was not just to make a transatlantic link based on musical form, but also to show how such dynamic musicking showcases the links between oppressed workers on these two continents: those living under wage slavery in Manchester and those under chattel slavery in the Americas (a link I will discuss using shanties as an example in Chapter 4). This radical musicking speaks to the truth of the transatlantic exploitation of labour and the fight against it, which was to reach its zenith during Lancashire's cotton famine of the early 1860s. An anonymous cotton spinner from Manchester makes this connection, and even claims that factory labour can be worse than slavery:

The negro slave in the West Indies, if he works under a scorching sun, has probably a little breeze of air sometimes to fan him: he has a space of ground and a time allowed to cultivate it. The English spinner slave has no enjoyment of the open atmosphere and breezes of heaven. Locked up in factories eight storeys high, he has no relaxation till the ponderous engine stops, and then he goes home to get refreshed for the next day; no time for sweet association with his family; they are all alike fatigued and exhausted.[35]

This polemical and arguably hyperbolic intervention speaks to the truth of the transatlantic exploitation of labour and the fight against it in this period. It is a testimony to the radicalism of a majority of Manchester's population that, despite the hardship caused by the blockade of cotton imports by Abraham Lincoln's government, many supported it wholeheartedly in order to defeat the Confederate South. In part at least, this story of transatlantic radicalism can be told through the music sung in the fields and factories thousands of miles apart.

In contradistinction to optimistic radical alliances between workers on different continents and in contrasting labour regimes, the exhibition also foregrounded more troubling narratives from the legacy of slavery. Nothing could be more mundane than Abraham Solomon's 1845 portrait of *Mrs Rosa Samuel and her Three Daughters*,[36] an everyday portrait of a Victorian family at ease with their place in the world. However, this family portrait belies the dark history of slavery that made the Samuel family's wealth. Rosa, the matriarch of the family, was born in 1809. She married her cousin Ralph Henry Samuel, a prominent member of the Jewish community in Liverpool, and a textile merchant who with his family also ran a successful cotton plantation in Rio de Janeiro, Brazil. The family made regular visits to their Brazilian plantation, unlike many plantation owners who were notorious absentee landowners and left their holdings entirely in the hands of often brutal overseers.

What makes their Brazilian connections so interesting is that they brought back with them four doll-like models, which were exhibited alongside the portrait.[37] These four brightly dressed models are fascinating 'mementoes' of the Samuel family's sojourns in Brazil (Figure 13). They offer unique insights into the dynamics of the slave–master relationship which have ramifications far beyond this one family's ideals and motivations. Made in the 1830s to mark Samuel's freeing of his slaves, they are brightly and ornately dressed in clothing that reflects their newly enfranchised status. We have no knowledge as to the motivation of Samuel in freeing his slaves long before emancipation in Brazil (1888); however, we can speculate that the legislation to free the slaves in the British Empire in 1833 gave him the impetus to emancipate those on his British-owned piece of soil in Latin America.

The figures themselves, although individualised and dressed imaginatively in their market-day best, are rather crudely modelled after caricatured images of Africans and could have been influenced by the nascent blackface minstrel depictions emerging in the circum-Atlantic world in the 1830s.[38] We can speculate that the models were played with by the daughters of the house, and reminded the whole family of their Brazilian holdings when they were back in Britain. One of the female figures carries a white baby, showing how closely involved in the family's life black slaves/servants were. Psychologically, they reveal the family's need for their African servants to be contained and confined in representations ordained by their master even after their actual emancipation. As such, these are memorial figures that have a reactionary effect, representing the family retaining control of their docile black servants. This reflects a continuing theme in black–white relations and representations: the infantilisation of Africans through slavery, imperialism and colonialism. As Jessica Adams succinctly adduces, such models of slaves, which were to become legion in the US as slavery was abolished, meant that 'slaves as animate property gave way to commodities as slaves'.[39] These objects bring with them many dilemmas for curators. Should we be preserving objects that potentially glorify a racist system that has ramifications for visitors today? As each model would take over £2000 to conserve, can such expense be justified for objects that are so tainted by their ownership and the troubled history of racial representation they exemplify? The curators wanted the exhibition to serve as a starting point for debate on these issues, but realised that the very unveiling of such troubling objects could prove problematic for many visitors.

Eventually, we used the very debate about the objects to enhance this section of the exhibition, adding labels that showed the discussion amongst the curators and comments from a critic of my interpretation of the objects. By doing this we hoped to show the open-endedness of the exhibition and the way that even our perceptions can be dialogised, both internally and externally, creating a debate rather than closing it by seemingly authoritative and all-encompassing interpretations. The public comment from a black British collector of such objects critiqued our politically charged conclusions about the models:

> It is my opinion they were made in the image of the slaves on the plantation who possibly cared for the children.
> There is no argument they are images of slaves, but I do not think the images are racist; on the contrary, I think they were made to remind the children of the servants they were closest to.
> These dolls are black with red lips but remind me of African dolls I have seen for sale in West African markets made with felt, wool and cotton cloth.
> Dolls made by Africans, in the image of the people around them, not intended to be racist.[40]

However, as can be seen by SuAndi's commentary below, some of the curators were even more radically disturbed by the images than I was. Her comments illustrate how the vigorous debate between curators during the show enabled our dialogism to have a fully public airing:

> If it had simply been a matter of choice without hesitation, I would have chosen to place these horrendous things back into the darkest corner of the collection cupboard. They do not resemble me or any other black person. Yet still I recognise that they are meant to be all of my people. Formed and shaped into raggedy dolls for the children of the plantation owner to drag behind them, much the same way as slaves were dragged into labour. To hide the past, to conceal those parts of it which displease, hurt

or offend is to collude with those who only want to speak of the past as a time of pride and glory. What civilised person is proud of how the British Empire was built? My fellow curator was right in his decision to include them. To trap them under glass like the very specimens they are. To have them stare out at the visitor with their beady dead eyes. They represent the silence of the slave.[41]

In this exhibition label, SuAndi undertakes a guerrilla memorialisation that uses the models to tell a story against themselves which highlights their collusion in the degradation of African peoples then and now. The display of the models is a necessary act of recuperation, but it is only through a thoroughgoing, communal and politically charged curating process that the multiple resonances of these objects were able to be brought out. SuAndi, who had wanted these models to remain in the collection cupboard, acknowledges the necessity of exhibiting them to narrate the most fully nuanced story of slavery possible. Exhibiting the horror here in British cities where the money was made is an essential aspect of any curatorial response to transatlantic slavery, as amnesia is far too much in the interests of reactionary forces that would prefer to downgrade Britain's involvement in such extreme exploitation abroad. The display of these models and the debates that ensued shows how guerrilla memorialisation should be a crucial aspect of any curating in the controversial subject of the transatlantic slave trade, whatever the cost in terms of controversy.

Also controversial in the exhibition were some of Godfried Donkor's images. I discuss in my final chapter his *Birth of Venus Triptych*, which offended the sensibilities of some visitors to the Whitworth Gallery with its pornographic depictions and negative associations. However, as I will show, it raised serious issues about commodification and about the crucial involvement of British cities in constructing the financial mechanisms for oppression on the other side of the Atlantic. Donkor's other collages in the exhibition are juxtaposed with prints by his eighteenth century hero William Hogarth, and they often have a similar satirical import to those of his precursor. For instance, in *Dessert* (2001) he juxtaposes the Prince Regent with a Caribbean servant woman who supplies him with tropical goods from the wealth-producing West Indies.[42] The voluptuous fruits are presented alongside her body, which the rapacious Regent desires to devour along with his dessert, as is indicated by his fork that he holds to his mouth like a phallic cigar. New and tropical pleasures came from the exploitation of Britain's colonies, and the famously self-indulgent Regent will satisfy all his appetites. Donkor shows here how racial exploitation follows directly on from imperial expansion. I juxtaposed this interior scene with the print *Toilette Scene (The Countess's Levée)* from Hogarth's series *Marriage à la Mode*, where the very inclusion of two black servants signifies wealth derived from colonial commerce, emphasised by the black character proffering tropically produced chocolate to the lady guest.[43]

Hogarth's use of black characters reflected a growing black population during his lifetime, especially in London, and as servants to the aristocracy throughout the country, so that by the end of the century there were several thousand black people in Britain. This black presence has often been omitted in popular British historical accounts, which have traditionally dated the arrival of a significant black population to the Windrush generation that settled after the Second World War. Donkor is fascinated by this earlier presence and uses collage techniques to insert an African presence where it has been elided, and foreground it where it has been sidelined. Examples include the Caribbean stick fighters in *London Mob* (2001) and the homage to the early black prize fighter in *Tom Molineux* and *Tom Cribb* (2001). In the exhibition, our juxtaposition of Donkor's work with that of his hero Hogarth shows how Donkor also strategically inserts black figures that pose questions regarding national identity and multicultural lifestyles of relevance to both Hogarth's time and his own. His collages work as memorials of an often-elided black presence. As Donkor, in talking about the resonances of his work, says:

> What I was interested in was mirroring with London's present, so what I was thinking about when I was making this piece was a typical rave or club now, how that would look as opposed to how it would look in the eighteenth century, so I was playing with those ideas.[44]

The dialogisation so apparent in Donkor's re-workings of late eighteenth and early nineteenth century iconic images worked alongside the curators' desire to make a show that opened up past images for creative reworking, either in the curatorial or the artistic process. The aim was to create an exhibition that challenged narrow ideas about Britishness by showing the longevity of an African presence in Britain.

Linking Britain to its ex-slave colonies in the Americas and to African roots and routes from there was a concern of much of the work in the exhibition. Althea McNish embodies this in her ancestry, life and praxis. A painter from early in her Trinidad childhood, McNish came to London as a student and made a career in textile and wallpaper design in the late 1950s. Bringing tropical colour to Britain, she became the country's only black textile designer of international repute. As a member of the Caribbean Artists Movement (CAM) she took part in its seminars and exhibitions, and organised CAM work for the BBC magazine programme *Full House* in February 1973, which proclaimed to the British public the importance of the Caribbean arts. McNish's career as a rare black and female presence helped develop recognition of multicultural issues in the hitherto conservative design world. As John Weiss argues, her use of cultural resources in London allied to her Caribbean background led to her unique hybrid style:

> It is noteworthy that Althea McNish and her fellow textile design students at the Royal College of Art carried on much of their studies inside the V&A Museum. The imperial collection of cultural resources had long been regarded as natural sustenance for the textile designer, and this respect for and reliance on exotic sources of imagery has its parallel in Trinidadian culture.[45]

Thus she uses imperial resources for new purposes. McNish's ancestry and life reflect the triangulation of the African diaspora. Her paternal ancestor came from Senegambia in the eighteenth century, before being enslaved in Georgia, fighting for the British in the war of 1812 and then settling in Trinidad in 1816. In recognition of this, her textiles were displayed in a triangular form speaking to Africa, the Americas and Europe. The rich tropical colours of the three textiles exhibited form a contrast with much British design of the time. All have a musical quality akin to the improvisation of African music and its stepchild, jazz. This, and the painterly technique, make for a unique Caribbean contribution to the world, bringing a legacy from the designer's homeland that colours Britain in a new vein. Nowhere is this more apparent than in the marvellously tropicalised 'Golden Harvest' (1959) (Figure 14), which was the result of a weekend spent in the countryside in 1957. Excited by the colour of the Essex cornfields glowing in the British sunlight, McNish developed drawings and watercolour sketches into a repeating design using both black monoprint and textured colour. As she says, 'My early exposure to the Caribbean environment led me to transform the tiny flowers of the British hedgerow into tropical exuberance.'[46] Taken alongside her other wonderful designs, this should warn us against a reductive view of black Atlantic arts that wants to make it either merely a critique of imperial legacy or consequence of it. McNish's exuberant textiles transmit their own powerful message about the limitations of such narrow views, showing that the legacies of trade and empire are both complicated and at times breathtaking in their simplicity.

Similarly, Sue Flowers's installation *One Tenth*, produced for the Lancashire Museum Service's Lancaster-based project 'Abolished?', talks to these complicated legacies and is in creative dialogue with that city's history.[47] In the city that was the fourth largest British slave port in the eighteenth century, Flowers' work is crucially involved in dialogising an extant museum collection, replete with the evidence of the 'crime'. Indeed, it comments acerbically on the building in which it is housed in: an oil portrait of Dodshon Foster (1730–1792) had always been centrally displayed in the old Custom House, now the Maritime Museum. Flowers, though, wanted to highlight not this figure's bourgeois respectability as a Lancaster merchant whose house and warehouse adjoined the building, but his criminal involvement in the slave trade. Her installation dialogises the portrait (which is retained in its usual place in the room) with a bright, evocative African flag which dramatically remakes the building's interior and, more specifically, by making images of Foster as a criminal and having them put behind bars in the windows (Figure 15). Flowers says:

> The installation attempts to subvert our daily understanding of Lancaster and its history. Here the wealthy merchant is transformed into a man of our times and becomes trapped into the very fabric of the building. Here one man is criminalised – reframed inside a building which represented his wealth and power. A new representation of the man is created in a new portrait and a series of images have become trapped behind the protective bars of the window frames.[48]

Flowers' installation also contains images of sugar and sugar cane to emphasise the goods that were exchanged for the slaves. At the centre of the room is a modelling of figures in a slave ship in the shape of sugar loaves (Figure 16). This reinterpretation of the infamous 1788 *Description of a Slave Ship* is linked directly to Foster's crime through an intentional numerical conceit, for the 55 loaves are representative of one tenth of the number of slaves taken on the voyages of his ship the *Barlborough* between 1752 and 1757. As Flowers comments:

> The whole of this work acts as a memorial to One Tenth of the enslaved Africans on the merchant ship the *Barlborough* and forms an epitaph to those who exploited them and the many more millions exploited internationally in the past and the present.[49]

The enslaved Africans are shown to be commodified by a slave trade that sees them as goods to be exchanged. The way in which enslaved Africans were made abstract by the Middle Passage is shown at its most extreme in the 550 numbered sugar cubes that overflow in another section of the installation (Figure 17). Here, the black numbers on the white cubes are dramatic, clean-cut evocations of the economics that denies humanity at the centre of the slave trade. Flowers, though, goes further, modelling Foster's head in fibreglass that resembles sugar, dramatising the way his criminal pursuit of wealth has dehumanised him, turned him into the very commodity he selfishly pursued. As Flowers says, 'the work acts as a memorial for the dead as much as an indictment of the criminal'[50] and this is its strength as a site-specific work of art that speaks to the ghosts of Lancaster's slave past in the very building where much of that trade was recorded. It is a supremely effective guerrilla memorialisation that dramatically intervenes in the narrative of the city and attempts to rewrite the story from the inside, right from the belly of the beast, in the Custom House which was built to feed the insatiable desire in Lancaster and its hinterland for slave-produced goods and the profits they engendered.

Lubaina Himid contributed another dynamic strand of the 'Abolished?' project with her installation *Swallow Hard: The Lancaster Dinner Service* (Figure 18).[51] It consisted of 100 patterned plates, jugs and tureens overpainted in acrylic paint with a variety of original designs. Himid's work is related to Judy Chicago's seminal installation *The Dinner Party* (1979), which had sought to portray the history of female endeavour in a sculpture made of 'china-painted ceramics and fine needlework symbolizing Western history through the lives of significant women'.[52] Himid's is a similar grand scheme, but with an altogether different and more satirical purpose. Her Lancaster dinner service is given added resonances by our knowledge that a common way to show conspicuous wealth in the homes of slave traders and plantation owners was through elaborate and expensive chinaware, as we saw in the Wye plantation discussed in Chapter 1. When, in 1824, the city of Liverpool wanted to thank its MP and plantation owner Sir John Gladstone for his services to the city's interests, including his support for the colonial authorities in their suppression of the 1823 Demerara rebellion, they presented him with a cash gift of £1400 and

> a dinner table service, plates excepted, of twenty eight pieces: two candelabra, two ice pails, two tureens ... to mark their high sense of his successful exertions for the promotion of trade and commerce and in acknowledgement of his most important services to the city of Liverpool.[53]

Himid's own dinner service is a guerrilla memorialisation in answer to establishment support for those labelled 'distinguished citizens'. Himid described the installation thus:

> There are views of the city, plants that always grew here; there are maps, slave ship designs and texts from sales of these ships which took place in the pubs and hotels. I have painted pages from account books, elegant houses, patterns from Mali, from Nigeria, from Ghana and all along the West African coast; these patterns, like the paintings of buildings and vistas, boats and documents all, cut across or weave in and out of the original patterns found on the old ceramics.[54]

Like Flowers's installation, Himid's was a site-specific artwork, this time at the Judges' Lodging's Museum in the centre of the city. This building too is haunted by the spectre of transatlantic slavery, with its slave-harvested mahogany a testament to this legacy. In an earlier exhibition here of her drawings, entitled 'Swallow', Himid had instructed viewers:

> While you look at the patterns, remember the text:
>
> To be sold to the highest bidder at the Sun in Lancaster on Thursday 2nd of September next the brigantine, *Swallow*, burthen about 70t with all her materials as lately arrived from Africa and Barbados. She was built in the year 1751 is well found and of proper dimensions for the slave trade. For particulars apply to Messrs Satterthwaite and Inman in Lancaster. *Williams Liverpool Advertiser*, 27 August 1756.[55]

Here, *Swallow* refers to a ship fitted out for the slave trade. However, the titles of Himid's exhibitions are never monological. 'Swallow''s dialogisms include the idea that these images are hard to swallow (an idea which was explored further in the Lancaster dinner service) or that they might need to be swallowed whole. Lancaster has not been able to swallow its history whole, and Himid's interventions here are designed to uncover the many-layered places and 'learn to make a metaphor for its past hidden history'. They are designed to show how the 'elegance and bustle of the city is interwoven with the horror of the slave trade'.[56]

As an example of this interweaving, the entrance hall of the Judges' Lodgings is dominated by a series of George Romney's portraits of Lancaster's slave trading families. The most prominent of these was Abraham Rawlinson (1738–1803), who was MP for the city from 1780 to 1790 and represented diligently the slave-holding interest. His letterbook contains the following 1792 correspondence, which reminds us aptly of the way pro-slavery propaganda worked to portray anti-slavery activists as antediluvian:

> The people in England want to lower the prices of sugar and yet continue presenting petitions from all quarters to Parliament to procure the abolition of the slave trade, many have left off the use of sugar, for the propose of putting a stop to the slave trade, if the custom become prevalent of eating and using nothing that has been touched by slaves, we may soon expect to see people in the state of their first nature, naked in the field, feeding like Nebuchadnezzar upon grass, what wonders their philanthropy of Enthusiasm will produce is unknown.[57]

Rawlinson's comments indict the abolitionists for their boycotts of slave-produced goods and portrays them as indulging in ridiculous grandstanding. Himid's multiple images answer back to such propaganda with polemics of her own against those historically responsible for the slave trade. Himid's installation dialogises the portraits in the Judges' Lodgings and the enslaving practices and pro-slavery propaganda the sitters promoted, but it does more than merely reflect their crimes, building a multifaceted picture of the town in the eighteenth century and placing it amongst the furniture of the museum. As she eloquently describes it, the installation is 'an intervention, a mapping and an excavation. It is a fragile monument to an invisible engine working for nothing in an amazingly greedy machine'.[58] One half of the installation was placed on the Gillow-made mahogany dining table on the first floor of the museum. Richard Gillow had a part-share in ships used in the slave trade; however, his major role in Lancaster's growing enrichment was through his furniture business. This used West Indian woods to manufacture fashionable pieces for the slave trading bourgeoisie in Lancaster, throughout Britain and for plantation houses in the Caribbean and North America. By displaying her dinner service on his table, Himid traces these links and critiques the amnesia that has hitherto meant that the conspicuous wealth made through slavery has been elided in the city. As she says:

> This dinner service will sit as if it has always been there, on the tables, the mantelpieces, the sideboards and the window sills of the Judges' Lodgings, telling the story of lost languages, the intense activity of commerce, the creative energy of influential traders and the alien-looking structure of British wild flowers.[59]

The variety of designs, sometimes combining image and text, confront the viewer with a colourful assemblage of images of eighteenth century Lancaster and its links to the world. Dialogising the slave traders are cartoon images redolent of the work of the savage caricaturists Isaac Cruikshank (1764–1811) and James Gilray (1756–1815) that show slave merchants vomiting and are tagged, for example, 'SICKENED BY ABOLITION' (Figure 19). These speak to the petitions from Lancaster townsfolk supporting the slave trade which show the town's continuing support for the trade right up till 1807. Elsewhere, a large carving plate tagged with 'The clergy eating the profits from the Slave Trade' shows four obese men of the cloth with glasses raised and knives and forks at the ready to tuck into their meal, exemplifying the way many churchmen supported the slave trade. The painting of such images on beautifully patterned plates make their own commentary on the conspicuous consumption engaged in by slave merchants and threatened by the abolitionists. Alongside these are tureens and jugs where 'the faces of the unknown black slave servants ask to be remembered'.[60] Subtly, Himid has given these anonymous figures an African name which is revealed when, for example, a tureen lid is raised. These slaves/servants show us 'inside the houses of Lancaster ship owners such as Dodshon Foster, William Lindow and John Satterthwaite'. There she imagines 'the lives of the almost invisible slave servants these men owned, brought from the plantations to work in quiet isolation in this chilly place.'[61] The tureens in particular rescue these people from the shadows of history and place them (colourfully and named) at home amidst their masters' rich furnishing and portraiture. Himid's purpose is to dialogise not just the Judges' Lodgings but the whole history of the city. Her dinner service continues the work in Lancaster begun by the Slave Trade Arts Memorial Project, which raised a memorial to the victims of the slave trade in 2005 (see Chapter 2), but does so in a different spirit. As Himid describes:

> the intervention will … help to explain what makes Lancaster the complicated place it is. It is a city in which traders became abolitionists and in which Quakers owned slave ships. There are beautiful buildings designed by men involved in horrible deeds. Behind doors in attics and underground are the hidden histories of a few almost invisible African people who were owned by families engaged in a legitimate but immoral strategy to make a lot of money fast. This work is not a memorial but more an encouraging incentive for everyone committed to restoring the balance, revealing the truths and continuing the dialogues.[62]

Himid's final sentence here speaks to issues that many of the curators and artists who produced work for the 2007 commemorations have grappled with: the fact that creating memorials is not just about passively remembering, but about using the past to make a difference in the present. Such guerrilla memorialisation creates new objects for museums or dialogises their old objects in juxtapositions that project hitherto hidden histories and help to create new contemporary realities. One of the major successes of the year has been that in small hitherto marginalised collections, like the Whitworth and Lancashire Museums, the dialogues that have been inaugurated have led to some inspiring and politically astute exhibitions and installations that deserve as much critical commentary as those that garnered the national headlines. As Gustavo Buntnix and Ivan Karp so aptly say of similar radical interventions, 'the peculiar friction thus generated is that of a history in the making, and of a prospective memory archaeology'[63] that can move the debate about race and representation and the legacies of slavery and imperialism in new and challenging directions. Such guerrilla memoriali-sation helps to reshape the archaeology of memory so that quiescence and amnesia are no longer curatorial options.

Notes

1. M. Wood, 'Packaging liberty and marketing the gift of freedom: 1807 and the legacy of Clarkson's Chest', in S. Farrell, M. Unwin and J. Walvin (eds), *The British*

Slave Trade: Abolition, Parliament and People (Edinburgh: Edinburgh University Press), pp. 203–223 (205).

2. J. R. Oldfield, *'Chords of Freedom': Commemoration, Ritual and British Transatlantic Slavery* (Manchester: Manchester University Press, 2007), p. 91.

3. J. Walvin, 'Public History And Abolition: A Review of *"Chords of Freedom"'*, *Patterns of Prejudice* 41, 3–4 (2007), pp. 398–399 (398).

4. M. Apted, *Amazing Grace* (London: Momentum Pictures, 2007).

5. Wood, 'Packaging liberty', p. 205.

6. Oldfield, *'Chords of Freedom'*, p. 92.

7. T. Bennett, 'Exhibition, difference and the logic of culture', in I. Karp, C. A. Kratz, L. Szwarja and T. Ybarra-Frausto (eds), *Museum Frictions: Public Cultures/Global Transformations* (Durham, NC: University of North Carolina Press, 2006), pp. 46–69 (63).

8. M. Postlethwayt, 'The national and private advantages of the African trade considered' (1746), in K. Morgan (ed.), *The British Atlantic Slave Trade: Volume 2* (London: Pickering and Chatto, 2003), pp. 195–328 (202).

9. Q. Cugoano, 'Thoughts and sentiments on the evil and wicked traffic of slavery ...' (1787) in V. Caretta (ed.), *Unchained Voices* (Lexington, KY: University of Kentucky, 1996), pp. 145–184.

10. W. St Clair, *The Grand Slave Emporium: Cape Coast Castle and the British Slave Trade* (London: Profile Books, 2006) p. 247. It is probable but not certain that the black servant depicted is Cugoana.

11. This object from the revolutionary era showed the cross-channel fertilisation of abolitionist ideas, as it used British abolitionist iconography as a means of showing its owner's radical sympathies with enslaved Africans.

12. P. Herbert, 'Saint Georges, le Chevalier de', in D. Dabydeen, J. Gilmore and C. Jones (eds), *The Oxford Companion to Black British History* (Oxford: Oxford University Press, 2007), pp. 426–427.

13. T. Hearne, *View of St. Christopher's: The Salt Pond, part of St. Christopher's and Nevis from the Shore at Basseterre, 1775–76*, Whitworth Art Gallery, Manchester. David Morris, the curator of prints at the Whitworth, first developed many of the observations I expand on in this section.

14. T. Hearne, *The Island of Montserrat from the Road before the Town, 1775–76*, Whitworth Art Gallery, Manchester.

15. D. B. Davis, *Inhuman Bondage: The Rise and Fall of Slavery in the New World* (Oxford: Oxford University Press, 2006), p. 247.

16. V. Carretta, 'Olaudah Equiano or Gustavus Vassa? New light on an eighteenth century question of identity', *Slavery and Abolition* 20.3 (1999), pp. 96–105.

17. O. Equiano, 'The interesting narrative of the life of Olaudah Equiano, or Gustavus Vassa, the African, written by himself' (1789), in V. Carretta (ed.), *Unchained Voices* (Lexington, KY: University Press of Kentucky, 1996), pp. 185–318 (223–224).

18. J. Ramsey, 'Notebook', in J. Pinfold (ed.), *The Slave Trade Debate: Contemporary Writings For and Against* (Oxford: The Bodleian Library, 2007), pp. 97–172 (115).

19. V. Carretta, *Equiano, the African: Biography of a Self-Made Man* (Harmondsworth: Penguin, 2006), p. 366.

20. J. Ruggles, *The Unboxing of Henry Brown* (Richmond, VA: Library of Virginia, 2003), p. 33.

21. Ruggles, *The Unboxing of Henry Brown*, pp. 127–128. In October 2009 the Yorkshire-based black artist Simeon Barclay undertook a reconstruction of this event, having himself posted from Bradford to Leeds and ascending from his box in front of Leeds City Museum. In an ironic twist, local train companies refused to convey him for health and safety reasons.

22. Ruggles, *The Unboxing of Henry Brown*, p. 133.

23. H. B. Brown, *Narrative of the Life of Henry Box Brown* (1851), ed. Richard Newman (Oxford: Oxford University Press, 2002). The curators were able to borrow an original copy of the 1851 edition from the John Rylands library in Manchester (where until the search undertaken after our inquiry it had been labelled 'missing'). This enabled a display of this text in its hometown for the first time in living memory.

24. Entertainments bill, 'Henry Box Brown showing a mirror of Africa and America at the Music Hall', 12–17 December 1859; 665/4/367, Shropshire Archives (Fig. 11). I would like to record my thanks to my undergraduate student Shukar Bibi, who discovered it during her research for my 'Commemorating abolition' class in 2008.

25. K. Chater, 'From slavery to show business', *Ancestors*, December (2005), pp. 32–33. Kathy Chater's discovery of census evidence that proves the longevity of his stay in Britain and Manchester is only slowly filtering through to the wider academic community. Her article makes Brown's entry in the 2007 *Oxford Companion to Black British History* decidedly arcane.

26. Ruggles, *The Unboxing of Henry Brown*, p. 168.

27. A. Rice and M. Crawford, *Liberating Sojourn: Frederick Douglass and Transatlantic Reform* (Athens, GA: University of Georgia Press, 1999). More recently, Fionnghuala Sweeney's *Frederick Douglass and the Atlantic World* (Liverpool: Liverpool University Press, 2007) has brilliantly continued and expanded this work.

28. S. Drescher, 'Public opinion and Parliament in the abolition of the British slave trade', in S. Farrell, M. Unwin and J. Walvin (eds), *The British Slave Trade: Abolition, Parliament and People* (Edinburgh: Edinburgh University Press), pp. 42–65 (48).

29. Both petitions had pride of place in the exhibition at Westminster Hall. A full transcript can be viewed at 'Parliament and the British slave trade', <www.parliament.uk/slavetrade> [accessed 15 November 2007].

30. Quoted in M. Sherwood, *After Abolition: Britain and the Slave Trade Since 1807* (London: IB Tauris, 2007), p. 50.

31. J. M. W. Turner, *Upnor Castle, Kent*, 1832–1833; and *St Agatha's Abbey, Easby, Yorkshire, from the River Swale*, 1798–99, both in the Whitworth Gallery, Manchester.

32. Anon, *Cotton pickers in the American South, 1895*, Bolton Museum and Archives Service.

33. W. Williams, 'Boll Weevil', in *Deep River of Song: Virginia and the Piedmont Minstrelsy, Work Songs, and Blues (The Alan Lomax Collection)*, CD (Cambridge MS: Rounder Records, 2000).

34. R. Palmer, *A Touch of the Times: Songs of Social Change* (Harmondsworth: Penguin, 1974), p. 224.

35. Quoted in E. P. Thompson, *The Making of the English Working Class* (Harmondsworth: Penguin, 1963), p. 201.

36. A. Solomon, *Mrs Rosa Samuel and her Three Daughters*, 1845, pencil sketch, Whitworth Art Gallery, Manchester.

37. 'Four Models of Freed Slaves', 1834–36, Brazilian maker, mixed media, Whitworth Art Gallery, Manchester.

38. W. T. Lhamon's *Raising Cain: Blackface Performance from Jim Crow to Hip Hop* (Cambridge, MA: Harvard University Press, 1998) delineates Jim Crow beginning in the 1820s in New York, so that the beginning of minstrelsy and its spread throughout the circum-Atlantic is now being placed earlier than the late 1840s, when scholars had previously situated it.

39. J. Adams, *Wounds of Returning*, p. 10.

40. Anon, label accompanying Brazilian models, 'Trade and Empire: Remembering Slavery' (exhibition), April 2008, Whitworth Art Gallery, Manchester.

41. SuAndi, label accompanying Brazilian models, 'Trade and Empire: Remembering Slavery' (exhibition), April 2008, Whitworth Art Gallery, Manchester.

42. G. Donkor, *Dessert*, from *Vauxhall Pleasure Series*, collage, 2001, Whitworth Art Gallery, Manchester.

43. W. Hogarth, *Marriage à la Mode*, Plate 4: *The Countess's Levée*, 1745, Whitworth Art Gallery, Manchester.

44. A. Rice, interview with Godfried Donkor on 'Commemorating abolition' website at www.uclan.ac.uk/abolition [accessed 27 July 2009].

45. John Weiss, 'Notes on Althea McNish', private email correspondence, May 2007.

46. J. Weiss, 'Notes on Althea McNish'.

47. S. Flowers, *One Tenth*, installation as part of the 'Abolished?' exhibition, Lancaster City Museums, July–October 2007.

48. S. Flowers and L. Himid, *Abolished?* (exhibition catalogue; Lancaster: Lancashire Museums, 2007), n.p.

49. Flowers and Himid, *Abolished?*, n.p.

50. Flowers and Himid, *Abolished?*, n.p.

51. L. Himid, *Swallow Hard: The Lancaster Dinner Service*, installation as part of the 'Abolished?' exhibition, Lancaster City Museums, July–October 2007.

52. J. Chicago, *The Dinner Party* (exhibition leaflet; Edinburgh: no pub.), August 1984.

53. Sherwood, *After Abolition*, p. 4.

54. Flowers and Himid, *Abolished?*, n.p.

55. L. Himid, 'Swallow', Judges' Lodgings, Lancaster, July–October 2006.

56. L/ Himid, 'Gallery talk', Judges' Lodgings, Lancaster, 17 October 2006.

57. A. Rawlinson and J. Rawlinson, 'The Lancaster Slave Trade', *Letter Book*, April 1792, Lancaster Library.

58. Flowers and Himid, *Abolished?*, n.p.

59. Flowers and Himid, *Abolished?*, n.p.

60. Flowers and Himid, *Abolished?*, n.p.

61. Flowers and Himid, *Abolished?*, n.p.

62. Flowers and Himid, *Abolished?*, n.p.

63. G. Buntinx and I. Karp, 'Tactical museologies', in I. Karp et al. (eds), *Museum Frictions: Public Cultures/Global Transformations* (Durham, NC: Duke University Press, 2006), pp. 207–218 (215).

1. Godfried Donkor, *Jamestown Masquerade* (2005).
Reproduced by permission of the artist.

2. Aaron Anthony House at the Wye Plantation, Maryland. Author's photograph.

3. Lemn Sissay and Michael Visocchi, *The Gilt of Cain* (2007).
Author's photograph.

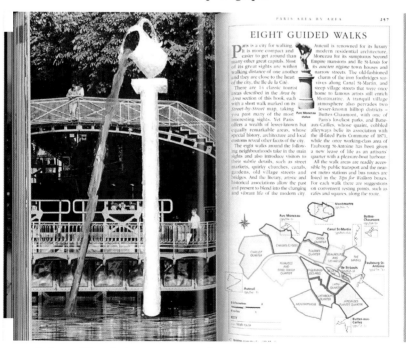

4. Lubaina Himid, *Paris Monument* from *What Are Monuments For? Possible
Landmarks on the Urban Map* (2009). Reproduced by permission of the artist.

5. Fabrice Hyber, *Le Cri, l'Écrit* (2007). Memorial in Luxembourg Gardens, Paris. Author's photograph.

6. Erwin De Vries, *Untitled* (2002). Memorial in Oosterpark, Amsterdam. Author's photograph.

7. Sambo's Grave,
Sunderland Point,
Lancashire.
Author's photograph.

8. Memorial at Sambo's Grave, Sunderland Point, Lancashire.
Author's photograph.

9. Kevin Dalton-Johnson, *Captured Africans* (2005).
The unveiling of the memorial at the quayside, Lancaster.
Photograph reproduced by permission of Paul Farina.

10. Manchester edition of
*Narrative of the Life
of Henry Box Brown* (1851).
Reproduced by permission
of the Whitworth Art Gallery,
Manchester.

11. Playbill for Henry Box
Brown's performance in
Shrewsbury (1859).
Reproduced by permission
of Shropshire Archives.

12. J. M. W. Turner, *Upnor Castle, Kent* (1832–1833), *St Agatha's Abbey, Easby, Yorkshire from the River Swale* (1798–1799) and anon., *Cotton pickers in the American South* (1895), hung by Emma Poulter at the exhibition 'Trade and Empire' (2007). Reproduced by permission of the Whitworth Art Gallery, Manchester.

13. Unknown artist, *Model of Black Servant, Brazil* (c.1830). Reproduced by permission of the Whitworth Art Gallery, Manchester.

14. Althea McNish, *Golden Harvest* (1959).
Reproduced by permission of the Whitworth Art Gallery, Manchester.

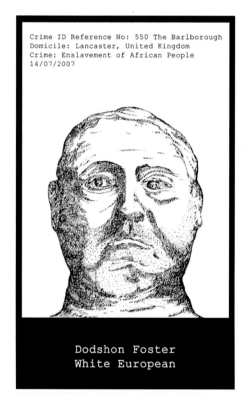

Crime ID Reference No: 550 The Barlborough
Domicile: Lancaster, United Kingdom
Crime: Enslavement of African People
14/07/2007

Dodshon Foster
White European

15. Sue Flowers, *Dodshon Foster as
a Criminal* (2007) from *One Tenth*.
Reproduced by permission
of the artist.

16. Sue Flowers, *One Tenth* (2007).
Reproduced by permission of Lancashire Museums Service.

17. Sue Flowers, *Sugar Cubes* (2007) from *One Tenth*.
Reproduced by permission of the artist.

18. Lubaina Himid, *Swallow Hard:*
The Lancaster Dinner Service.
Reproduced by permission of the artist.

19. Lubaina Himid, *The Vomiting Toff*
from *Swallow Hard:*
The Lancaster Dinner Service.
Reproduced by permission of the artist.

20. Lubaina Himid, *Cotton.com* (2002).
Reproduced by permission of the artist.

21. Statue of Abraham
Lincoln in Manchester.
Author's photograph.

22. *Memorial Gates*, Hyde
Park, London (2002).
Author's photograph.

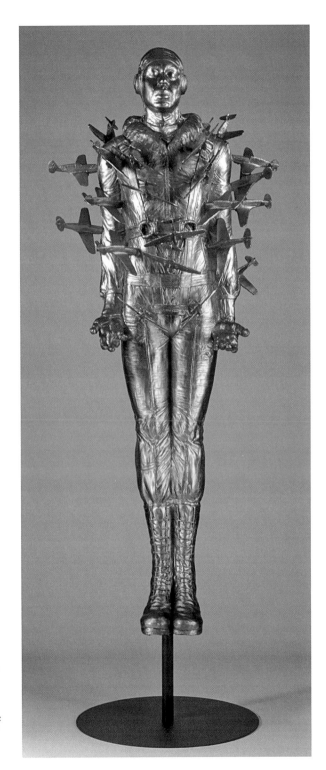

23. Michael Richards, *Tar Baby vs St Sebastian* (1999). Reproduced by permission of the Studio Museum of Harlem.

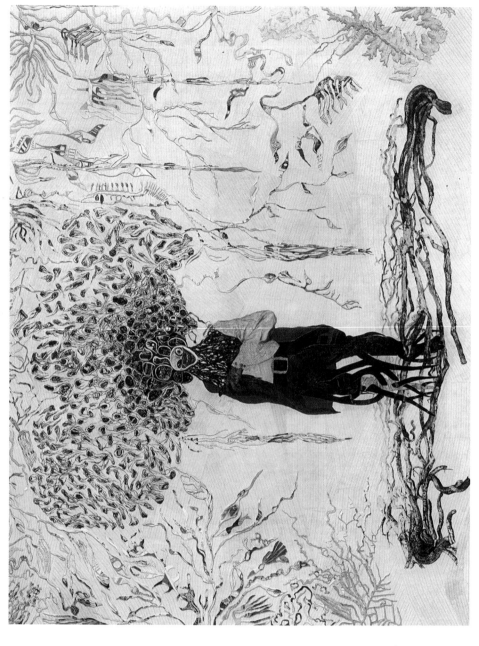

24. Ellen
Gallagher, *Bird
in Hand* (2006).
Reproduced by
permission of
Tate Galleries.

25. Godfried Donkor, *The Birth of Venus* (2005).
Reproduced by permission of the artist.

26. Lubaina
Himid, *Naming
the Money* (2004).
Reproduced by
permission of the
artist.

4

The Cotton that Connects, the Cloth that Binds: Memorialising Manchester's Civil War from Abe's Statue to Lubaina Himid's Cotton.com

We cannot truly tell ourselves a free story till we tell ourselves that we are truly the children of the Middle Passage. It is a story that brings to bear upon our daily lives the full indebtedness of our identities. When we return to the scene of our telling where whites once sought to seal the sign of ownership in African flesh we will find always before us the signs of African American artistry ineradicably embedded in the body of American thought. *Aldon Lynn Neilsen*[1]

Aldon Lynn Neilsen's wonderfully elliptical description of the depth of US culture's debt to African peoples in the context of the transatlantic slave trade is only lacking in its narrow insistence on the American hemisphere. For, in the wake of Paul Gilroy's[2] epochal turn to a thoroughgoing context of the black Atlantic, we should widen Nielsen's epigraph to insist on the term 'African Atlantic' preceding 'artistry' and on the notion of the 'transatlantic' when we discuss the intercultural in the context of slavery and its aftermath.

Neilsen's comment speaks to the interconnectedness of African diasporan and white communities throughout the circum-Atlantic, and it is this indebtedness that I would like to explore in this chapter, which will discuss the commodities that these different proletariat groups produced and the kinetic cultures that connected them around the circum-Atlantic in the eighteenth and nineteenth centuries and to this day. A wonderful artistic invocation of the sometimes serendipitous, but always highly charged nature of the inter-relatedness of people and products across far-flung geographies was imagined by the Brazilian artist and environmental activist Maria Thereza Alves in her installation *Seeds of Change: Bristol 2007*, created for the 'Port City' exhibition at the Arnolfini in Bristol. Here she used 'ballast flora', a category of plants that were 'the product of seeds which were brought to this country in the ballast of ships'[3] to dynamically comment on Bristol as a key player in the transatlantic slave trade. She engaged with local communities and used these 'ballast seeds' to germinate plants on small plots. She described the experiment as:

> an attempt to establish the histories of complexities of ballast flora and the potential of individual histories that these plants were witness to, previously isolated from their intimate connection to the economic and social history of Bristol.[4]

This 'ballast flora' traces links that foreground the history of slavery and colonialism and show Bristol's involvement in both. The installation at the Arnolfini included plants from Africa and the Americas that had been found as ballast seeds in Bristol's Avon riversides. The installation illustrates some of these plants and shows them as conjuring up the histories of colonised peoples, whose contributions to the wealth of Bristol have long been elided:

> The people of the Susu, Gola, Limba, Mende and Yalunka tribes were among those enslaved on Bance Island in Sierra Leone and taken by Bristol slave ships to Jamaica to be sold in order to replace the indigenous Arawaks... These ships would then continue onto the Carolinas to bring slaves to replace the indigenous workforce there, the Cherokees... Ballast taken from Jamaica ... or the Carolinas and therefore from anywhere along the East Coast, where Cherokees traded, could mix with seeds accidentally coming from any of the villages which were attacked by slavers in Sierra Leone. Among the villagers were the Sasu who were originally from Guinea ... The Limba are autochthonous to Sierra Leone. The Gola are from Liberia. The Mende were originally from the Sudan and were traders with neighbouring countries such as Liberia, Ivory Coast and Guinea. Seeds from any of these places could have arrived in Bristol and been unloaded in the ballast dumps at the Wapping Quay, which is now the site of the Industrial Museum.[5]

The work wonderfully evokes a trading globalisation that implicated Bristol (and more widely Britain) in the exploitation of peoples in Africa and the Americas. Taking Alves's methodology of tracing seeds and plants and showing the implications of their movement for peoples in the circum-Atlantic, this chapter will move northwards. Specifically, it will examine links to that key driver of the industrial revolution in north-west England, the commodity of cotton. Cotton, crucially involved in the slave trade as raw material produced by slave labour and trade good used by merchants to purchase slaves, was also used by Africans to display their cultural difference through dynamic colour and pattern, and by working class Europeans as everyday material. W. E. B. Du Bois described the dynamism of cotton in terms of race and class in the slave economy with a succinctness that resonates: it is 'a fibre that clothed the masses of a ragged world'.[6] This 'ragged world' is seen in all spheres of the circum-Atlantic, as can be illustrated by the voyage of the US slave ship *Horizon* to Mozambique under the captaincy of Alexander McClure in 1803–1804 (an illegal voyage, as the South Carolina legislature at the time banned foreign slave imports). McClure's voyage led to the deaths of nearly 300 of the 534 slaves on board, which was no doubt exacerbated by his inattention to their welfare as he collected plant and other samples on layovers on his voyage. However, as the *Charleston Courier* relates, these samples were much appreciated back home.

> Alexander McClure, Esq., who arrived a few days ago from the East-India in the ship *Horizon*, has not been inattentive during his absence, to the interests of his country: for during his stay at the Isle de France, Mozambique and at the Cape of Good Hope, he with great pains, collected a variety of seeds of useful plants which have not heretofore been introduced into this country. The most valuable of these we believe to be the seed of the Bourbon Cotton, which is in such request among English manufacturers, as to induce them to give nearly double the price for it that is given for the best Cotton raised in this State. We understand that Mr McClure intends to distribute this seed amongst some planters here and in Georgia, with a request that they will use their endeavours to cultivate it, and naturalise it to our climate.[7]

Cotton was vital for the development of slave-based economies, and the exploitation of new strains of the plant (following the development of the cotton gin in 1793) enabled the American South to become increasingly dominant in the marketplace. Cotton as tropical commodity here is shown as vital to a globalising of the economy that was to have ramifications for the development of Europe, Africa and the US. The north-west in particular was to come to rely increasingly on the availability of massive amounts of cotton to keep its economy running. In the crisis caused by the American Civil War that led directly to the cotton famine in Manchester and the other Lancashire mill towns, many workers' support for emancipation, despite the hardships it brought them, is a utopian theme explored in this chapter.

Cotton and its resonances will be explored through an investigation of the African-born, British-resident Lubaina Himid's work. In *Revenge* (1992), Himid developed a body of work that created an African diasporan take on the Middle Passage. Her work has always sought to put back together the dismembered bodies of African figures from the Western fine art tradition, and to show an African culture surviving the Middle Passage nightmare. Nowhere is this more evident than in her stunning refiguring of a transatlantic journeying in *Between the Two My Heart Is Balanced* (1991), which is currently on permanent display in Tate Britain. Elsewhere, I discuss the political ramifications of the painting's display in Tate Britain;[8] here, though, it is her use of cloth I want to foreground. Maud Sulter contends of this series:

> [the paintings] weave around the concept of fabric. The making of cloth, the creation of patterns, women's clothing and fabric, the existence of fabric as a form of black women's creativity. Lubaina has chosen fabric to be the ground, the arena for the battle with imperialism.[9]

It is the paradoxes of cotton which make it so valuable for Himid. In her later work *Cotton.com* (2002) (Figure 20), Himid crucially foregrounds the intersections of these various experiences with the commodity. Made especially for an exhibition concerning urban memory in Manchester, Himid chose to use the material responsible for the city's wealth as the prime source for her exhibit. The work itself consists of a hundred small black-and-white paintings, each decorated with a different design borrowed from textiles, ranging from small fish through leaves and fingerprints to abstract oval patterning. The paintings are displayed in a grid pattern stretching to the ceiling of the Cube Gallery, which itself is a redesigned old cotton mill; hence the work layers its narrative of the past on the very bricks that contained that past.

Cotton.com, like *Revenge*, deals with the warp and weft of cloth as it moves around the Atlantic triangle, crucially showing that the making of the cloth always involves the labour (forced and so-called 'free') of black and white men and women and children in the new and the old worlds. Cotton is the motor for economic progress, but at what cost to those who produce it and its products? In the paradoxical circular economy of the Atlantic, driving modernity forward in Manchester is achieved at the cost of the survival of the stagnant, often feudalistic slave system in the cotton fields of the American South. My point is not that the slave system was monolithically feudal or that modernity infused all aspects of the developing factory system; in fact, there are many similarities between them, as slavery at its most efficient (for example, in the use of a factory system for the production of sugar) had proved a template for the development of capitalist organisations of labour. Robin Blackburn compares the two forms of labouring, asserting that 'industrial discipline is similar to plantation discipline';[10] Himid's point (and mine here) is that similarities in labouring elided the difference between the slave and the factory labourer; that indeed, thrusting Old World modernity is built on the labour of both the slaves and Manchester workers.

As Karl Marx realised, cotton was vital to the economic wellbeing of Britain, and the American Civil War (1861–1865) threatened its continuing prosperity, bringing to light its dependence on wage slaves in Britain and chattel slaves in the Americas:

> The second pivot [on which English modern industry relied] was the slave-grown cotton of the United States. The present American Crisis forces them to enlarge their field of supply and emancipate cotton from slave-breeding and slave-consuming oligarchies. As long as the English cotton manufacturers depended on slave-grown cotton, it could be truthfully asserted that they rested on a twofold slavery, the indirect slavery of the white man in England and the direct slavery of the black men on the other side of the Atlantic.[11]

It is the similarities between these two exploited peoples and their reactions to their conditions that Himid explores in *Cotton.com*. Robin Blackburn makes the point that 'the pace of capitalist advance in Britain was decisively advanced by its success in creating a regime of extended private accumulation battening upon the super-exploitation of slaves in the Americas.'[12] Himid wanted to explore this phenomenon to highlight 'on whose back' such buildings as the giant cotton mills in Manchester had been built.[13] It is not only historical exploitation that Himid illustrates through her work. Its title, *Cotton.com*, highlights its interest in speaking to more modern forms of labour that, especially in contemporary developing countries, include child labour and 'super-exploitation'. Arlene R. Keizer makes this point well, showing that overplayed distinctions between slavery and wage labour have often elided essential similarities. She says:

> It is too easy to think of slavery or conditions similar to slavery as anomalies in the modern or postmodern world. If one accepts the idea that North American and Caribbean slavery was, in later stages, a capitalist socio-economic formation in many respects, it is then necessary to refigure the theories about subject formation under capitalism to include the effects of consistent physical abuse... Doing so will not only illuminate the past; it will also illuminate the present working conditions of many factory and prison workers in the developing and overdeveloped world.[14]

Himid's work is similarly multi-faceted, speaking to the making and trading of cotton historically and in its contemporary context. Both lead to the super-exploitation of a globalised proletariat. Himid represents the de-individualisation of such a proletariat by hanging the paintings in a grid-like system. What all of the paintings also share are repetitions of the core motifs in the mode of patterned cloth. These speak to the indexical patterning of communication across a range of forms, from ancient hieroglyphics to the constant chatter of texting and internet communication in the modern era. Hence, it reflects literally the (post)modernity of its title

– a web-analogous *Cotton.com* – but also shows how these modes had their earlier forms. Moreover, the repeated forms (indeed the stacked paintings themselves, with their repeated black-and-white designs) speak to slavery through their similarity to the stacked slave bodies on ships immortalised in *Description of a Slave Ship* (1789).[15] The frenzied rush of communication and the repeated patterns of cloth on the cotton are echoes of the black-and-white regimented order captured in that iconic description of the Liverpool ship *Brookes*. Yet like the *Description*, *Cotton.com* hints at the presence of slaves without immediately individualising them: abstracted and diagrammatised, Himid's work talks of presence, but simultaneously shows absence.

Such 'absent presence' works on two levels. Firstly, and obviously, the work speaks to the ghosts of Manchester's past, both the Mancunian factory workers and the enslaved wealth creators across the Atlantic. More interestingly, Himid's work also illustrates the way goods such as cotton elide the narrative of their creation in becoming a mere commodity form. As Stephen Best reminds us in discussing 'the paradox of the commodity form',

> its 'value in exchange', as Marx theorised, appears neither entirely material and within reach, nor entirely ideal and elusive, but fugacious (and a tantalisingly absent presence) in that 'we know it exists yet we don't know 'where to have it.'
> Or perhaps the problem is that it can be had anywhere.[16]

The labour, both slave and free, which has gone into the making of finished cloth is hidden beneath the individually painted patterns in floating signifiers that Himid wants to pin down so that the presences of the workers that made the cloth are not entirely absented, so that it cannot 'be had anywhere', or if it is, that its roots and routes are not elided.[17]

Himid teases out these presences and illuminates their paradoxes by her contextualising of the piece through its location and her addition of textual elements. In her initial conception, Himid wrote texts for each of the paintings. These texts were imagined communications between the cotton workers in Manchester and the plantation workers in the Carolinas. In the work in the Cube gallery, only one of these communications survives and faces the paintings. Its survival seems to speak to the erasure of the other 99 texts, exemplifying the way that the work of history destroys written and other evidence, but that some record of exploitation survives. Expressed by a slave, the remaining text reads: 'He said I looked like a painting by Murillo as I carried water for the hoe gang, just because I balanced the bucket on my head.'[18] Himid has commented recently that this text could be seen as an 'ironic take on how slaves were being looked at by those making records'.[19] I think Himid here, as well as making a point about the prosaic construction of slave identities through record-keeping, also has an aesthetic point to make. This elliptical statement explicates the way art has historically been complicit in exploitation like slavery by aestheticising it. The slave's labour is the occasion for a voyeuristic moment of recognition which places his/her balletic movements in an aesthetic frame that helps to remove it from its everyday, prosaic mode of labour. Of course this leisure is only for the voyeur, whose delight is at the expense of the labouring slave. However, Himid also makes the point of agency through these visual and verbal communications, disrupting everyday notions of silencing by showing the labourer's human responses to the mechanistic, repetitive and dehumanising labour shared by slaves and factory workers.

Such agency is illustrated by cotton workers on both sides of the Atlantic, who reconfigure their workplace, meant to be a space of discipline and punishment, as an arena for playful communication. For instance, in a factory in Kentucky, slaves did a little jig and 'at the same time walk(ed) backward and forward about their spinning, with great regularity, and in some measure keeping time with their steps'.[20] In a sense, this example and Himid's work reply to the rhetorical questioning of a slave's human potentiality by the writer A. J. Verdelle:

> What intellectual acrobat will you find stooped in the cotton fields with sore and bleeding hands and split and bleeding feet? How much mental energy greets those sore and swollen hands and feet? How can anyone's thoughts possibly leap? What lessons of pain or grace will the stooped fieldworker teach the young ones? How much hope burns in the abject? Who can healthily remain conscious, awake?[21]

The slaves do manage to retain individual and collective humanity through their cultural resources (field hollers and communal singing) and hard-earned family connections that survive despite the horrors of the cotton field and the factory. It is this survival and the slaves' conscious rebellion against their enslavement that Himid celebrates through the vibrancy of the patterned cloth communications. Thus although on the surface the work might seem to resemble such works as the *Description*, with individuals reduced to ciphers, Himid in fact shows how the invisibilised lives are not as controlled and alienated as they might at first seem. Hence, the work reflects their triumphant survival of such harsh conditions.

Most of the other elided texts are more prosaic, and their excising was at least in part a pragmatic decision by Himid in response to the gallery's space constraints. They illustrate, however, the way that communications between these working class Mancunians and their fellow workers in the Carolinas are pared down to the bare minimum by the force of their exploited circumstance. The elided texts were found texts from slave and worker's narratives that outlined the full range of experiences in the factories and plantations, such as:

> We saved on the rent because my brother his wife and their four children came to live with us.

> We on the hoe gang have our food in the field and only stop work long enough to eat.

> I never heard her screaming because the noise of the machines drowned her out.

> He was caught by the dogs and kept in irons till there was a chance to sell him.

> The dust and floating cotton in the air is making him cough more than ever.

> His little brother was taken naked from his bed by the overlooker one morning and kicked all the way to the factory.

> There was a nursery for suckling at the quarters.

> Most of the time we eat porridge, bread and potatoes, sometimes we go without.

> He ran away, was caught, then whipped.

> We cost $1000 dollars each and you can buy land for $1 an acre.[22]

These texts exhibit a shared transatlantic experience of drudgery and exploitation that links Lancashire factory workers to Carolinian slaves. The spare autobiographical statements make more explicit Himid's political purpose in *Cotton.com*. She insists that the varied forms of exploitation in a transatlantic economy elide differences between free and chained labour in systems which depend on one another and where child labour, violence and hunger are the accompaniment to unremitting toil. Moreover, Himid is insistent on the actuality of these transatlantic communications, even if they are partial and contingent. She explained to me how she imagined the disparate groups empathising with each other's position as cogs in the capitalist machine:

> I imagined the cotton workers in these buildings taking the cotton off the barges that had come up the ship canal and finding little bits of fabric, perhaps finding a bit of cloth, or a bit of hair, some kind of thing that had accidently found its way from the cotton picker's body or clothes or field

or whatever into these bales and managed to find its way back across the Atlantic, up the Manchester Ship Canal. There you get this whole bale of cotton off and you have to card it and thin it and then imagine all the thoughts you might have had.[23]

If one aspect of the conception of the piece was about actual physical links between the workers, even if as evanescent as the presence of human hair in the transplanted cotton, Himid combines this with a seeming anachronistic conceit which the title of the work alludes to. She transposes the postmodern communication modes of mobile phones and email to the mid-nineteenth century world of postal mail and non-literacy in vernacular folk cultures. She is interested in the way that in texting and emailing, something significant can be said extremely pithily so that 'big stories are condensed into tiny amount of texts'.[24] This big story of slavery and historical and modern international capitalism can likewise be explicated in condensed form by those who are its victims as they talk to one another. Himid continues:

> It was two things – it was imagining that finding of the bits in the cotton and imagining thinking how that other person lived their life and how the workers in Manchester might talk to, have a conversation with the cotton pickers in Carolina and what those cotton pickers in Carolina might try to tell those Manchester cotton workers. Of course, I would hope it would not be a kind of 'my lot is worse than yours' but much more of a kind of: 'Do you see the situation we are in? We're all being done over here, stitched up here: perhaps we could try to communicate here, try to undercut, undermine this in some way.'[25]

The political nature of the work might not be immediately apparent as the abstract quality of the individual paintings might seem to be merely about the aesthetics of design and the beautiful variety of patterns that working with cotton can create. Himid carefully disabuses the viewer of such simplistic reading of the work. Her praxis here, to quote Sarat Maharaj's incisive discussion of earlier pieces, is to 'work through the field of non-representational art, turning its abstract purism against itself, turning it inside out into programmatic statement.'[26] Ultimately she shows how the patterns relate to her conception of the conversations between workers and slaves which make up the weft and wave of the designs themselves:

> The abstract patterns are actually conversations. Each one had a text but the pattern represents the sound of conversation, like listening over a telephone exchange or reading lots of communicated email messages or text messages but seeing them all at once. And because some of them are black on white and some white on black, there's no distinction between

English patterns or African patterns or African American patterns, they all are patterns that are borrowed from all those sources. That's the point I am trying to make; it's very naive but we have to keep talking to each other to say it's like that, but it's not quite like that. Or 'Yes, this did happen, his leg did get chopped off because he was too near the piece of machinery' is not better or worse than 'His leg got chopped off because the dogs were chasing him because he tried to escape'. It's real and it happened and it needs saying; it's not about competing to say who had it worse, the working class British or the slaves. No, all of us are part of the same rip-off/forms of exploitation.[27]

The patterns then reflect the ongoing conversations between exploited workers and chattel slaves; through these patterns Himid says she wants 'to make real the idea of dialogue, communication, exchange and collaboration in a sort of monument to similarity and difference shot through with political banter.'[28] Himid agreed with me during our interview that an exemplary mode of such interracial banter were the shanties often learnt by white sailors from black dock-workers in the South and then transplanted throughout the Atlantic world.

These lyrics, as they developed through the nineteenth century, exemplify a significant and often elided black American and Caribbean contribution to the cultural life of the black Atlantic. The songs describe African Atlantic diasporic movement and its contribution to the development of a black Atlantic tradition of routed freedom. A song like 'Roll the Cotton Down' relates the move from labouring for poor pay in the racist South to an escape to sea, where the rewards were greater. The centrality of cotton in this famous shanty attests to the importance of the material in the transatlantic economy and shows how apposite Himid's use of it is as symbolic for black–white relations historically. Sung by cotton stowers in such towns as Mobile, Alabama, to describe a wished-for liberation out to sea, it became what Stan Hugill calls a 'halyard and capstan song', performed at sea to celebrate the move away from the South:

Was ye ever down in Mobile Bay,
Screwin' cotton by the day?

Oh, a black man's pay is rather low,
To stow the cotton we must go.

Oh, a white man's pay is rather high,
Rock an' shake 'er is the cry.

Oh, so early in the mornin', boys,
Oh, afore the day is dawnin', boys.

Five dollars a day is white man's pay,
So bring yer screws an' hooks this way…

Oh, tier by tier we'll stow 'em neat,
Until the job is made complete.

Oh, Mobile Bay's no place for me,
I'll pack my bags an' go to sea [I'll sail away on some other sea][29]

Such songs were not only sung by black people, but were part of an interracial tradition of shantying that allowed white sailors who had similar narratives of displacement to sing them with feeling too, despite the obvious dichotomies caused by racial inequality pointed to in the lyrics. It is such linked yet different experiences that Himid draws attention to in *Cotton. com*. According to Hugill, 'the wharves of Mobile and such places were the meeting ground of white men's songs and shanties and Negro songs and work songs.'[30] Evidence abounds that black workers sung such call and response melodies in the plantation fields, but even more intriguingly for my argument here, black slaves working in factories during the dawn of Southern industrialisation showed their propensity for making up songs to ameliorate the drudgery of work. In a hemp factory in Lexington in the 1840s, an observer witnessed around a hundred slaves 'drown the noise of the machinery by their own melody; the leader would commence singing in a low tone – "Ho! Ho! Ho! Master's gone away". To which the rest replied with rapidity, "Ho! Ho! Ho!"'[31] The transfer of a work song aesthetic from a rural plantation to the factory floor emphasises the mass circulation possibilities of antebellum African American musicking that reached its apotheosis in shantying. As Joseph Roach contends, 'since the late seventeenth and eighteenth centuries, local cultural productions have been hybridised routinely by the hemispheric circulation of collectively created forms.'[32]

In the 'work song exchange' or 'shanty mart'[33] in the Gulf ports, songs such as 'Roll the Cotton Down', whose origins go back to such plantation songs and their development through factories and ports, gained a currency far beyond their black origins. However, the lyrics of the song attest to these origins in strictured life on shore, and the importance of sea travel in transcending them. The shanties show a black tradition of song-making which delights in a movement away from the slave South (though they might occasionally regret the loss of lovers, family and familiar home-places such travel occasioned). Shantying reveals the life experiences of Africans in the diaspora literally on the move. As Bolster describes, 'Sailors linked far-flung black communities and united plantations with urban centres',[34] and one of the ways they achieved this was through cultural forms such as song.

Unaccounted for in traditional histories, the songs these black and white dock-workers and seafarers have passed down reveal the enhanced freedom they discovered in travelling the circum-Atlantic. They can reveal for us stories that traditional historiography has omitted, and point to a rich cultural heritage of inter-continental and inter-racial musical exchange that was at its peak in the mid-nineteenth century. Such communicative patterns exemplify the cogency of Himid's anachronistic conceit. Although email and text messages are only possible in Himid's imaginative universe for these nineteenth century working class whites and the black chattel slaves, they, in fact, communicated their similitude and difference through shared oral traditions like shantying. Himid describes this shantying mode, with its origins in plantations, as 'a beautiful example of conversation and song turning into another song'.[35] As Marcus Rediker describes, it is not just commodities that these different proletariat groups produced, but also kinetic cultures that connected them around the circum-Atlantic:

> The workers of the Atlantic produced commodities that moved with the planetary currents around the world, but, so, too, did their experience, which often flowed from American slave huts, Irish cottages, and the rolling decks of deep-sea vessels, across the Atlantic, back to the metropoles of Europe.[36]

Originating in the Caribbean, in the US southern states and at sea on the wild Atlantic, shanties are the prototype of a mobile, sea-chopped, African-derived, diasporic communicative mode that Rediker talks about here, and that Himid seeks to approximate in her abstract patternings and their text(s).

There is, however, a more direct agenda in Himid's work that relates to a specific historical moment when the links between Manchester, the American South, and the cotton it produced were foregrounded dynamically. The period of the American Civil War (1861–1865) and the subsequent shortage of cotton produced tremendous privation for the economy of Lancashire and for its workers. This privation was so extensive that the period came to be known as the 'cotton famine'. In some Lancashire cotton towns, unemployment due to the absence of raw cotton was extreme. For instance in Burnley during the summer of 1862, 10,000 out of 13,000 operatives were out of work.[37] The privations of the cotton famine reached most northern communities, as is related in a recently rediscovered publication, *The Life of the Late James Johnson, Coloured Evangelist: An Escaped Slave from the Southern States of America, 40 Years Resident in Oldham* (1914). This pamphlet details the wandering of Johnson on his arrival in Britain in December 1862 at the height of extreme unemployment and attendant misery in many places:

I was worse now than ever – cotton stockings and a pair of slippers in bleak December, friendless and homeless, roaming the streets of Liverpool. I walked over to Southport, and finding nothing to do, walked by Ormskirk to St. Helens, on to Warrington, thence to Manchester; again on to Wigan, Huddersfield, Leeds, York, Beverley and Hull, where I took to singing, dancing and rattlebones, which I found was easier than begging.[38]

Johnson's solution to privation was to become an itinerant entertainer, using his cosmopolitan cultural resources to aid him. His narrative of itinerant poverty shows the widespread privation caused by the cotton famine. In researching for *Cotton.com*, Himid was encouraged to reflect on this moment of Civil War and attendant poverty as pivotal in Britain and Manchester's relationship with cotton and its exploitative mode of production on both sides of the Atlantic. The site of memory Himid fixed on to galvanise her thinking was the memorial bronze statue to Abraham Lincoln by George Grey Bernard, unveiled in Manchester in 1919 (Figure 21). Its inscription of 'an address from the working people of Manchester to his Excellency Abraham Lincoln', urging him to end slavery and expressing support for the embargo of cotton despite the privation caused to Lancashire workers, and Lincoln's reply praising the Lancashire workers' internationalism, are emblematic for Himid of the political stand taken by many working class Lancastrians in the wake of the Civil War.[39] She stresses the significance of the inscriptions as indicators of a fervent dialogue that promoted a transatlantic radicalism and a utopian idealism that needs to be remembered in these 'apolitical times':

The statue was important because it can/could be referred to in one to one verbal conversations about 'Cotton.com'. It brought a discussion about a historic/past event into a contemporary context and in a very everyday, even banal way it made the idea of 'Cotton.com' seem more about reality than a dreamy, might-have-been idea. The important part for me is the text and not the figure, although of course you need the figure to draw you towards the text. The text is wearing away and difficult to read now, and the effectiveness it does have lies in what you can do with it rather than what it is, how you can use it to bring political discussion into the conversation in these somewhat apolitical times.[40]

The statue, in a sense, provides the template for the work, showing the possibilities for the circulation of ideas transatlantically and their continuation through the figure of Lincoln and his conversation with the workers memorialised on the plinth. Himid's description of 'apolitical times' is attested to by the furore over the re-siting of the statue in 1986 from Platt Fields in Rusholme to the centre of the city, when the inscriptions were altered and extended, much to the chagrin of the local press. Apart from an 'extended history lesson' told through the extracts from the speech of a Manchester worker and Lincoln's reply, the alteration from 'working men' to 'working people' was seen as a flagrant example of political correctness and lampooned in the *Manchester Evening News* report.[41] However, the presence of women and children in the cotton mills attests to the accuracy of the contemporary neologism. That Manchester's daily local evening newspaper should marginalise the significance of the ceremony to rededicate the memorial says much about the apolitical nature of Thatcherite and post-Thatcherite Britain which Himid alludes to above.

To add insult to this contemporary injury, the addition of a memorial plaque to Princess Diana in front of the statue in 1998 is thoroughly inappropriate: What is the link between a privileged aristocrat and the history of transatlantic radicalism? This strange juxtaposition thoroughly undermines the radical intent of the statue, foregrounding celebrity rather than historical importance. Himid, though, is intent on the statue and its inscription rather than the somewhat apolitical contexts of the latter decades of the twentieth century. Ironically, it is the reporting of the earlier 1919 handover of the statue from Americans in Cincinnati to the city of Manchester that more accurately approximates the valences of the statue Himid wants to emphasise. John A. Stewart from the Anglo-American Committee had then first drawn attention to the importance of the statue being in Manchester rather than in London, where it had originally been intended to stand close to the Houses of Parliament. He said:

> The sentiment of London was quite against the Northern States, but Lincoln found in John Bright and Cobden and in all the men of great affairs in Manchester warm friends and sympathisers. It is owing not a little to the way in which the English cotton spinners stood by us which enabled us to preserve the Union and bring the war to a successful conclusion. For that reason we are very grateful.[42]

The statue, then, narrates a key tale of transatlantic radicalism, and it is this that attracts Himid to it even if these radical roots have been obscured by some aspects of its re-siting. Himid's *Cotton.com* has a general contextualisation of the circulation of cotton and its meanings during the late eighteenth and nineteenth century. Nevertheless, it speaks to cotton as a commodity in the globalised present, but most specifically it has as a specific contextualisation the cotton famine, when solidarity between working class 'slaves' and American black chattel slaves helped to defeat the forces of Southern reaction.

The imagined communications in *Cotton.com* had their actual historical counterpart in the radical messages sent from industrial workers in support of the overthrow of slavery. Meetings of workers in favour of the North reached their apotheosis during a massive meeting in the Free Trade Hall, Manchester on 31 December 1862 to support the Emancipation Proclamation. This mass working class meeting of several thousand adopted an 'Address to Lincoln' that stressed the links between radicals in Britain and those opposed to slavery in North America:

> The vast progress you have made in the short space of twenty months fills us with hope that every stain on your freedom will shortly be removed, and that the erasure of that foul blot upon civilisation and Christianity – chattel slavery – during your presidency will cause the name of Abraham Lincoln to be honoured and revered by posterity... If you have any ill-wishers here ... they are chiefly those who oppose liberty at home.[43]

This message also stressed that the forces of reaction in Britain that supported the Confederacy were those conservative forces that opposed working class emancipation at home. Lincoln's reply acknowledged the sacrifices of the working people of Manchester:

> I know and deeply deplore the sufferings which the working people of Manchester and in all Europe are called to endure in this crisis... I cannot but regard your decisive utterances on the question as an instance of the sublime Christian heroism which has not been surpassed in any age or in any country. It is indeed an energetic and re-inspiring assurance of the inherent truth and of the ultimate and universal triumph of justice, humanity and freedom.[44]

Lincoln's empathy with the starving workers of Lancashire was not expressed only in words, but also found practical form in the sending of relief ships with supplies to the stricken region, most notably the *George Griswold*, which arrived in Liverpool in February 1863 with over 13,000 barrels of flour, pork, corn, rice and $30,000 in cash for the distressed operatives.[45] Such gestures helped to cement the allegiance of cotton operatives to the North's cause, despite the economic difficulties and privation supporting it caused them. As we can see from his speech above, the sacrifices of the Lancashire workers were used by Lincoln to internationalise the struggle against the South and promote it as part of a universal struggle for human rights. Radicals in the north-west of England went further, however, making links between the oppressed working class in Britain and the chattel slaves in bondage in the South. For example, John Turner from Ashton, just outside Manchester, the working class secretary of the local branch of the Union and Emancipation Society, described slaves as 'working men and women who are defrauded of the fruits of their labour and the ownership of their own bodies, because they are guilty of having a skin not coloured like our own'.[46] He then made the link between slavery across the Atlantic and oppression at home, answering the Confederate supporters who were propagandising that slavery was beneficial to the Lancashire economy and hence its workers, by foregrounding the institution as a key 'working man's question, for if it was right for slavery in one part it was right in another; and it behoved the working class to give no help to scoundrels who wanted their work done for nothing'.[47] From elsewhere in Lancashire, in Rossendale, a 'Working Man' in 1864 considered 'the slave, the property of the employer', whilst not thinking 'it right for the black man to be the white man's chattel'.[48] The discourse of slavery links the industrial and the plantation slaves.

Himid's work is a representation of this babble of radical communication that linked struggles for freedom across the Atlantic. However, it was not just radical working class Britons who spoke, but also escaped slaves who toured Lancashire and the rest of Britain to condemn the Confederacy. Probably the most famous of these was William Andrew Jackson, who escaped bondage as the coachman of Southern leader Jefferson Davis and used his vernacular rhetorical skills to continue the war on the foreign front by propagandising on behalf of the Union. Such live exemplars of transatlantic performative acts illustrate the multifarious nature of the communication Himid reflects in her work, which had a profound effect in radicalising the Lancashire working class. One Union supporter in Bristol portrayed Jackson as an 'oracle,' opining that 'there is no gainsaying him'.[49] The cotton might not literally speak its messages, but the toilers in cotton spoke to one another in the transatlantic exchange of ideas in which the escaped slave held a privileged position as experienced informant and counter-propagandist who spurred Lancashire radicals on in their own fight for justice. As one observer from Mossley near Manchester said:

> The eternal negro found eloquent defenders amongst the white slaves of Lancashire – some even going so far as to kiss the ruby lips of the past-forging, God-fearing, temperance-promoting, runaway coachman of Jeff Davis.[50]

Jackson himself would make specific the links between mill-owners in Lancashire and plantation owners in the South, naming Davis as an exploiter of both black slaves and white workers. He said of Davis that he had 'never met anyone who had worked more zealously to keep his race and the "poor white trash" in bondage'.[51] He inculcated in his British audience the story of Davis's exploitative ways by aligning his treatment of slaves with that of their fellow workers in the States. By 1865 and the end of the war, working class northerners could speculate on better times ahead. As Richard Blackett explains, an Ashton man captured this optimism in the wake of the victory of Union forces by describing how the war's result might impact on the fight for franchise reform in Britain:

> We have a general impression amongst us that the once despised and enthralled African will not only be set free, but be enfranchised and in spite of his master; and when the slave ceases to be and becomes an enfranchised free man, that the British workman's claim may be listened to.[52]

Such misplaced optimism, shown in both British and US contexts by the continuation in the late nineteenth century of unbridled capitalism in Britain and the development for African Americans of debt peonage and disenfranchisement in the Southern US, should not blind us to the important links made between the struggles against racial and class oppression during the 1860s. Not all Manchester workers were able to see beyond their own desperate situation to support the slaves against their masters, but many were. The ferment of opinion, oratory and debate was a highpoint of the transatlantic exchange of ideas, and at its centre was cotton and its trading. Himid's *Cotton.com* comments retrospectively on this era when radical working class whites in Manchester dramatically juxtaposed their exploitation with that of those black slaves who had produced the cotton bales they worked on, not in a competition to see who was most heinously exploited but in a transatlantic gesture of solidarity.

The importance of the physical cotton to this narrative is emphasised by the arrival of the first cotton bales at the port of Liverpool after hostilities had ended, when they were placed on a cart 'trimmed with flowers and bunting' and paraded through the streets accompanied by a picture of Abraham Lincoln.[53] Cotton here becomes the cipher for the feelings of the people dockside at the end of privation, and was symbolic of the victory of the progressive forces whilst providing an acknowledged link between labourers in Britain and the US.

Himid sees her piece as a kind of rescuing of the lives of cotton workers in Lancashire and the Carolinas from forgotten history, filling the silences and gaps created by physical distance and barriers to communication with the texts that approximate a conversation which was sometimes had but often imagined. The Civil War created opportunities for new conversations, but these are often forgotten in a brash postmodern world intent on marginalising Manchester's radical past. Dionne Brand talks of such lapsed memories, describing how in Canada as in the UK, effective remembering is key to the development of social justice in the here and now:

> Only the brazen can say, 'I was not here, I did not do this and feel that'. One hears that all the time in Canada; about what people feel they are and

are not responsible for. People use these arguments as reasons for not doing what is right and just. It never occurs to them they live on the cumulative hurt of others. They want to start the clock of social justice only when they arrived. But one is born into history, one isn't born into a void.[54]

Himid insists on the responsibility of all of Manchester's citizens for its chequered past, disavowing a static response to the challenges of race and class that Lincoln's statue opens up for reactionary forces. Paul Ricoeur warns that 'remembering … quickly veers off into commemoration with its obsession of a finite completed history.'[55] Brand, like Himid, wants to dialogise the past to create empathy with history's victims that will work against such apolitical 'completion'. Himid's piece does not allow the forgetting and elision such completion would engender; ultimately it chimes with the empathetic sentiments of the abolitionist orator George Thompson who, in a meeting at Stockport in 1861 at the start of hostilities, pleaded that working men should think beyond their own selfish interest:

> I hope you will not allow any temporary suffering to lead you to give your sympathies to the enemies of human freedom on the other side of the Atlantic; I hope we shall prove there is something we love better than cotton, that is liberty of the human race.[56]

Like Thompson, Himid asks her audience to look beyond the materialistic to the people who harvested and wove the cotton, and their radical message which she believes still has relevance in the twenty-first century. Their liberty had been crucially undermined by the operation of the transatlantic cotton economy; however, hidden in the weft and weave, in the fabric of the communications Himid allows us to be privy to, are the possibilities of the exchange of information and stories that are the beacon for a more enlightened world. The stories Himid uncovers emphasise her own radical politics that, like those of her nineteenth century forebears, moves beyond essentialist identity politics with all its limitations to show the connections between racial, sexual and class politics across the Atlantic and the possibilities for a praxis that moves beyond the tyranny of binary difference. Kobena Mercer describes the importance of such a politics that reaches beyond ghettoised nationalism:

> The challenge is to be able to theorise more than one difference at once: to abandon the logocentric hierarchies of binary thinking so as to enter into the over-determined spaces in between in which relations of identity and differences are actually lived. As a half-caste negro homosexual intellectual, located somewhere in the professional-managerial class, is my marginal identity really more worthily oppressed than the homeless and

unemployed white male youth who I encountered begging in the West End of London on my way home from work?[57]

Himid's work here is an exemplary attempt to make such a radical, multidirectional politics work and theorise both race and class at one and the same time. *Cotton.com* ultimately remembers those who created Manchester's wealth despite exploitative economic conditions over centuries. Her piece is an exemplary act of rememory; a remembrance of what is forgotten in many traditional histories which seeks to reinvigorate our way of thinking about Manchester and about transatlantic relations between peoples. Himid, in a quotation I have used elsewhere in this study, articulates what I believe is her praxis in *Cotton.com*: the excavation of what is not immediately apparent as present. She says:

> I was trying to find a way to talk of a thing that is not there, sort of inside the invisible if you like. I am interested in the politics of representation, how when something is there you can talk about it, write about it, paint about it, but when something isn't there what can you say, how can you make something of it, how can it not have been in vain, if you like. So that idea for memorialising came from trying to visualize the invisible.[58]

Himid's recovery of the unrepresented in *Cotton.com* is paradoxically achieved by attention to the material, the harvesting and manufacture of which is responsible for the transatlantic effacement of these exploited workers. Fabric, the site of exploitation, is, through its patterned wonder, also the possible site of communicative emancipation. Painting on the cloth that binds produces the patterns that are potentially liberatory. Filling in the erasures of history is an endeavour of particular importance to the unrepresented. The anti-essentialist message of *Cotton.com* is that those silenced were not just the non-literate African American slaves, the cotton pickers in the Carolinas, but also the cotton workers thousands of miles away in Manchester. Himid's marvellous conceit is that despite the miles they spoke (and continue to speak) with an articulation and radicalism that resounds today through the fabric of her work. They created lasting memorials that helped build transnational, transracial identities and alliances that give us hope for the development of radical class and racial politics in our more apolitical times.

Notes

1. A. L. Nielsen, *Writing Between the Lines*, p. 171.
2. P. Gilroy, *The Black Atlantic: Modernity and Double Consciousness* (London: Verso, 1993).

3. T. Trevor, 'Maria Thereza Alves' in *Port City: On Mobility and Exchange* (Bristol: Arnolfini, 2007), pp. 66–75 (66).

4. Maria Thereza Alves quoted in Trevor, 'Maria Thereza Alves', p. 66.

5. Maria Thereza Alves quoted in Trevor, 'Maria Thereza Alves', pp. 70–71.

6. W. E. B. Du Bois, *Black Reconstruction* (Millwood, NY: Kraus-Thomson, 1935), p. 84.

7. *Charleston Courier*, April 22 1804, quoted in J. A. McMillan, *The Final Victims: Foreign Slave Trade to North America, 1783–1810* (Columbia, SC: University of South Carolina Press, 2004), pp. 104–105.

8. A. Rice, *Radical Narratives of the Black Atlantic* (London: Continuum Press, 2003), pp. 72–77.

9. M. Sulter, 'Without Tides, No Maps', in L. Himid (ed.), *Revenge: A Masque in Five Talbeaux* (Rochdale: Rochdale Art Gallery, 1992), p. 24.

10. R. Blackburn, *The Making of New World Slavery: From the Baroque to the Modern 1492–1800* (London: Verso, 1998), p. 565.

11. Quoted in Sherwood, *After Abolition*, p. 56.

12. Blackburn, *The Making of New World Slavery*, p. 572.

13. A. Rice, 'Exploring inside the invisible', p. 24.

14. A. R. Keizer, *Black Subjects in the Contemporary Narrative of Slavery* (Ithaca, NY: Cornell University Press), pp. 44–45.

15. Reprinted in M. Wood, *Blind Memory: Visual Representations of Slavery in England and America 1780–1865* (Manchester: Manchester University Press, 2000), p. 18.

16. S. M. Best, *The Fugitive's Properties: Law and the Politics of Possession* (Chicago, IL: The University of Chicago Press, 2004), p. 17.

17. This discussion about the way art memorialises presence in a world that has historically enforced African Atlantic absence from the historical record can be compared to the way jazz music does the same, which I discuss in Chapter 5.

18. L. Himid, *Cotton.com*, 'Fabrications', Cube Gallery, Manchester, 2002. Interestingly, Murillo had a black slave/servant, Sebastian Gomez (See H. W. Debrunner, *Presence and Prestige: Africans in Europe, a History of Africans in Europe Before 1918* (Basel: Basel Afrika Bibliographien), 1979, p. 40.

19. Himid, 'Gallery talk'.

20. S. White and G. White, *The Sounds of Slavery: Discovering African American History Through Songs, Sermons and Speech* (Boston, MA: Beacon Press, 2005), p. 180.

21. A. J. Verdelle, 'The truth of the picnic: writing about American slavery', *Common-Place: Representing Slavery: A Roundtable Discussion* 1, 4 (July 2001), http://www.commonplace.org [accessed 10 February 2006].

22. L. Himid, '*Cotton.com* texts', manuscript, 2002.

23. Rice, 'Exploring inside the invisible', p. 24.

24. L. Himid, email correspondence, September 2003.

25. Rice, 'Exploring inside the invisible', p. 24.

26. Quoted in D. A. Bailey, I. Baucom and S. Boyce, *Shades of Black: Assembling the 1980s Black Arts in Postwar Britain* (Durham, NC: Duke University Press), p. 275.

27. Rice, 'Exploring inside the invisible', p. 24.

28. N. Rudd, 'In the city', in M. Crinson, H. Hills and N. Rudd (eds), *Fabrications: New Art and Urban Memory in Manchester* (Manchester: Cube Publications, 2002), pp. 4–9 (8).

29. S. Hugill, *Shanties from the Seven Seas: Shipboard Work-Songs and Songs used as Work-Songs from the Great Days of Sail* (Mystic, CT: Mystic Seaport, 1994), p. 124.

30. Hugill, *Shanties from the Seven Seas*, p. 17.

31. White and White, *The Sounds of Slavery*, p. 180.

32. J. Roach, *Cities of the Dead: Circum-Atlantic Performance* (New York, NY: Columbia University Press, 1996), p. 12.

33. Hugill, *Shanties from the Seven Seas*, pp. 17 and 258.

34. J. Bolster, *Black Jacks: African American Seamen in the Age of Sail* (Cambridge, MA: Harvard University Press), p. 6.

35. Rice, 'Exploring inside the invisible,' p. 25.

36. M. Rediker, 'The red Atlantic; or, "a terrible blast swept over the heaving sea"', in B. Klein and G. Mackenthun (eds), *Sea Changes: Historicizing the Ocean* (London: Routledge, 2004), pp. 111–130 (116).

37. D. Hollett, *The Alabama Affair: The British Shipyards Conspiracy in the American Civil War* (Bebington, Merseyside: Avid Publications, 1993), p. 37.

38. J. Johnson, *The Life of the Late James Johnson, Coloured Evangelist: An Escaped Slave from the Southern States of America, 40 Years Resident in Oldham England* (Oldham: W. Galley, 1914), p. 13.

39. Full transcript in T. Wyke, *Public Sculpture of Greater Manchester* (Liverpool: Liverpool University Press, 2004), pp. 88–89.

40. Himid, email correspondence. The text is now cleaned and restored, benefitting from the interest aroused by the 2007 commemorations.

41. See Wyke, *Public Sculpture of Greater Manchester*, p. 91.

42. See Wyke, *Public Sculpture of Greater Manchester*, p. 91.

43. R. J. M. Blackett, *Divided Hearts: Britain and the American Civil War* (Baton Rouge, LA: Louisiana State University Press, 2001), p. 81.

44. Wyke, *Public Sculpture of Greater Manchester*, p. 89.

45. Hollett, *The Alabama Affair*, pp. 64–65.

46. Blackett, *Divided Hearts*, p. 32.

47. Blackett, *Divided Hearts*, pp. 32–33.

48. Blackett, *Divided Hearts*, p. 96.

49. Blackett, *Divided Hearts*, p. 133.

50. Blackett, *Divided Hearts*, p. 180.

51. Blackett, *Divided Hearts*, p. 222.

52. Blackett, *Divided Hearts*, p. 243.

53. Blackett, *Divided Hearts*, p. 3.

54. Brand, *A Map to the Door of No Return*, p. 82.

55. Ricoeur, *Memory, History and Forgetting*, p. 408.

56. Blackett, *Divided Hearts*, pp. 177–178.

57. K. Mercer, 'Back to my routes: a postscript to the 1980s', in J. Proctor (ed.), *Writing Black Britain 1948–1998: An Interdisciplinary Anthology* (Manchester: Manchester University Press, 2000), p. 286.

58. Rice, 'Exploring inside the invisible,' p. 24.

5

'Black Music Across the Ocean Waves'
Toni Morrison, Jackie Kay and Jazz
as African Atlantic Memorial

...the notion that black language leads toward music, that it passes into music when it attains the maximal pitch of its being. This belief contains the powerful suggestion that music is the ultimate lexicon, that language when truly apprehended aspires to the condition of music. *Kimberly Benston*[1]

 Music is our witness and our ally. The beat is the confession which recognises, changes and conquers time. Then history becomes a garment we can wear and share, and not a cloak in which to hide, and time becomes our friend. *James Baldwin*[2]

My parallel is always the music, because all the strategies of the art are there. All of the intricacy, all of the discipline... I use the analogy of the music because you can range all over the world and it's still black. I don't imitate it, but I am informed by it. Sometimes I hear blues, sometimes spirituals or jazz and I've appropriated it. *Toni Morrison*[3]

This chapter will discuss the way that music as a form encodes aural memories that have been fundamental to the doughty survival of African Atlantic communities in the face of slavery, racism and oppression, and the way that writers have acknowledged the power of music and utilised it in their novels. Musical performance has a malleability which enables it to speak especially to and for a diasporan people. As Joseph Roach asserts:

Genealogists resist histories that attribute purity of origin to any performance. They have to take into account the give and take of joint transmissions posted in the past, arriving in the present, delivered by living messengers, speaking in tongues, not entirely their own. Orature is an art of listening as well as speaking; improvisation is an art of collective memory as well as invention; repetition is an art of re-creation as well as restoration. Texts obscure what performance tends to reveal; memory challenges history in the construction of circum-Atlantic cultures, and it revises the yet unwritten epic of their fabulous co-creation.[4]

Roach's rich explication illustrates how the music of the African Atlantic carries its historical message across the oceans; its improvisatory nature prevents ossification and brings aural memorials of past homespaces to enable the survival of living cultural forms and the creation of new ones despite extreme dislocation. For African Atlantic writers across the diaspora, such well-travelled music is used as the 'ultimate lexicon' for interpreting and expressing the memories of these local and global histories. For instance, Jackie Kay's novel *Trumpet* (1998) utilises the resources of the African American musical tradition to tell a story of black Scottish identity. As her main character, jazz trumpeter Joss Moody, solos, he constructs a black Atlantic identity. Kay uses the multifarious lexicon of a jazz aesthetic learnt from African American performers such as Bessie Smith and Toni Morrison to express her character's diasporan identity. She describes Moody performing:

> When he gets down, and he doesn't always get down deep enough, he loses his sex, his race, his memory. He strips himself bare, takes everything off, till he's barely human. Then he brings himself back, out of this world. Back from way. Getting there is painful. He has to get to the centre of the whirlwind, screwballing in musical circles till he is very nearly out of his mind. The journey is so whacky, so wild that he sometimes fears he'll never return sane. He licks his chops. He slaps and flips and flies. He goes down, swirling and whirling till he's right down at the very pinpoint of himself. A small black mark. The further he goes the smaller he gets. That's the thing. It's so fast he's speeding, crashing, his fingers going like the hammers, frenzied, blowing up a storm. His leather lips. His satchelmouth.[5]

The combination of short sentences, sentence fragments and repetitions build riffs and counter-riffs that construct a bopping jazzy prose style. Kay's final image of 'leather lips' and 'satchelmouth' aligns her black Scots trumpeter with the legendary Louis Armstrong, showing the African American origin of the art form Joss Moody is revelling in. It is the origins of this music – its dynamic forms, its memorialising function – that I want to explore in this chapter before returning to a closer examination of *Trumpet* and Toni Morrison's novels *Sula* (1973) and *Jazz* (1992).

In Toni Morrison's first novel, *The Bluest Eye* (1970), there had been a telling acknowledgement of the power of African American musicians to express the very soul of black Americans. In talking about Cholly, the working-class African American who rapes his own daughter, Toni Morrison writes:

The pieces of Cholly's life could become coherent only in the head of a musician. Only those who talk through the gold of curved metal, or in the touch of black and white rectangles and taut skins and strings echoing from wooden corridors, could give true form to his life… Only a musician would sense, know without knowing that he knew, that Cholly was free. Dangerously free.[6]

Note how the group imagined has the instrumentation of a typical jazz quartet – brass, piano, drums and bass – which shows how Morrison, in calling on an African American musicking tradition, thinks of jazz as central to that tradition. Overall, this passage illustrates that despite all her formidable talents as a writer, Morrison is forced to concede that African American musicians are the artists who could best express Cholly's deep despair. Morrison's concession of the higher ground to the musical tradition over the literary should not surprise us, as influential African American cultural commentators in the 1960s (when she was writing the novel) were continually downplaying their literary tradition and valorising what they saw as a much more vital musical tradition. For Africans in the diaspora, music has traditionally been by far the most important mode for building a safe, stable identity in a hostile world. Joseph Roach has talked eloquently of this diasporan music that emerged in the new world, as a new form, related to African music but with its own cadences; he discusses Benjamin Latrobe's 1819 description of musicking in New Orleans, using it as emblematic of the complex genealogies of the music:

[this] convergence of dance and musical forms, clustered feats of daring and invention, which were deeply indebted to Africa, yet no longer of it – living proofs of its impermanence and unforgettability. They emerged from the margins of circum-Atlantic performance culture, from 'in back of town', a displaced transmission, rising, phoenix-like, from the ashes of diaspora and genocide on the wings of song.[7]

This combination of 'impermanence and unforgettability' in a music that has travelled across oceans and through traumatic historical waters makes for a musicking that has both deep roots and complex routes that can articulate the African Atlantic culture it comes from in ways that writing in particular finds very hard to match. Both Frederick Douglass[8] and W. E. B. Du Bois[9] in their writings in the mid-nineteenth and early twentieth centuries had situated this musical tradition (and especially the 'sorrow songs' or spirituals) as central to early African American folk culture; however, black nationalists of the 1960s went much further.

Critics from the Black Arts Movement, such as those collected in the landmark collection *Black Fire* (1968),[10] insisted that writers must use the cultural resources of the African American musicking tradition and create works true to that. Indeed, one of the editors of the collection, Amiri Baraka (Leroi Jones), was in the forefront of the movement to foreground the black musical tradition as vernacular example to both black and white writers years before he edited *Black Fire*. In a 1962 address to the American Society for African Culture, he lambasted Eurocentric poetic models and posited more usable ones; rather than listening to 'second-rate English poetry with the notion that somehow it is the only way poetry should be written. It would be better if such a poet listened to Bessie Smith sing "Gimme a Pigfoot" or listened to the tragic verse of a Billie Holiday, than be content to imperfectly imitate the bad poetry of the ruined minds of Europe.'[11] For Kay too, thousands of miles away in Scotland, Bessie Smith became a crucial figure in the construction of her identity as an African diasporan woman artist in the fullest sense: 'Bessie was bisexual, and had lots of relationships with men and women. She was one of the most important voices of the 20th century. I grew up in Scotland without many black people around – except my brother – and Bessie became part of my family. I looked at her and saw some reflection of myself.'[12]. Bessie Smith became a crucial part of Kay's useable past that she was unable to access from the staid British popular music traditions that were on offer as she grew up in central Scotland.

Overall, the valorisation of iconic figures in the jazz world by both Morrison and Kay, and their use of jazz forms, is an apt reply to these nationalist critics' demands that black writers should create literature which distances itself from European forms by a willed use of black vernacular and/or musical traditions. They are also part of a community of black women writers in the post-Civil Rights era (for example, Toni Cade Bambara, Ntozake Shange and Alice Walker) who responded to this black nationalist agenda and who privilege black music. Talking about her novel *The Salt Eaters* (1980), Bambara has said how she was involved in the 'avoidance of a linear thing in favour of a kind of jazz suite',[13] whilst Shange has acknowledged that 'we give the musicians more space to run with / more personal legitimacy than we give our writers.'[14] Most appositely, Walker, in a 1973 interview with John O'Brien, discussed the relationship of her writing to the musical tradition: 'the most I would say about where I am trying to go is this: I am trying to arrive at that place where music already is; to arrive at that unselfconscious sense of collective oneness: that naturalness, that (even when anguished) grace.'[15] Morrison and Kay, in their later discussions about music, echoed Walker's idealisation of the mode. For instance, the form of *Trumpet* echoes that of jazz, as Kay discusses: 'There's a solo, with improvisations by people [in the novel]; one refrain made to play different ways. Jazz is fascinating, because it's always fluid, it has the past in it – work songs, slave songs, blues. Jazz is a process of reinventing itself.'[16] For Kay, jazz is a polyglot form that can speak to her diasporan African Atlantic routes. The use of the vernacular by Kay and Morrison is, however, not purely a response to the polemics of their generation but, like Walker's, an engagement with the long history of black culture. Morrison's earlier encounter with a jazz aesthetic is mapped thus:

> I try to incorporate into that traditional genre, the novel, unorthodox novelistic characteristics – so that it is in my view Black, because it uses the characteristics of Black art. I am not suggesting that some of these devices have not been used before and elsewhere – only the reason why I employ them as well as I can.[17]

These 'unorthodox novelistic characteristics' come from roots in the oral culture of African Americans. To an extent, Morrison's avowal of an aesthetic forged from the oral tradition of her ethnic group is a conscious distancing of her literary craftsmanship from that of Anglo-American writers. Denise Heinze suggests such a distancing, contending that 'Morrison frequently alters, substitutes, or replaces the white aesthetic by presenting or creating a black aesthetic of difference.'[18] The more vernacular and African American her prose style, the less easily she is assimilated into a mainstream that limits her.

This privileging of the vernacular through their use of a jazz aesthetic also situates Morrison and Kay's work in a very specific tradition of African Atlantic writing for which Richard Wright had proselytised decades earlier when he, as Paul Gilroy describes, contrasted 'the unwritten and unrecognised culture of the Negro masses' in bitter opposition to the 'parasitic and mannered outpourings that sprung from the pens of the sons and daughters of the bourgeoisie'.[19] Wright adduced that it was through vernacular forms that true racial wisdom had flowed, and his nationalist vernacular agenda set a tone which the black arts critics were to follow. At the centre of this nationalist vernacular tradition is the musical tradition. The novelist and critic Gayl Jones posits music as the central oral mode feeding into black literary expression in her illuminating study *Liberating Voices*. In it, she eulogises the musical tradition thus: '[the] fearless and courageous and thoroughgoing way of dealing with the complexity of the black experience… music is probably the only mode we have used to speak of that complexity.'[20] It is not only the sturdiness of this musical expression that makes it so central to African American artistic endeavour, but also the unbroken chain of the performative culture that means it can speak of the tortured routes of a diasporan people across the Atlantic and of its roots in African traditions. As Lars Eckstein eloquently expresses it:

This unique and largely unbroken continuity of musical expression suggests the realm of music has to be considered as a central *lieu de mémoire* in the African diaspora. The different variations of call-and-response patterns or the blues mood do not signify individual, specific historical events as such; nevertheless, they rely on specific cultural codes which are grounded in a collective historical experience, and are well able to 'evoke' – albeit with a degree of vagueness – the occurrences and consequences of black Atlantic slavery.[21]

In these terms, African Atlantic musicking is the key mode of transmission of a diasporic, routed culture. Thus it is imperative in a study on memorialisation in the African Atlantic arts that the musical mode is explored and given equal weight to that of the written and visual arts traditions. Some of the most effective memorials in the black Atlantic have been and continue to be musical performances, and it is these that Morrison and Kay call on in their novels. In doing so they are responding to the specific nuances of the black diaspora, wherein the operations of a brutal transatlantic slave trade meant an extreme cultural displacement which music and its transplanted memory in part ameliorated. Édouard Glissant has recently articulated this:

> The Africans had lost everything; they had nothing, not even a song. In jazz, black Americans had to recompose, through memory and through extraordinary suffering, the echo of what Africa had for them. Jazz came about not through a book, but through a flight of memory.[22]

Central to the oral tradition, musicians themselves have always been aware of their role as cultural commentators, as makers and keepers of memory and community history, seeking to express not only their feelings but those of their community too. The jazz clarinettist Sidney Bechet, for example, constantly interlaces his story with that of his people, remembering especially one of the motivations for his playing of the blues being a man he met in prison in Galveston, Texas:

> He was like every man that's been done a wrong. Inside him he'd got the memory of all the wrong that's been done to all the people. That's what the memory is... When I remember that man, I'm remembering myself, a feeling I've always had. When a blues is good, that kind of memory just grows up inside it.[23]

Such remembering is vital in African Atlantic cultures where modes for passing on a history needed to be developed in the face of limits put on education and movement. African Americans in particular have used their musical culture as a tool to encode and distribute ideas and memories, to literally create aural memorials. The constant interaction between the individual musician, his community and his lived history was so foregrounded for Bechet that he was conscious of it whilst playing. Bechet again illustrates the effectiveness of his music as a tool for remembering when he says:

> You're playing a number... maybe you don't know it's about that. But then, later you're thinking about it and it comes to you. It's not a describing music, nothing like that. Maybe nobody else could ever tell it was about that. But thinking back you know the music was how you felt about remembering that time on the street...[24]

This intimate relationship of jazz music with a personal and communal history is not confined to the early practitioners of the form. The bebop pianist Hampton Hawes, for instance, believes that his music carries the memories of his slave grandfather's pain as well as knowledge of his own oppression by racism:

> Maybe my grandfather was whipped for real, but they whip me too, man; only they whip me mentally. I'm just as fucked up as he was so that when I play, the same shit is going to come out of me as came out of him when he had to hum to get some strength in his body to finish picking all that cotton.[25]

For Hawes, then, his music connects the memories of African Americans across generations. It is not only individual memories that jazz musicians encode in their musical performances; the very structures of jazz allow them to reach out towards a communal history of remembrance. For instance, the jam session, the workshop of the improvising jazz musicians, will often use tunes familiar from the jazz repertoire, turning them inside out and gaining new sounds and meanings from the old material. Such literal defamiliarisation, so that what has seemed a seminal performance becomes only the raw material for experimentation the next time an improvising musician uses it (which could be the next decade, or the next day), posits jazz as an extremely mobile and malleable form. As Stanley Crouch contends, 'different nights, different moods, and different fellow musicians can bring about drastically dissimilar versions of the same songs.'[26]

The constantly inventive nature of jazz performance is obviously useful for Morrison and Kay, who want to signify past interpretations of African Atlantic history and create new meanings. The history of reworking jazz standards in each new era gives black writers a model for their own project of 'remembering', not only bringing back to mind, but also as in the opposite of dismembering: putting back together again. Each new 'bringing back to mind' reconstructs the past anew, and is often in opposition to the past recorded literally by some white historians. For instance, Morrison's reservoir of stories, like a jazz musician's reservoir of tunes, is not there to be faithfully played note for note (or in her case to be told exactly as they are handed down) but to be reinvented so that they have relevance for the present and can reinterpret the past, free from a historiography which belittles African American achievement. In *Beloved* (1987), for instance, she reinvents the story of Margaret Garner (a runaway slave who in 1856 had murdered her child to prevent her from being re-enslaved) so that it is not framed by a white abolitionist interpretation but rescued for African American posterity as a positive story of literal rememberment; whilst in *Jazz* (1992) she uses a portrait by James Van Der Zee of a dead black girl in a coffin and weaves a subtle and engaging narrative around her lifestory. Similarly, Kay in *Trumpet* (1998) reworks the story of the white transgendered US jazz pianist Billy Tipton through the story of her black transgendered trumpet-playing Scottish hero Joss Moody. The development of the jazz form through the reworking of pivotal tunes could thus be seen as paradigmatic for the many black writers who use and reinterpret historical moments and oral stories from their own community and broader African Atlantic cultural forms.

Kimberly Benston alluded to such reworkings and discussed their relationship to the myth of Orpheus in his landmark 1977 essay 'Late Coltrane: a re-membering of Orpheus', which establishes a means to discuss African American creativity with reference to this foundational myth. The reworking of stories can be seen in this light as a literal re-memberment. Benston talks of 'the mystery of the Orphic dismemberment and restitution: the destructive-creative threat to and recovery of Expression itself'.[27] Morrison and Kay could be seen to literally reinvent stories and create new expressive means to do it.

More polemically, by invoking a jazz culture, Morrison and Kay wish to call upon the oppositional values which are at the core of the tradition. The values of the culture have often been antithetical to white European Protestant values, emphasising libidinal freedom and critiquing the culture of an ordered, bourgeois lifestyle. In many historical periods (for example in the 1920s when the music was labelled Bolshevistic by some critics) jazz culture functioned as a critique of dominant value systems. Such oppositional moments are a consequence of various formal elements in the music:

> In European terms it is a profoundly revolutionary music… Its composition in performance by the improvising group, horizontal-variational development with an eschewal of architectural form, different concepts of timbre, pitch and tone production, the principle of perpetual polyrhythms and rhythmic counterpoint, all of these are antithetical to European practices.[28]

Christopher Small adds to this depiction of jazz music being intrinsically non-European and subversive by stressing the functional, rhythmic, communal and improvisational modes recurrent in jazz culture. Such modes, when included in a performance, are fundamentally subversive of the values of industrial society. Small says of jazz that at certain times in its history it was a natural medium of rebellion for whites and African Americans:

> [it was] an embodiment or carrier of values which called into question those of white American culture of the past and present, jazz was a natural medium of rebellion against the standards of prosperous middle class America which had given the young everything except what they really needed: communality, warmth and emotional honesty.[29]

Paul Gilroy also emphasises this radicalism in black Atlantic musical expression by positing it as playing an important role in producing a 'distinctive counter-culture of modernity'.[30] Formal elements such as antiphony, improvisation and intentional non-closure are particularly antithetical to the values of an industrial society. The direct oral/aural transmission which is a function of antiphony helps to keep culture decentralised, creating 'a network of listening individuals and groups all working on equal terms with one another'.[31] In this world of mutual respect, memories can be shared and worked with through the music. Antiphony, or call and response, breaks down the hierarchies existent in high art forms of music, where the composer and conductor hold powerful sway over orchestras that are forced to play the notes as written by the former and communicated by the latter. As Small says of early New Orleans jazz, '[the] mutual human care and consideration that would enable the ensemble to give a performance that would satisfy the community of listeners and dancers'[32] is paradigmatic of the needs of African Americans in an unsure world. Stanley Crouch links such performance to a quintessentially democratic ideal and ideology, which valorises the individual and allows him or her to assert this individuality through group performance:

> The demands on and the respect for the individual in the jazz band put democracy into aesthetic action. Each performer must bring technical skill, imagination, and the ability to create coherent statements through improvised interplay with the rest of the musicians ... each player must have a remarkably strong sense of what constitutes the making of music as opposed to the rendering of music, which is what the performers of European concert music do. The improvising jazz musician must work right in the heat and passion of the moment, giving form and order in a mobile environment, where choices must be constantly assessed and reacted to in one way or another. The success of jazz is a victory for democracy...[33]

Such a radical paradigm of democracy in action militates against seeing the jazz performance and indeed jazz history either merely in terms of stellar soloists or indeed of communitarian ensembles. As if to prove the limitation of either polar extreme, the major metaphor used to describe jazz music is 'conversation'. As Paul Berliner has asserted, 'effective conversation is so valued in the aesthetic system of jazz that artists typically strive to embody it in their performances, lest their playing be unworthy of the tradition.'[34] By 'conversation' the musicians mean those with each other, with the tradition, and with the dancing or listening audience. Charles Mingus, in talking about his famous duet with Eric Dolphy on 'What Love' (1960), where the two presented an extended and very emotional vocalised interplay, said: '[the] conversation developed out with Eric past Bird... we used to really talk and say words with our instruments... we'd discuss our fear, our life, our views of God.'[35]

Jazz music, then, as Ingrid Monson so succinctly posits in her essay on John Coltrane, makes the metaphor of conversation central because it contains not texts to be distributed by higher beings, but socially interactive processes of communication which allow audiences and musicians the space for singular or collective creative improvisation and interpretation.[36]

It is this continual dichotomy that makes jazz culture an attractive mode for Morrison and Kay to use in their work. Though at the heart of a transatlantic US culture, its values provide a constant questioning 'other' to the certitudes of the hegemonic beliefs of Eurocentric culture. The paradox is, of course, that these seemingly alien values are actually core values of US culture. Freedom and individualism, enshrined in the Declaration of Independence and the Constitution, are debased in the modern capitalist state rife with poverty and racism. A thriving jazz culture reaffirms in every performance the importance of these core democratic values and passes them on as aural memorials that enable key ideals to be assimilated and shared.

Such values coming from a melding of African and American cultures lead to a constant dialogue in the music between core African and European cultural values. Morrison and Kay constantly debate the worth of these two value systems in their work, so jazz is the obvious form to invoke as they interrogate them. It is this doubleness – its closeness to roots and flirtation with high art forms – which makes jazz particularly appealing to black writers. Its essential malleability makes it a highly valuable analogous form. At certain points in jazz history when its vernacular base was threatened by attempts to make the music sound more 'legitimate', more like Western art or pop music, some protagonists in the culture have resisted these attempts at watering down the sound by going back to the bluesy roots of the music to create sounds that distance it from appropriation by the mainstream (for instance with the advent of bebop in the mid-1940s).

This process is a particularly apposite one for exploring Morrison's and Kay's modes of writing. In their novels, both writers make words their own, appropriating them from the language of the majority culture and shifting their focus. They decentre and de-form literary language, making it appropriate for telling a blue/black tale. This is rather like the jazz musicians who add to traditional sounds by incorporating distinctive oral modes from their vernacular roots and using these to distance their music from the mainstream.

Examples of such vernacular forms influencing and changing the history of jazz are multifarious. From Louis Armstrong's insistence on playing blues trumpet whilst all around him white and mainstream musicians sought accommodation with the classical tradition, to Ornette Coleman's emphasis on the blues as being at the centre of his avant-garde free-form improvisatory piece 'Free Jazz' (1960), jazz musicians have constantly reinvigorated their tradition by reference to the vernacular. An extremely effective and immediately transparent instance of such vernacular signifying can be seen in Ethel Waters' 1932 recording of the popular song 'I Can't Give You Anything But Love' which, as Ann Douglas relates, is given a unique rendition by Waters: 'she sang the first stanza in a crisply cultivated and white feminine manner then shifted into a perfect imitation of the palpably masculine, sexual and Negro Louis Armstrong (who'd recorded the song in 1929), complete with slurred diction, down-and-dirty growls, off-beat swagger, and scatting.'[37]

This performance shows how African American performers take the raw material of Anglo-American expression and create a wholly new form from its ruins. Ralph Ellison described the debt Anglo-American culture owed to the African American thus: 'American culture owes much of its distinctiveness to idioms which achieved their initial formulation through the cultural creativity of Afro-Americans.'[38] Michele Wallace is more polemical and notes that such practices, which have come to be called deconstructive by literary critics after Derrida, have been central to African Atlantic aesthetic practice for centuries:

And if only for the record, let me state clearly here that only a black person alien from black language use could fail to understand that we have been deconstructing white people's language and discourse... since 1619. Derrida did not invent deconstruction, we did. That is what the blues and signifying are all about.[39]

Morrison and Kay understand this central deconstructive mode in African American expression, its roots in black history and in musical forms such as jazz and the blues. More perceptive white critics have noted the quick-wittedness of such African American appropriation and invigoration of white cultural forms; even a white member of the plantocracy such as Duncan Clinch Hayward was forced to bow to the wisdom of his slaves: 'I used to try and learn the ways of these Negroes, but I could never divest myself of the suspicion that they were learning my ways faster than I was learning theirs.'[40] African American culture thus creates new indigenous forms by playing around with the raw material extant within the dominant culture. Charles Hartman has characterized jazz as resounding 'with a mixture of voices'.[41] Thus it is jazz culture's constant reinterpretation of given material which is as much its lifeblood as the invention of new tunes.

Hartman's idea of a 'historical echo-chamber' is a useful shorthand phrase to describe this central facet of jazz culture; he contends that jazz

embraces neither pure reduplication, nor pure invention. It desires neither the pure resurrection of the stilled voice of the composer – which a performance of Beethoven might think of itself striving toward – nor the soloist's voice sounding in pure isolation. Inevitably it resounds with a mixture of voices. We can call this mixture a 'dialogue' – remaining aware of a possible confusion, since the relation among players within the group performance also accepts the same metaphor. Nor does the mixture confine itself to two voices, the composer's and the soloist's. Many voices may speak together in oblique relation to each other, and at a wide range of volumes.[42]

Hartman's paradigm for jazz performance situates it as having unique relationships between the jazz player and his or her history; to dramatically over-simplify, we might constitute the three major features of this paradigm as the tune, the tradition and the present performance. Jazz, then, is a form in constant dialogue both diachronically and synchronically. Each musician is in dialogue with his or her improvising fellows and with those who have preceded him or her in the tradition. Such a mode has obvious resonances for black writers who wish to have a relationship to history that validates the individual tale-teller, their dialogue with past versions of the tale and their performance of the tale in a listening community. This all matters far more than the abstract facts of the tale to writers like Morrison and Kay whose novels, in this way if no other, exhibit a thoroughgoing jazz aesthetic. In Western critical parlance, such important cultural activity has been labelled 'dialogising'. Russian language theorists have highlighted the contested nature of language (and of course music could be characterised as a language), showing how words are not neutral but value-laden. Mikhail Bakhtin, for instance, could be talking of the radical vernacular intentions of many African American artists when he talks of the need to take language from the powerful and 'make it one's own':

> The word in language is half someone else's. It becomes one's own only when the speaker populates it with his own intention, his own accent, when he appropriates the word, adapting it to his own semantic and expressive intention. Prior to this moment of appropriation, the word does not exist in a neutral and impersonal language, but rather it exists in other people's mouths, in other people's contexts serving other people's intentions: it is from there that one must take the word and make it one's own.[43]

The example of Ethel Waters taking a pop song created in an Anglo-American form and dialogising it, making it into an African American form by adapting it to her own semantic and expressive intentions, is paradigmatic of black Atlantic artistic praxis. Similarly, to make the word one's own, to appropriate the literary tradition for their own vernacular purpose, is the radical intention of writers like Morrison and Kay.

The language of the literary tradition has often been used to serve the powerful, but Morrison and Kay's intention is to use it to relate the untold stories of a people who had been denied the power of literary language through legalised oppression (through slavery and later the Black Codes), racism and other more insidious economic and cultural repression. Caliban replied to Ariel in *The Tempest*: 'You taught me language and my profit on't / Is I know how to curse.'[44] Morrison and Kay employ the master's language to undertake a similar vernacular response. Their radical intention, though brilliantly codified by Bakhtin and articulated centuries earlier by Shakespeare, does not principally come from Russian language theorists, canonical playwrights or even deconstructionists, postmodernists or poststructuralists, but from the core traditions of African Atlantic people who had to 'make a way out of no way' and did so by taking the words out of white people's mouths and adapting them for their own purposes.

The avowal of such an oral mode by Morrison and Kay highlights their constant efforts to validate such a black aesthetic. Jazz music, with its oral traditions and its encoding of African American cultural and social history, is one of the central and most effective modes African Americans use to harbour important aspects of their past, to effectually remember. Such remembrance at its most effective is never ossified and content to play familiar changes which have been worked out well in advance, but an attempt to reinterpret the old tunes in ways relevant to today, to literally create aural memorials that acknowledge the past whilst creating new expressions. Bechet recognised the importance of the constant replenishment of jazz through reinterpretation of standard tunes and said of critics being too obsessed with nostalgia:

> They get to think in a memory way about this jazz; but these people don't seem to know it's more than a memory thing. They don't seem to know

it's happening right there where they're listening to it, just as much as it ever did in memory.[45]

Bechet contrasts a stagnant 'memory thing', which holds a jazz tune and replays it *ad nauseum*, with the living culture of actual jazz music which serves as such an effective paradigm for black writers' constantly inventive, yet deeply rooted, storytelling craft in which remembering is so central. The jazz culture's own tradition of rememory and the musical modes it uses to harbour remembrance provide these writers with an effective paradigm which they are able to use in their writing. There are dangers in eulogising the oral tradition over the literary because it may run the risk of sentimentalising non-traditional cultures, positing them as more radical than they were or are; but in the face of the current hegemony of written cultures over oral cultures, calling on the latter can often have a radicalising effect on the former, as Berndt Ostendorf says:

> [a] traditional oral culture which is conservative when taken for itself may provide a counter-cultural alternative when it meets with the myths of an alienated literate consciousness.[46]

Using such a paradigm and applying it to Morrison and Kay, they could be seen to be suffusing their texts in vernacular forms derived from a jazz and African Atlantic aesthetic which provides a counter-cultural alternative to traditional literary practices. As I have hinted throughout the discussion of dialogisation, it is not only white language and aesthetic practice which is subject to healthy appropriation. African Atlantic culture is internally dialogised, so that aesthetic forms are constantly being signified on and altered. One of the most transparent signifying practices within African Atlantic culture is that known as 'second lining'. This practice developed in the late nineteenth century around parades where bands played as crowds of brightly costumed revellers danced down the street. Bechet was himself a 'second liner' and describes the function of the second line in his autobiography:

> And those that didn't have money, they couldn't get in the parade. But they enjoyed it just as much as those that were doing it – more, some of them. And those people they were called 'second liners'. They had to make their own parade with broomsticks, kerchiefs, tin pans, any old damn thing. And they'd take off shouting, singing, following along the sidewalk, going off on side streets when they was told they had no business being on the sidewalks or along the kerbs like that... They'd be having their own damn parade, taking what was going on in the street and doing something different with it, tearing it up kind of, having their fun. They'd be the second line of the parade.[47]

Such second lining 'was not merely infantile: it was the primary class in the folk academy of a people's music'.[48] This can be attested to by the roll call of musicians from all periods in jazz history whose first lessons were learnt on the second line: Jelly Roll Morton, Louis Armstrong, Lester Young and Ed Blackwell were all students in the second line. Note too the description of home-made instruments – 'any old damn thing' – which were used to create a hubbub. Such use of found instruments to create cacophonous sound, different from, but feeding off, the mainstream band, shows a vernacular response to a more refined sound at the very heart of jazz practice. The second line 'tears up' and has fun with mimicking the parade, creating its own different and parallel ritual. This paradigm of mainstream music in the tradition being constantly open to revision from the margins of the discourse, which becomes the mainstream only to be second lined itself in later times, attests to a malleable tradition with its roots deep in a playing and listening community, which itself creates aural memorials that are sustaining because of their vibrant currency.

Second lining existed on both secular and religious parades, playing an especially crucial role in funeral parades where its ability to change mood after the parade left the cemetery, in response to musical directions from the band, contributed much to the dignity and efficacy of the ceremony. Bunk Johnson, an early jazzman, describes such an occasion, the funeral of a mason:

> …then we'd march away from the cemetery. Then we'd go right on into ragtime – what the people call today swing – ragtime. We would play 'Didn't He Ramble', or we'd take all those spiritual hymns and turn them into ragtime… We would have a second line there that was 'most equivalent to King Rex parade – Mardi Gras carnival parade. The police were unable to keep the second line back – all in the street, all on the sidewalks, in the front of the band, and behind the lodge, and in front of the lodge. We'd have some immense crowds following. They would follow the funeral up to the cemetery just to get this ragtime music coming back.[49]

The achievement of such joyous revelling in a funeral context has been much commented on, and the use of a jazz mode by writers is an homage to such an effective aesthetic mode. Also attested to is its functionality at funerals, wherein African Americans are given the strength to continue despite oppression, racism and personal and communal tragedies through taking part in a ceremonial in which jazz music plays the central role. Participants here create effective memorialisation through improvisation and performance. As Joseph Roach has described, the commemoration becomes crucial for the whole community as it continues after the grieving family have moved away: 'after the body is cut loose – sent on its way in the company of family members – a popular celebration commences less like a forgetting than a replenishment.'[50] Such kinetic memorialisation is crucial to oral African Atlantic cultures as a means of articulating important events which were historically not recorded in writing or in statuary. Each ceremonial at a funeral would repeat the same mode of community memorialising whilst the specific communal improvisations would honour the individual being mourned, thus combining communal ritual with respect for the dead loved one and their family. This combination of collective and family memorialisation is in the service of a 'symbolic embodiment of loss and renewal'[51] that is crucial to the survival of community values, and where better to affirm this than at the funeral of an individual where 'the body of the deceased performs the limits of the community called into being by the need to mark its passing'?[52] The jazz funeral thus creates an effective aural and performative memorial that uses the resources of the music to enable communal mourning and transcendence. It enables the community to effectually remember the individual mourned and celebrate the continuity of the cultural praxis that so effectively commemorates their life and death. As Anne Whitehead asserts:

An image of the past is, then, not simply conveyed and sustained by ritual performances; it is also brought to life in the present and relived through direct embodiment and gestural repetition.[53]

This intersection between the past and the present enables effective memorialisation through the dynamics of a community commemoration that leaves its imprint on individuals as a form of body memory which can be called on in the future when needed again. Jazz, as a part of the ceremony, enables the creation of an aural memorial that is effective in sustaining African Atlantic culture across geographies and chronologies.

The jam session is another of the modes used to effectually remember and the communal nature of the experience is central. The social and improvised nature of jazz means that African Americans can share their history through the dynamics of musical performance. Ben Sidran, in talking about Charlie Parker's concerts, says:

he'd play a phrase and people might never have heard it before, but he'd start it and the people would finish it by humming it. It would be so lyrical and simple it would just seem the natural thing to play.[54]

In such instances, the call and response between performer and audience is so naturalised that it is often confusing as to who is calling and who responding. This instinctual antiphony is effortlessly achieved because of a shared cultural history. The continuity between these kind of occurrences in a mid-twentieth century context, and in those modes which were part of the nineteenth century plantation experience for African Americans, in which slaves shared their experience through improvised songs, illustrate great continuity in the musical traditions of black Americans. The shared racial memory of audience and performers meant that at times of great social pressure music could provide an important unifying force. As Burton Peretti says, 'jazz performance[s] [were] public rituals: they were the focus of social energy among migrating blacks.'[55] In the rent parties of the 1920s and the jazz suppers of the 1930s, jazz players and audiences performed ritualistic social melding in opposition to the atrophication, commodification and alienation of modern capitalist America. The informal jazz scene provided socialisation into a difficult and new urban environment for many migrating African Americans, keeping them in touch with their rural and Southern past.

Such rituals continued even when jazz music became less popular in the African American sub-culture, being replaced by rhythm and blues and, later, soul music. A performance of John Coltrane is emblematic of the kind of continuing interaction between jazz musicians and a black audience;

> You have the element of rage in any black person which comes out in many forms. In John Coltrane it is the erratic response, the sudden swirling change of direction ... clarity of protest which comes out in artistic form. The work of art becomes a vehicle for frustration and howling out against injustice we all receive. A composer like John Coltrane creates a tremendous excitement with a live black audience when he begins to communicate this primordial rage and the audience howls in unison ... it's like a catharsis and after it's over one is purged again so you can go back out and cope with it – life.[56]

Other instances the commentator mentions as symptomatic of such cathartic experiences for African American audiences are in the congregations of black churches and in the concerts of great soul artists such as James Brown. Within this wide spread of artistic responses, jazz is seen as a central healing force in African American culture, achieving a spirit of community despite oppression by channelling rage at racism and injustice into artistic response in order to militate against its harmful affects. The jazz musician in this paradigm acts as a spokesperson, or more aptly a griot, for their community, encoding in the music an effective message (often a rememory of hard times gone) easily read by the audience, who add to the musician's knowledge through their cathartic responses during the performance. As the African American poet Michael Harper says, there is 'a tremendous amount of history, metaphor, cultural information and detail in the music of black America'.[57] As a repository of so much of value to African Americans, it is little wonder black writers want to quaff from the reservoir of jazz history. Kay, in particular, values the music for its ability to link her to her diasporic history and has described eloquently the importance of jazz music in an African Atlantic context where it is vital for constructing identity and linking to wider cartogrophies than are available for black Britons in other artistic spheres:

And because I didn't have access to being able to write, or wasn't confident enough to write in, Caribbean voices or African voices, then it seemed that music was a lovely bridge for that. So I have written a lot about jazz and jazz itself interests me because it's such a fluid form and it comes from the blues, and I like the idea that black music has shifted and changed. It's like identity in that way – identity's something that's fluid, it's not something that's static and fixed and I'm really interested in writing about identity and how fluid it is, how it's not something that we can just say, this person is that kind of person and they stay that kind of person for ever. So music just has been I suppose a wonderful metaphor, a wonderful live constantly changing thing to try and grapple with and write about.[58]

Music allows Kay access to an international black culture and historical architecture that helps frame her texts, providing a form in which to write an African Atlantic identity despite her physical distance from the specific wellspring of African American culture. The jazz culture's centrality for African Americans and black people in the diaspora is in its ability to express their needs and desires in the here and now, and in the context of their cultural tradition and history in its widest contexts. For the jazz singer and pianist Nina Simone, the jazz performer literally equals blackness:

Jazz is not just music, it's a way of life, it's a way of being, a way of thinking. I think that the Negro in America is jazz … it's not just music. It's the definition of the Afro-American black.[59]

Jazz can define the African American because of its ability to express both the secular and the sacred definitions of African American thought. The music can trace its origins back to the black church of antebellum America and reconstruction, as well as to African religious traditions. The church context is where many African American musicians learnt the structural patterns that underpin jazz music. As Charles Keil says:

Constant repetitions, coupled with small but striking deviations – statements and counterstatements, all of which equal soul. It is a pattern that a negro child in the rural South or the urban ghetto learns by heart, normally in a church context, and it is as old as the oral traditions and call–response patterns of West African poetry and music.[60]

Leroi Jones stresses too that the instrumental voicings of early jazz come from singing voices in early African American churches. From here too come models for riffs and breaks which jazz musicians were able to adapt for their more secular contexts. This melding has extended to the material used in jazz performance from the earliest times to the present; from Louis Armstrong's numerous performances of 'When the Saints' and Sam Morgan's 'Over in the Gloryland' (1927) to John Coltrane's hymn 'A Love Supreme' (1964) and Albert Ayler's 'Truth Is Marching In' (1967), the sacred mode has influenced a large number of jazz performances. Such a synthesis was not without its controversial aspects, as many religious African Americans objected to the use of sacred melodies in a music they believed belonged to diabolic forces. Rudi Blesh intervenes appositely in this argument:

> though the music of the church singer is like the blues, and that of the congregation is one of the sources of jazz, nevertheless, to the religious negro such kindred music is sinful or worldly. Yet all are essentially the same music.[61]

Jazz musicians seem to concur with Blesh's view of the proper malleable nature of the form as a soundtrack to both the secular and sacred concerns of African Americans. An anecdote from Nina Simone illustrates the sacred underpinning of even such good-time jazz music as boogie-woogie:

> Mother and them were so religious that they wouldn't allow you to play boogie-woogie in the house, but would allow you to use the same boogie-woogie beat to play a gospel tune. I just don't agree with this attitude because our music crosses all those lines. Negro music has always crossed all those lines.[62]

The close association of the secular and sacred is emphasised by reports of Buddy Bolden, the founding father of jazz, melding the two traditions in his hugely influential performances. Dude Bately said of him, 'If Bolden stops on the hymn, the good lord wins; if he stops on the blues, the devil wins.'[63] From such performances and testimonies, expanding over the whole history of jazz culture, music can be seen as being at the crossroads of African Atlantic worldly and other-worldly concerns, providing a malleable form which can be picked up and used whenever necessary. From New Orleans funerals to uptown brothels, from rent parties to the public performance of spirituals in a jazz setting, jazz music synthesises the secular and sacred experiences of diverse characters whose life experiences differ markedly, thus providing a common musical style which is available to them all, and creates memorialising performances that help to build African Atlantic identities throughout the diaspora.

Despite its strength historically for African Americans, jazz has often been misunderstood and designated as merely entertainment music; for Morrison, though, it is 'speech, balm, consolation *and* entertainment',[64] and by her championing of the jazz tradition she seeks to rewrite such damning historiography. In effect, she could herself be seen as a functioning second line to jazz musicians, responding to their calls from her own position in the literary world, interpreting their concerns and feelings for a (sometimes) different audience. Her oft-stated claim that the music is no longer enough on its own to sustain African Americans is justification for her role as interpreter of her musical heritage to a modern audience. As she says:

> The book [*Jazz*] is a jazz gesture. Jazz is improvisational. You must be creative and innovative in performance. Even errors take you on to a new level of attainment. Writing is another form of music. There was a time when black people needed the music. Now that it belongs to everybody, black people need something else which is theirs. That's what novels can do, what writing can do. I write in order to replicate the information, the medicine, the balm we used to find in music.[65]

As Morrison gains an aesthetic mode from jazz, so she interprets a misunderstood and often maligned musical culture to the world. Morrison's writing is a 'jazz gesture' in a modern world which negates the achievements of jazz. Morrison literally writes as a means of re-invoking the potent, but disappearing, jazz culture which she sees as essential to her people.

The increasing marginality of jazz in US culture is partly caused by the centrality of improvisation to its aesthetic, which is a mode that has had little credibility in Eurocentric aesthetic praxis in the twentieth century. However, this mode creates much of the creative tension which makes jazz such an exciting and vibrant music, for the musician must negotiate between the freedom which being able to improvise gives him or her and the awareness of form necessary to make a coherent aesthetic statement. Musicians such as Coltrane did not achieve their epoch-making performances by just turning up on stage and blowing, but put in years of practice so that it would appear spontaneous. As Gunther Schuller contends, a famous Armstrong solo such as 'West End Blues' (1928) 'did not suddenly spring full-blown from his head. Its conception was assembled bit-by-bit over a period of four or five years.'[66] Morrison understands such aesthetic practice and in talking about Coltrane's performances with me she said: 'black people are very interested in making it look as though no thought went into it. And the jazz musician's the classic person. I mean the hours and hours of work so that you can be so imbued with it, so you can actually stand on stage and make it up.'[67]

The need to make the creative act look effortless, as though no sweat went into its creation, is an important legacy of the jazz tradition for Morrison.

In fact, Morrison draws on the improvisatory mode at the centre of the jazz aesthetic because of its awareness of form rather than its supposed lack of it, and in doing so is thoroughly attuned to core African American aesthetic values. Ted Gioia, in analysing jazz performance, posits it as exhibiting a 'retrospective' rather than a 'blueprint' method of composition (the best example of the latter method is the architect who draws up full plans before the building is constructed). Thus, in an actual composition the jazz performer 'always looks behind at what he has already created', so that 'each new musical phrase can be shaped in relation to what has gone before.'[68] Thus creation as process rather than as product is achieved in jazz by repetitious rhythmic figures such as riffs, which help the musician to structure his improvisations with reference to what has already been created.

Improvisation is a style that lies at the heart of African American vernacular tradition and differentiates it from mainstream musical modes. Stanley Crouch talks of such a performative jazz achievement as being 'fresh to Western art': 'These musicians hear what is played by their fellow performers, are inspired to inventions of their own, hold their places in the forms of the songs, and send tasks to their muscles that must be executed so swiftly that all functions of mind and body come together with intimidating speed.'[69]

The centrality of improvisation in the jazz aesthetic means that jazz performance always has an evanescent quality; such evanescence comes from the status of jazz as an oral art form, and true to such forms, jazz evades attempts to notate it. David McAllester comments: 'Just as the ethnographer starts to write down what he sees, the clear outlines of the culture as it was a moment ago start to get wavery.'[70]

Many jazz performances elude attempts to pin them down, glorying in an aesthetic of sheer presentness and making attempts at full appropriation very difficult. Of course commodification through the selling of records and the marketing of performers shows the penetration of capitalism into jazz culture; however, the music at its most creative eludes the dominant hegemonic forces of Eurocentrism and capitalism that try to appropriate cultural forms from marginal cultures. In this way the music can be seen as quintessentially subversive. Kimberly Benston links this quality to core African American praxis thus: 'the root of the black writers' elevation of music to a position of superiority among the arts lies in the music's aversion for fixed thoughts and forms.'[71] Jazz performers delight in their musical culture's radicalism, which is predicated on its continual rebirth and on evanescence. As Billy Higgins says:

> The only good thing about music today is that they haven't really exploited jazz because they can't hold onto it. As soon as they think it's here – it's

there. What more can I say about jazz? Nothing! The music says it all. Take the pencil away, the paper and everything and just hit it.[72]

Jazz music's willed, improvisatory aesthetic glories in a non-intellectualised climate where the mystique of the performance and the performers is an achieved one. Witness the amount of legends in jazz-lore and the accent throughout on oral rather than literary history amongst musicians themselves. There is a playful obscurantism about jazz musicians when they discuss the history of the music. Thus Thelonius Monk, when he describes the scene at Minton's where bebop, according to jazz mythology, was spawned, says: 'I've seen practically everyone at Minton's, but they were just there playing. They weren't giving any lectures.'[73] Of course, technically Monk was right, there were no 'chalk and talk' men at Minton's; however, it was undeniably a revolutionary laboratory of sound where new techniques in rhythm, harmony and melody were practised, shared and taught.

Both Higgins and Monk are obviously playing up the non-intellectualised side of jazz to stress its mystical, other-worldly and non-Western qualities. In fact, they could even be said to be masking the complexity and difficulty of jazz performance behind a smiling insouciant primitivist face, to be literally signifyin(g) on an Anglo-American need to intellectualise, rationalise and explain. However, whether contrived or real (and really it is a combination of both), jazz culture's non-intellectualised strain is very useful for Morrison, and later Kay, who want to emphasise an African Atlantic culture which makes the complex appear simple, the protagonist exhibiting a grace throughout the most difficult of feats. Morrison, in her interview with me, made a direct link from such feats to her own writing when she talked of the improvising musician and the grace of her people:

> *Rice*: John Coltrane practises hours and hours every day so that his playing appears spontaneous.

> *Morrison*: Of course, and it looks natural. People do it in sport. It's all style and effortless gesture. And I like to write like that, as though it were a whole clause. When I do it right it looks artless and it looks like it's not writerly, non-writerly. Sometimes I haven't done it very well and you can see the work but, whatever, I don't want your literary precedents to help you.[74]

The precedents she does want to help you come from the bedrock of her own oral culture, from the improvisatory nature of the jazz culture which has influenced her beyond measure. However, it is not just the absolute presentness of the jazz experience that interests Morrison, it is the combination of this with a remembrance which locates almost all jazz performances in a lived history. It is the way the music delights in a lived, seemingly infinite past, just as it wallows in new improvisatory turns; for instance, the way in which when Eric Dolphy in 1961 played 'God Bless the Child', Billie Holiday's 1941 performance of the tune was only just beneath the surface.[75] Even more pertinently, Albert Ayler's revision of the famous tune 'The Saints Are Marching In' into what he called 'Truth Is Marching In' (1967) served not to bury the old tune but to resurrect it, to show its meaning for the present and to create an aural memorial of the continuity of struggle and its development in African American culture. What had been a millennial tune, played after funerals in New Orleans to celebrate the continuation of life, had become in Ayler's version a political anthem for the 1960s. Ayler consciously made this link in an interview with Nat Hentoff, used for the liner notes of the album, in which he discussed not only the New Orleans roots of the tune, but also the importance of Louis Armstrong, whose version of the tune was a seminal one in jazz history:

> In a way we're trying to do for now what people like Louis Armstrong did at the beginning. Their music was a rejoicing. It was a rejoicing about beauty that was going to happen ... now the truth is marching in as it once marched back in New Orleans.[76]

Ayler, who could be said to have articulated the goals of the Civil Rights movement in spiritual terms, obviously found in the old tune resonances for the continual fight for African American justice. As he told Hentoff in the same interview:

> In my music I'm trying to look far ahead. Like Coltrane, I'm playing about beauty that is to come after all the tensions and anxieties. I mean the cries of love that are in the young and that will emerge as people seeking freedom come to spiritual freedom.[77]

It is fitting that Ayler and his brother Donald had played 'Truth Is Marching In' at Coltrane's funeral earlier in 1967, and the juxtaposition of a version of the old religious marching tune with all its historical resonances at a memorial to a player of so-called 'anti-jazz' shows the actual continuity of the jazz tradition through the free jazz period. The brothers here created a moving and thoroughly apposite memorial to Coltrane using their version of the old New Orleans funeral marching tune. Ayler's use of this tune is also important because of the way it harks back to a collectivity that existed in the early days of jazz, which practitioners of the 1960s sought to emulate. The very form of the tune – with collective improvisation, polyphony and a rhythmic marching sound so the hearer can imagine a procession – emphasises its collectivity and functional nature. These dynamic musicians simultaneously create aural memorials which are both beautiful and pedagogic. Hence, though it is correct to stress the evanescence of the jazz performance, jazz protagonists often seem to be working against such temporality by emphasising the latest stage of a historical tradition in which they are steeped, and creating from it performances that are a legacy to generations to come. Morrison and Kay use this combination of the diachronic and the synchronic in their novels, where characters in long oral narratives, happening in the present, have an easy facility to jump backwards in time to fill in gaps and provide explanations. They remember the past through improvisatory riffs situated in the here and now. As Eckstein has noted in talking about Morrison's *Beloved*, in a succinct analysis that can also be applied to other jazz-influenced novels including Kay's *Trumpet*:

> The broken beats of the blues, spirituals and jazz that the novel takes up are so much part of the everyday black life that they establish a secure foundation for the exploration of suffering and pain. In the expressive tradition of African American music, in the security of off-beat phrasings, history becomes graspable without being destructive and its stories thus become speakable.[78]

It is the very everyday nature of African Atlantic musical expression that enables it to articulate traumatic history without being overwhelmed by it. Obviously, such powerful and efficacious expression is key for both Morrison and Kay in preserving and describing histories, the values of which have been undermined by their being largely confined to an oral mode devalued in our literate culture. As Ingrid Monson asserts, 'the transformative resources in African American musical practices invert, challenge and often triumph over the ordinary hegemony of mainstream white hegemonic values.'[79] Their triumph as aural memorials reaches its apogee in famous versions like the Ayler brothers' funeral performance; however, as Morrison and Kay show in their novels, such memorials are central to the understanding of the formation of cultural identities for diasporan Africans, not only in the US but throughout the circum-Atlantic. As Paul Gilroy shows, the power of music in African Atlantic culture is its ability to continually reflect on and memorialise a triumphant survival in the face of racism and colonialism:

> The contemporary musical forms of the African diaspora work within an aesthetic and political framework which demands that they ceaselessly reconstruct their own histories, folding back on themselves time and again to celebrate and validate the simple unassailable fact of their survival.[80]

It is this survival that Morrison celebrates in all her novels. Jazz culture, with its easy acquaintance with the dangers and pleasures of evanescence and remembrance, becomes for Morrison an essential mode. She shows that creating memorials that encode this traumatic history, and the survival of it, is possible in even the most marginalised communities. One of the most apposite illustration of this comes in her second novel, *Sula* (1973). Here the ways in which the two major protagonists, Sula and Nel, cope with loss are commented on. It is telling that when Nel thinks of how to cope with her husband Jude's death, she thinks back to the keening cries she heard at a child's funeral. She describes her rememory of the funeral thus:

> She thought of the women at Chicken Little's funeral. The women who shrieked over the bier and at the lip of the open grave. What she had regarded since as unbecoming behaviour seemed fitting to her now; they were screaming at the neck of God, his giant nape, the vast back-of-the-head that he had turned on them in death... The body must move and throw itself about, the eyes must roll, the hands should have no peace, and the throat should release all the yearning despair and outrage that accompany the stupidity of loss.[81]

Their way of dealing with that loss is to cry out their collective pain. This keening helps them come to terms with this new absence, shows their human presence surviving such loss and remembers effectually the life that has gone. It provides a framework within which loss can be dealt with: a quintessential African Atlantic communal framework that the jazz tradition celebrates and exemplifies, as shown by the example of funeral parades. The community creates an aural memorial to the lost individual that is both appropriate and moving. The musical performance is evanescent, however, as shown by Nel's rememory of it here; despite this, it serves as a powerful tool to help those who subsequently have to cope with loss. The problem for Nel is that she cannot at this stage let herself go enough to mourn the loss of Jude in this way; the howl of outraged pain is unable to burst through:

> Hunched down in the small bright room Nel waited. Waited for the oldest cry. A scream not for others, not in sympathy for a burnt child, or a dead father, but a deeply personal cry for one's own pain. A loud, strident: 'Why me?' She waited. The mud shifted, the leaves stirred, the smell of overripe green things enveloped her and announced the beginning of her very own howl.
> But it did not come.[82]

Such a cry would resemble a field holler, the cry by which slaves showed their deep private despair in the antebellum South. This cry is best expressed in the modern jazz tradition by Abbey Lincoln's howls on the 'Freedom

Triptych' on Max Roach's *We Insist! Max Roach's Freedom Now Suite* (1960), or the screams of outraged fury in Archie Shepp's performance on *Poem for Malcolm* (1969).[83] As Mae Gwendolyn Henderson says, with specific reference to a female holler, these howls 'serve to disrupt or subvert the symbolic function of language, creating space for black women away from racism and sexism'.[84] However, in *Sula,* Nel cannot unleash such a howl because she does not have a strong enough sense of self. Her recognition of self is shown to have developed after a Jim Crow incident on a train journey south, when she distances herself from her mother's fawning response to a racist conductor and decides to harness her own resources in the face of societal constraints. However, this self-worth has been undermined by life in a community where she was secondary to her husband. This early recognition scene is pivotal, however, because, like much of the rest of the scene on the train, it is cut back to in later passages:

> There was her face, plain brown eyes, three braids and the nose her mother hated. She looked for a long time and suddenly a shiver ran through her.
> 'I'm me,' she whispered, 'Me.'
> Nel didn't know quite what she meant, but on the other hand she knew exactly what she meant.
> 'I'm me. I'm not their daughter. I'm not Nel. I'm me. Me.'[85]

Nel has moved from this tentative rejoicing in 'me' to the plaintive state after Jude has left in which she cannot even cry, 'Why me?'[86] Instead of a deep cry that brings up welled-up sorrow which would connect her to others who cry in despair in an oral and aural culture of remembrance, Nel is locked into a visual symbol of alienated lonely despair which is irritating and constantly foregrounds the messiness of her loss:

> And finally there was nothing, just a flake of something dry and nasty in the throat. She stood up frightened. There was something just to the right of her, in the air, just out of view. She could not see it, but she knew exactly what it looked like. A grey ball hovering just there. Just there. To the right. Quiet, grey, dirty. A ball of muddy strings, but without weight, fluffy, but terrible in its malevolence.[87]

The ball is a symbol of absent presence (ironically resembling the spider's web which Sula had envisaged her being trapped by) which Nel cannot escape. Its always being 'just there' is emphasised by its repeated occurrence in the passage, which is stressed by words connected with vision. If this image is a marker of how Nel is unable to come to terms with her loss because of a lack of self-awareness and an alienation from the core oral traditions of her people, the irony is that Sula is used by Morrison as illustrative of how loss can be coped with through musical catharsis. Sula has been left by her lover, Ajax, the first man she has ever really cared for. Robert Grant notes the parallelism of the friends' desertions: 'both characters are depicted experiencing very similar reactions to loss and loneliness; specifically both women must confront an intimate absence and emptiness that memory, paradoxically, both emphasises and assuages.'[88] Morrison, in a conscious repetition of the themes surrounding Jude's disappearance from Nel, describes how Ajax's presence seems to continue after his absence, only this time the discussion is much more overt:

> Every now and then she looked around for tangible evidence of his having been there. Where were the butterflies? the blueberries? the whistling reed? She could find nothing, for he had left nothing but his stunning absence. An absence so decorative, so ornate, it was difficult for her to understand how she ever endured, without falling dead or being consumed, his magnificent presence.[89]

Sula's despair is compounded by her discovery that Ajax has left only his driver's licence, which shows that she never even knew his real name. Namelessness or false naming is a constant theme in African American literature and Morrison cannot resist a brief riff as Sula laments not knowing her lover's real identity:

> Sula stood with a worn slip of paper in her fingers and said aloud to no one, 'I didn't even know his name. And if I didn't know his name, then there is nothing I did know and I have known nothing ever at all since the one thing I wanted was to know his name so how could he help but leave me since he was making love to a woman who didn't even know his name.'[90]

The riff here on 'knowing his name' cuts back to Nel's cry about Jude committing adultery despite the fact that 'he knew me', but more than this it shows the precarious nature of the knowledge of anyone. If a person can be present one moment and absent the next, and when he was present you did not even know his given name, then there is little wonder that blues songs of lament are those which dominate love relationships in this community. The object of desire is gone and the weeping, keening response is a typical one in black musical praxis. Language is not adequate to express such loss, yet Morrison invokes jazz and the blues here to express the pain of separation from the object of desire and to create a sustaining aural memorial. The blues song of remembrance is instrumental to the grieving process, and it is such a song that Sula articulates as she grieves, which helps her to cope with her loss:

When she awoke, there was a melody in her head she could not identify or recall ever hearing before. 'Perhaps I made it up,' she thought. Then it came to her – the name of the song and all its lyrics just as she had heard it many times before. She sat on the edge of the bed thinking, 'There aren't any more new songs and I have sung all the ones there are.' She lay down again on the bed and sang a little wandering tune made up of the words *I have sung all the songs all the songs I have sung all the songs there are* until, touched by her own lullaby, she grew drowsy, and in the hollow of near-sleep she tasted the acridness of gold, felt the chill of alabaster and smelled the dark, sweet stench of loam.[91]

Contrast this passage, alive with sound, with Nel's visual dissonance. Sula is able to devise such a song because of her strong sense of self. The constant riffing on song and the act of singing stresses the power of the musical tradition, as does Sula's improvisatory construction of a new song from the apparent despair of there being no new songs. It is being touched by her own lullaby, created from the musical traditions of the African American community, that enables her to move to the images at the end of the passage which cuts back to those describing her and Ajax making love. Here she has envisaged paring away his skin and finding gold, alabaster and loam. Her rememory of it now mourns Ajax's absence. It does more than that, however; it makes him present through a blues remembrance, an aural memorial. The song both highlights Ajax's absence and remembers his presence as gritty reality rather than romanticised fantasy. The loam, alabaster and gold are now seen simply as minerals with negative as well as positive qualities. In a sense the song reinstitutes Ajax's presence as loss, as a means to cope with that loss. Remembrance negates absence most completely for that flickering time that the song continues, and such a revelation leads us directly to the mode that is at the centre of the jazz aesthetic: evanescence.

Improvisation as a major defining feature of jazz gives it a quality of evanescence that makes it quite different to Western art music, where notation is more important. This quality of evanescence is best captured in Eric Dolphy's wonderfully elliptical comment recorded on his *Last Date* album: 'Once you hear music, when it's over, it's gone, in the air – you can never capture it again.'[92] It is this evanescent mode in improvised music that is used to work against absence, to encode the remembrance which works to reinstitute presence even if it is only at the level of memory. This happens whilst simultaneously, of course, the music by its own immediate disappearance 'in the air' expresses the quality of loss in a way that a physical or written memorial would struggle to express so eloquently. Sula's improvised song is paradigmatic of such an aesthetic process of a memorial that is effective precisely because it is ephemeral. Such disappearance is part of the mystery Kimberly Benston highlights in talking of the 'Orphic utterance momentarily stilled', to which only the renewal of music can respond. Thus Sula's song is quintessentially in the Orphic paradigm, as it acknowledges the limitations of musical expression whilst insisting on the need for it. Or as Benston expresses it, '[a] voice that temporarily ceases singing in the face of mystery, only to embrace a new strain that will henceforward echo this silence, but in song'.[93] Such songs provide a memorial function to which Morrison's novels pay homage.

Morrison's use of such a mode here shows her deep knowledge of the effectual nature of musical praxis in African Atlantic culture and its function as 'balm and consolation', as described in *Sula*. The music has multi-faceted functions in the culture which Morrison celebrates throughout her novels. Its dynamic quality is described wonderfully by Morrison herself:

> Music makes you hungry for more of it. It never really gives you the whole number. It slaps and it embraces. The literature ought to do the same thing. I've been very deliberate about that. The power of the word is not music, but in terms of aesthetics, the music is the mirror that gives me the necessary clarity.[94]

The necessary clarity is imaged best by a jazz tradition which provides an analogous form for Morrison's writing rather than an exact parallel. It shows her that a radical difference is necessary to create a form that will be sufficiently detached from the mainstream to retain aesthetic independence whilst being close enough to be understandable. Jazz provides the analogous form, the aesthetic she can use. Audre Lorde famously said, 'You cannot use the master's tools to destroy the master's house';[95] Morrison, by deliberately eschewing traditional literary form and utilising a vernacular from her own people's tradition, demonstrates her deep understanding of Lorde's feminist and radical intervention. Morrison is using a radical style, and through it embracing ideologies radical in the context of US letters. As she terms it herself, it is this very act of 'contemplating chaos'[96] that is a catalyst for the creation of radical new forms. A. Yemisi Jimoh highlights how a philosophical approach from jazz enables Morrison's radicalism:

> Jazz philosophy embodies the idea that there is space for one to go beyond the margin into the unknown in order to change the rules within the existing structure, to present the unpresentable, to say the unsanctioned. In this space, 'contemplating chaos' becomes possible and living in it is necessary for triumph or survival. Through music, Jazz creates a space for this survival or triumph even when these concepts seem impossible.[97]

A jazz aesthetic is a mode most appropriate for the telling of stories from deep in the past that Morrison is only just now (right at the moment she does it) telling out loud. By quaffing from this radical musical tradition she is creating dynamic literary memorials that have an enhanced power to remember and effectively memorialise African American tragedy and survival.

Of course, it is by now a commonplace to suggest that the only great indigenous art that the US has exported to the world is jazz music. This musical tradition forged in African American communities in the South at the turn of the century and taken northward in the 'great migration' of the succeeding decades articulated the aspirations and longings of a people denied their full rights in US society. Morrison takes these bare bones of simultaneous historical fact – the growth of the new musical form, jazz, and the great migration – and makes of them a narrative of rare power and imagination, calling it simply *Jazz* (1992). It is jazz music that creates the memorialising moments that fully tell that story, and describes how new identities were created.

The migration from the rural South was shown to be forced by economic hardship and racism, which left many African American sharecroppers little hope but escape to the fabled riches of the Northern cities. Morrison tells in flashbacks the horrendous story of foreclosures, which broke the spirits of so many African American families who had hoped for so much after their hard fight for freedom. One of her characters, Violet, reminisces about the time when 'white men came'

> talking low, as though nobody was there but themselves, and picked around in our things, lifting out what they wanted – what was theirs, they said, although we cooked in it, washed sheets in it, sat on it, ate off it. That was after they had hauled away the plough, the scythe, the mule, the sow, the churn and the butter-press.[98]

Morrison stresses that many African Americans, despite being legally free in the postwar South, were so enmeshed in an economic system of peonage that their freedom was a mirage. This reminiscence, told from a child's perspective, highlights the absurdity of a system wherein African Americans, after the overthrow of plantation slavery, had the illusory power of owning their own bodies whilst at the same time being in total thrall to a system which owned all their means of sustenance. In such passages Morrison powerfully evokes the rural distress that led to migration northward to cities whose wealth was emerging as a source for black southern folklore. *Jazz* articulates the promise of these cities and the disappointment of many African Americans at the poverty and racism they found in these 'promised lands'. The excitement of the move North and subsequent adjustments to the reality of life in the metropolis are conveyed by the musical form that accompanied African Americans northward: jazz music. In the early years of the century it was transported on the steamboats of the US's great rivers from New Orleans to St Louis, then on to Chicago to 'infect' the whole urban North by the end of the First World War.

Jazz, though, is not just an historical leitmotif used by Morrison to give her novel authentic colour, but a sign of the difference between African American art and the Anglo-American art it shadows. As Morrison attested to me in an unpublished portion of a 1988 interview:

> The point in black art is to make it look as a jazz musician does, unthought out, unintellectual, as it were. So the work doesn't show, to be able to do it on the spot. And that's a double-edged sword because if a black person does something extremely well, white people say, 'Well, it's natural' or 'It's magic' or something ridiculous like that.[99]

Morrison seeks to build on this improvisational tradition by appropriating those aspects of it which can be applied to writing. Whilst doing this, she acknowledges the limitations of her art form; she told me, 'It has actually to be written – I have all these illusions about it being oral, but it has to work quietly on the page. It is a book and I can't do it to every reader.'[100] Hence, jazz music cannot serve as a totally transparent model for the writer because of the gigantic gulf in medium between the mainly referential system of words and the more non-referential musical mode. Morrison's work is irredeemably frozen to the page when it is published, whereas the jazz musicians' tunes can be refined and redefined in successive performances both by themselves and others. In an inverted boast to Claudia Tate, Morrison acknowledged the limitations of her art form thus: 'I only have 26 letters of the alphabet; I don't have colour, or music. I must use my craft to make the reader see the colour and hear the sounds.'[101]

Despite these limitations, Morrison attempts to mirror the improvisational jazz aesthetic that links her to her African American musical contemporaries and precursors. In *Jazz*, the main narrative is outlined in the first few lines of the novel and concerns a series of unsavoury incidents in the city. It is the 1920s, and Joe Trace has murdered his young girlfriend Dorcas, who has been unfaithful to him. He feels he has been driven to adultery by his wife Violet, who has taken to sleeping with a doll. Stung by jealousy, she attempts to mutilate Dorcas's corpse at the funeral; meanwhile, Dorcas's guardian Alice refuses to inform the authorities of Joe's guilt.

These bare bones of the plot are revealed at the very beginning, and thereafter the novel is an attempt to explicate these violent and distressing events, to flesh out the characters and explain their motives. The urban and rural pasts of the protagonists are described, and they are all allowed to voice their own perspectives on the reasons for the actions they undertake. The major narrative then, which is actually voiced by an articulate, gossiping everywoman, is defined and redefined by the varied narrative perspectives of the characters themselves. Morrison's technique here establishes a template that Kay will follow in the construction of her novel *Trumpet*, as we will see later. Morrison, in a foreshadowing of Kay's discussion of her novel's various solos, explained the way she hoped this would work:

> When I was working out how this story would be told I decided to use the central narrative as you would the concept of jazz. Like a melody you play on, with various other narratives told by other people, other musicians as it were, giving their interpretation.[102]

The numerous voices sound against one another in the same way individual musicians play against each other as a way of establishing their own unique sound in a jazz ensemble. We hear Joe referring to his orphaned childhood and his search for his mother, and then of Violet's mother's suicide after being dispossessed of her house, as described in the reminiscence of foreclosure mentioned earlier. We hear Alice talk of watching a demonstration for civil rights with a young Dorcas, who has recently been orphaned by the St Louis riots of 1919, and Violet speaks of the almost mythical character Golden Gray whose privileged, fatherless white background does not prepare him well for the news that he actually has a living black father.

In this way Morrison valorises each of the characters, allowing them to tell their own versions, before creating a collective one at the end of the novel. The gossiping everywoman is unnamed, and her narrative acts as a kind of chorus that the novel continually cuts back to. This voice is, however, not omniscient and has only an equal say to that of the characters directly involved in the story, foregrounding the democratic nature of the type of jazz performance I believe Morrison is invoking here. All have a chance to be heard, and in order to come to a collective understanding of the dreadful events they are all party to, they must first listen to all the justifying solo voices and measure them against their own. Here then, Morrison mimics the group nature of jazz music, showing how a singular artwork is constructed from several solo voices. As can be seen from the examples above, many of the narrators cut back to the rural past as a means to understanding their present, rather as jazz musicians cut back to the original tune as a starting point and reference point for their whole improvisation. The use of such a mode is commonplace in jazz performance and is explicated by James Snead thus:

> In black culture the thing (the ritual, the dance, the beat) is there for you to pick it up again when you come back to get it. If there is any goal in such a culture, it is always deferred; it continually cuts back to the start,

in the musical meaning of cut, as an abrupt, seemingly unmotivated break (an accidental da capo) with a series already in progress and a willed return to a prior series.[103]

Such continual cutting back by the characters to the pasts that created them leads to a circuitousness which mimes jazz's non-linearity. Morrison creates no clear climactic point in the novel, always returning her characters to the past as a way to understand the present, rather as a jazz musician cuts back to older renditions of the tune to reinterpret it in his or her own improvisation. Satisfaction comes to the reader or audience not in a climactic moment but, in contradistinction, by the willed absence of a climax. As Morrison said herself in an interview published in 1983:

> Classical music satisfies and closes. Black music does not do that. Jazz always keeps you on the edge. There is no final chord. There may be a long chord, but no final chord… There is always something else that you want from the music. I want my books to be like that – because I want the feeling of something held in reserve and the sense that there is more, that you can't have it all right now.[104]

My stress on Morrison's African American technical virtuosity and the stylistic difference it engenders in her work is not intended to deny the importance of the polemical stands she takes on such issues as the power of black women historically, the debilitating effects of miscegenation in a racist culture, and the importance of class in African American society, but rather to show how the use of a jazz aesthetic allows her to comment on these issues with greater incisiveness. For instance, Morrison's critique of the middle-class African Americans' denial of their shared roots in Southern black society with working-class blacks is given added potency by the use of a jazz mode to explicate it. Here Alice is ruminating on the significance of a demonstration she witnessed on Fifth Avenue, which has disturbed her and seems to explain the racist oppression she has suffered:

> [A] melody line she doesn't remember where from sings itself, loud and insistent in her head. 'When I was young and in my prime I could get my barbecue any old time.' They are greedy, reckless words, loose and infuriating, but hard to dismiss because underneath, holding up the looseness like a palm, are the drums that put Fifth Avenue into focus.[105]

These drums illustrate the serious side of the music which operates alongside and underpins the 'dirty get-on-down music' Alice and her middle-class friends despise so much. It is a link to their historical roots, which Morrison believes would give them greater ability to deal with the prejudice and discrimination they daily endure. Their denial of the whole jazz experience because of a prudish dislike for its juke-joint excesses leaves them alienated from its potential to enhance ethnic solidarity, and means it cannot provide them with a route out of their lonely despair. The drums can 'put Fifth Avenue into focus' for such middle-class African Americans, but only if their priggishness and fear of the sensual can be overcome. In this way jazz music is quintessentially memorialising, having the function of linking these African Americans to a past that would be nourishing for them would they but embrace it. The music's memorial function is to engage these alienated city-dwellers with a Southern past that, despite its travails, did provide an ethnic solidarity and cultural wellspring that enabled survival. A useable identity is only possible, Morrison asserts, by remembering that past and the music that encodes it; the memorialising function of jazz provides the most efficacious bridge to that wellspring.

In this novel, it is not only the humans who are illuminated, for at times the city itself seems a character and in her description of it Morrison creates a breathless, staccato style by a willed non-use of punctuation to illustrate the fast-moving, noisy nature of the city experience itself. The free-form amalgam of city signs is used to build up an effective jazzy description:

> The city is smart at this: smelling and good and looking raunchy; sending secret messages designed as public signs: this way, open here, danger to let colored only single men on sale woman wanted private room stop dog on premises absolutely no money down fresh chicken free delivery fast.[106]

Whilst Morrison's prose resembles jazz at the sentence level, at the same time the whole novel is structured using a jazz aesthetic. No chapter ending is left to hang without the succeeding chapter picking up on the last phrase to begin to build a new solo. Thus Joe Trace's explanatory solo about his past ends with, 'And let me tell you, baby in those days it was more than a state of mind',[107] and this cue is immediately taken up by the major narrative voice at the beginning of the next chapter: 'Risky, I'd say, trying to figure out anybody's state of mind.'[108] This leads to a seamlessness that recalls the best of jazz performance, which despite being a series of disparate solo interactions works as an aesthetic whole. Jazz musicians often pick up on the musical traces of the previous soloist as they launch into their own definition of a piece, so creating communal work out of individual memory. Morrison, here, is consciously using their technique of antiphony to structure her novel.

The most important technique Morrison appropriates is the riff, which structures whole long passages of all her novels. Henry Louis Gates Jr explicates the riff thus:

The riff is the central component of jazz improvisation. It is a figure musically speaking, a foundation, something you could walk on. A short phrase repeated over the length of a chorus.[109]

The way Morrison utilises this form linguistically is by repeating a word or short phrase to create a kind of musical poetry in the narrative. Thus Felice, who tells Joe and Violet of Dorcas's final few hours alive, reaches an understanding of Violet's need to mutilate Dorcas to cure herself, and this is marked in the text by an extended riff about the importance of integrity:

I thought about … the way his wife said 'me'. The way she said it. Not like the 'me' was some tough somebody, or somebody she had put together for a show. But like, like somebody she favoured and could count on. A secret somebody you didn't have to feel sorry for or have to fight for. Somebody who wouldn't have to steal a ring to get back at whitepeople and then lie and say it was a present from them.[110]

The repeated 'somebody' is the figure Morrison 'walks on', using it to structure the short passage. The repetitions make for a lyrical prose style which mimics the jazz sound created by the wilful use of the repetitions of notes and phrases. This particular riff is redolent for Felice, who is coming to an understanding of the importance of a ring stolen from 'whitefolks' by her mother as an emancipatory gesture. She had not understood the full importance of it until her discussion with Violet, which has persuaded her that it was not the theft that was the crime but the covering lie her mother used to protect herself. The passage also echoes back to (cuts back to) a conversation in which Alice had told Violet that she should pick the targets of her wrath with more discretion:

Fight what, who? Some mishandled child who saw her parents burn up? … Or maybe you want to stomp somebody with three kids and one pair of shoes. Somebody in a raggedy dress, the hem dragging in the mud. Somebody wanting arms just like you do…[111]

Violet has learnt to respect her own 'somebody', her 'me', rather than attacking another's. Felice and Violet's growth as characters is reflected by the use of 'somebody' as a positive quality now and the riff, repeated and redefined as the novel unfolds, is key to an understanding of this development. When the reader hears the echo they are immediately reminded of the less positive use of the riff earlier, and can judge the development that has been made by the characters' sharing of their stories.

Jazz is full of such riffs, though many of them are less self-contained than this one and are spread over several paragraphs, creating long and involved jazz passages. One of the most important riffs for an understanding of the novel is the extended one that Violet introduces around the notion of 'cracks', which are dark fissures in 'the globe light of [her] day' showing her scenes she is excluded from. It is the healing force of musical interplay with Alice, her acknowledgement of her history as told through jazz, that will dissolve these 'cracks' and allow her to piece her life together again.

The healing force of jazz is ironic in the context of the 1920s when Dorcas was murdered, for she is cut down at a party to the accompaniment of raucous jazz music. Morrison's novel faces up to the ambivalences of the musical form, showing how its values were degraded and demeaned within the market-place of the 'jazz age'. That these values are built on sand is shown in phrases that undermine the romance of the juke-joint party: 'This is the place where things pop. This is the market where gesture is all.'[112] In the arms of the lover whom all the other girls want, Dorcas's contentment is shown to be based on a false, consumerist value system that is ultimately destructive. The use of the word 'pop' here reflects the debasement of African American music, translated into pop by being frozen into a record, and its commodification as just another tune for the seduction of minors.

Despite showing this use of jazz within the market-place, Morrison is always at pains to stress its origins in vernacular black culture, carrying the memories of its Southern origins and hence undermining the version that would have it bursting into life in the cities as a direct reaction to the post-war zeitgeist. Thus when she portrays musicians jamming on the rooftops she is at pains to emphasise the rural origins of the tune:

> You would have thought everything had been forgiven the way they played … the brass was cut so fine … high and fine like a young girl swinging by the side of a creek, passing the time, her ankles cold in the water … The young men with brass probably never saw such a girl, or such a creek, but they made her up that day. I could hear the men playing out their maple-sugar hearts, tapping it from four-hundred-year-old trees and letting it run down the trunk …[113]

The original inspiration comes from a pastoral Southern scene, and the image of maple trees is decidedly rural too. Morrison is signifying on traditional ideas of the jazz age, which enclose it hermetically in a city context. For her the jazz is made by a transplanted people whose bridge to a defining past is as important as their present sorrows. By denying themselves entry to such sounds, Alice and other middle-class blacks deny their African American heritage, and their consequent alienation is a theme Morrison emphasises through her dialectic on the jazz tradition. But she does more than this, describing how the music encodes cultural memories that would be lost without its memorialising function. Now routed far from the South, jazz is a crucial aural memorial to a Southern history which is in danger of being forgotten in the brash new urban spaces of the Northern cities. Morrison asserts that despite its existence in this twilight world of sordid sex and materialistic ideology, jazz provides a bridge to past history and a map out of present troubles, compulsively inveigling itself even into the most stony middle-class, devil-music-hating of African Americans:

> The tunes whistled through perfect teeth are remembered, picked up later and repeated at the kitchen stove. In front of the mirror, near the door one of them will turn her head to the side and sway, enchanted with her waistline and the shape of her hips.[114]

Even the performative gesture of a slight movement is shown here to encode a memory of the past that has helped to frame an identity to cope with the urban present. The sway here is a literal body memory that enables Alice to reconnect with her past. Such an 'incorporating practice' of memory 'sedimented or amassed in the body' creates a performative and aural memorial of the Southern past.[115] Alice, despite her 'better instincts', is attracted to a quality in the music that is present both in the juke-joint and in the drum music used on a demonstration for negro rights, and finds herself singing a melody line. The music, then, was (and is) 'multi-lingual', providing languages for experiences ranging from sex through loss to politics. It was not merely the accompaniment to libidinous practices and drunkenness that white-owned places such as the Cotton Club emphasised, but also a reservoir of expressive resources for African Americans to quaff from. Morrison signifies on the accepted views of jazz and undermines them through her narrative, which emphasises the positive value of the jazz inheritance. As with Bechet, she believes that, 'The music had the role of teaching the people what to do with the freedom they now had, that they didn't have before.'[116] It does this through its riffs on an African American rooted and routed history, which it encodes in these aural memorials.

For Morrison then, jazz is used not merely to add colour to her work, but is its driving inspirational force, encompassing aesthetic values that underlie the history of her 'tribe'. *Jazz* exemplifies this through an extended riff on the compulsive, 'finger-snapping', 'clicking' rhythm of African American life which, despite conservative white American attempts to confine it to the ghetto, breaks free to affect the language, culture and music of Anglo-America. The everywoman narrator images Joe and Violet for us:

> For me they are real. Sharply in focus and clicking. I wonder do they know they are the sound of snapping fingers under the sycamores lining the streets?... the clicking is there. In the T-strap shoes of Long Island debutantes, the sparkling fringes of daring short skirts

that swish and glide to music that intoxicates them more than the champagne.[117]

Morrison shows how many aspects of the 'swinging twenties' were caused by the enhanced African American presence in the city. Jazz is a form that, in Scott Saul's words, 'celebrates and worries the idea of freedom'[118] so that the new experiences of blacks in modernity are crucially figured by it. Morrison's jazz aesthetic, exemplified by this clicking and finger-snapping presence, becomes, in her own words, 'something else you must figure in before you can figure out'.[119] And such critical figuring becomes imperative, not only to understand Morrison's work and African American culture but also to fully understand the US culture it shadows. By such 'colonisation in reverse', Morrison uses the full resources of the jazz aesthetic to refigure US cultural history in her own ethnic image. This is finally the great triumph of *Jazz*: to mirror in prose the aesthetic triumph of the African American music it celebrates. Jazz music, by creating aural memorials, helps sustain African Americans on the move in ways that no other artform can equal, and this is why Morrison uses it to frame and tell her people's story. It is a measure of jazz music's sturdy transatlantic strength that the black Scots novelist Kay is able to utilise it too.

Despite links across the diaspora, however, it is important – before we discuss Kay in the context of a jazz aesthetic developed by black writers in the US – that we inject a note of healthy scepticism about unproblematic encounters between African American and UK culture, as Kay's mode of writing is just as much about revealing the unique contribution of black Britons to the diaspora as it is about showcasing the cross-cultural and globalising form of jazz music. Ignorance of black British history is endemic amongst leaders of the black Atlantic cultural community. For instance, there can hardly be a more iconographic African American male spokesperson in the late twentieth and early twenty-first centuries than the film-maker Spike Lee. Yet his profound lack of knowledge about black British history is revealed by his response to questions from an audience when he visited Britain in 1999. I want to quote the encounter to show the flavour of a condescending, neo-colonial response to European blacks. In response to a question about the difficulties facing black British actors and asking whether he might be able to do anything for them, Lee responds,

> I've been coming here since 1986 and every time I come I get asked this same question. 'Spike, what can you do for us?' Nothing's changed. How many years have black people been here? Fifty?[120]

Lee's startling ignorance here (there has been a black presence in Britain since Roman times) is very revealing and is commented on by the exiled

American Tara Mack, who admits to having had similar prejudices herself. Her further comment, however, is pertinent to the relationship of black Britons to African Americans. She says,

> It always amazes me how much black people in Britain seem to know about and identify with black Americans. Sometimes I want to say, you do realise that black Americans are barely aware you exist?[121]

The mid-twentieth century is key to the development of the fascination of those diasporan Africans with an African American culture that has an exoticism and dynamism that their own more liminal presence on European shores sometimes makes them in awe of. Kay and other black cultural workers show how Spike Lee is wide of the mark in his limited knowledge about the presence of blacks in Britain, which long predates his late twentieth-century blinkers.

In my 2003 study *Radical Narratives of the Black Atlantic*,[122] I traced some of these black historical presences in the UK: from Scipio Kennedy in Ayrshire in the early eighteenth century, through Sambo's brief sojourn in Lancashire in 1736, and the London mendicant Joseph Johnson who begged with a ship on his head in the early nineteenth century, to Pompey, the major-domo to Wilfred Scawen Blunt, who lived in rural Sussex from 1866 to 1885. Such lesser-known figures are set alongside characters like Olaudah Equiano, Robert Wedderburn and Mary Prince, whose radical interventions helped to define and make a place for a black British presence that thoroughly undermines Lee's crass generalisation about black Britons being a recent phenomenon. Historical black figures are constantly being discovered in the most obscure corners of the UK, in communities that have generally been thought of as completely white. Of course this should not surprise us, as trading relations between Britain and the West Indies in the slave trade and afterwards meant that people moved as well as goods. For instance, in the small coastal town of Wigtown in south-west Scotland, a black woman, Margaret McGuffie, the daughter of the provost no less, lived between 1841 and 1894 in the big house, then called Barbados Villas, named for her birth-place. Her presence is attested to by still extant legends about the 'dark lady of the big house' and by her name on the family obelisk in Mochrum churchyard, several miles away.[123]

Kay is acutely aware of this history of black British (and indeed Scottish) presence, which predated the Windrush generation (so called after the *SS Empire Windrush*, which brought the first significant post-war boatload of West Indians across in 1948), and it is to her fiction I want to turn to interrogate the interaction of a black British literature imbued with knowledge of a sustained historical tradition and with the weighty presence of African American characters, themes and style.

Kay has established the long tradition of black presence in the UK as her starting point:

> I think the history that children are taught in schools, British history or Scottish history or English history, doesn't really include black people, and yet black people have been part of this country's history long, long before the *Windrush* that everybody seems to talk about as a marker date.[124]

Despite her avowed intent to foreground black British presence, Kay's *Trumpet* is just as concerned with investigating pivotal moments of African American intervention in UK culture and, in part at least, with the liberational possibilities of the African American form jazz in a UK (and black British) context.

The novel tells of Millie MacFarlane, a white Scots woman who is blown off her feet by the jazz music played by her African-Scottish lover Joss Moody in the 1950s. Almost all the reviews and academic criticism of this novel have concentrated on the sensational story at the centre of the novel: that Joss was born a woman, Josephine Moore, and hid this from his[125] adopted son and his fans until it was revealed at his death. Kay brilliantly resituates the true story of the life of the white US pianist Billy Tipton to tell the similar cross-dressing story of her fictional character. This is such a fascinating scenario that it was bound to engage critics of the book; however, I want to concentrate on what the novel can tell us about the tiny black community in Scotland in the middle of the twentieth century and afterwards, about the racial dynamics of a small Celtic country, and the relationship of the UK to an African American culture that was in the 1950s extending its global reach through its most successful global export, music. Joss's dual parentage, half Scottish and half African (like Kay herself), is revealed in Millie's early description of him having 'skin ... the colour of Highland toffee'.[126] However, Joss exhibits his identity principally not through Scottish or African cultural forms but through US music. Joss and Millie's wedding is played out not to a soundtrack of Scottish ceilidh music or UK pop tunes, but to the fresh tunes coming from the US, principally the African American forms of blues and jazz. As I will show later in this study, just as the working class Yorkshirewoman Joyce in Caryl Phillips's *Crossing the River*, and the girls in *Picture Post* article from Bristol, are described as in awe of African Americans and their musicking, so Millie is portrayed jitterbugging at her wedding with her Scottish-African lover to sounds from across the Atlantic:

> Joss takes me up in his arms and kisses me. Everyone claps and hoots. Then we dance. A circle of people, a human wall, swiftly forms around us. All gamblers' eyes on us. Joss takes my hand and we spin. I twirl under his

arm; swing under his legs. He lifts me high in the air. He jumps enjoying himself now. It is the 28th of October 1955… We dance for ages. We dance as if we are in a movie. Everyone grabs the limelight as if their dance was a solo spot. 'Shake, Rattle and Roll'. 'Bill Bailey'. 'Take the A Train', 'Why Don't You Do Right?', 'Blues in the Night'… The Moody Men are in their element, changing music all the time.[127]

The complex and inter-generational nature of this adoption of African American musicking is exemplified by Millie's mother's reaction to it. Millie describes her mother dancing with the bridegroom:

My mother dancing with Joss is quite a picture. If she only knew. The Moody Men start singing songs that have just come in from America like new trains arriving, steaming at the station. Old Mason Dixie line. It is not my mother's idea of wedding music.[128]

Mrs MacFarlane's narrow prejudice is exposed not just in her reaction to the foreign music played at the wedding. She is not happy about her daughter's choice of husband either, and Kay's description of this is told through Millie's narrative and illuminates a Scottish racism that undermines the mythology of welcome encapsulated in Robert Burns's signal Scottish phrase, 'A man's a man for all that.' This racism comes not out of proximity to a large black presence but from a generalised absence of different races in some areas of the UK. Kay brilliantly dissects such racism:

When I told her I was marrying Joss, she said she had nothing against them, but she didn't want her own daughter. People should keep to their own. It wasn't prejudice, it was common sense, she said. Then she said the word, 'Darky'. I don't want you marrying a 'Darky'.[129]

This description works as an incisive exemplar of racialised thinking. Mrs MacFarlane is unable to finish her sentences, unable to mouth the prejudice she feels. These fragments show her fighting to maintain her dignity in the face of her prejudice. She cannot utter the fully racialised thoughts because she realises they come from an ignorance that her bourgeois aspirations make her disdain in others. Yet her horror at her own daughter's future miscegenation emboldens her to say what she thinks and to utter the word 'Darky'. In a sense Mrs MacFarlane's horror is the flipside of her daughter's fascination. The delight in difference that attracts Millie is the horror of the other that repulses her mother. This polite racism that hides behind elision and feigned politeness is so powerful when written because it is still typical of many places in the UK in the twenty-first century. Kay relates how many Scots still find it hard to acknowledge their own black citizens. In conjuring the racism of the 1950s, Kay speaks to her own experience of growing up in Scotland in the latter half of the twentieth century, where she felt like a stranger in her own land because of the questioning of her origins. As she explains it, in Scotland, 'Everyone kept asking me, "Where are you from?" even though my accent sounded exactly like theirs.'[130] An anecdote she tells illustrates her point:

> I went to sit down in this chair in a London pub and this woman says, 'You cannae sit doon – that's ma chair.' I said, 'Oh, you're from Glasgow aren't you?' And she said, 'Aye, how did you know that?' I said, 'I'm from Glasgow myself.' She said, 'You're not, are you, you foreign looking bugger?'... I still have Scottish people asking me where I am from. They won't actually hear my voice, because they are so busy seeing my face.[131]

Joss Moody has a similar problem of finding his identity in a Scotland that has no place for an African presence, that builds its Scottish identity in part at least through a racialised mythology of Celtic whiteness. Joss discovers identity through his art form, jazz music, a Scots-African using an art form intimately associated with African Americans to mould himself in a predominantly white UK. As Colman, his adopted son, rather disparagingly narrates, Joss is enthralled by his heroes across the water:

> All the black guys his father loved to talk about were American, black Americans. Black Yanks... You spend your whole time worshipping black Yanks: Martin Luther King, Louis Armstrong, Fats Waller, Count Basie, Duke Ellington, Miles Davis. Black Yanks all of them.[132]

Moody plays the music of black America with his own signature because black America, with its large population and dynamic home-grown cultures, has a cultural cogency far removed from the marginality of black Europeans in the 1950s and 1960s. It is whilst playing African American music that he comes to terms with the ambiguities of his seemingly fractured identity. But it is not only his gender ambivalence that he plays out, but also his position as a black person on the fringes of a predominantly white Europe. Kay describes the ambivalent ways in which identity is worked out on these fringes through musical performance: 'I think the wonder part about certain pieces of music is that when we're listening to them (or playing them) we can lose ourselves in them, but we can also find ourselves in them; that music defines us, but it also help us to lose our definitions.'[133]

For black Africans in Europe, far from the wellspring of black diasporan traditions, music is crucial in broadening out from often narrow and chauvinistic national definitions. Kay's discussion here shows the paradoxical nature of music, which helps to create new realities at the same moment as it inscribes memory of a thoroughly routed, defining past. Here she describes eloquently the combination of improvisation and memorial history that is so important in the jazz tradition and helps to frame African Atlantic identities. Like Morrison, she shows how the music creates aural memorials that have resonances at home and in far-flung geographies of the black diaspora, that reach back to the past to create meaning in the here and now. Such a diffuse diasporan identity created, here at least, through music is figured by Kay as being typical of black Scots and other black Europeans, but not necessarily problematic: 'I like the in-between land, and what I am really interested in writing about is how that affects people, when they feel they belong and they don't belong, when they fit in and they don't fit in. A lot of us have that experience, being slightly outside of things.'[134]

Kay makes Moody's in-betweenness, his black Atlantic 'hybridity and intermixture'[135] explicit in describing how when he plays a solo, he is working out, and through, his identity, expressing his own specific history and that of diasporan African strangers in an unwelcoming land. Jazz, paradoxically, enables Moody to be at home when thinking about Scotland:

> So when he takes off he is the whole century galloping to its close. The wide moors. The big mouth. Scotland. Africa. Slavery. Freedom. He is a girl. A man. Everything, nothing. He is sickness, health. The sun. The moon. Black, white. Nothing weighs him down... He just keeps blowing. He is blowing his story. His story is blowing in the wind. He lets it rip. He tears himself apart. He explodes. Then he brings himself back. Slowly, slowly, piecing himself together.[136]

Moody here self-invents, but does so on the basis of his own African diasporan identity, of having a home somewhere else that he is in exile from as well as a home in Europe where he is a stranger. Charlotte Williams succinctly describes this paradox: 'diaspora peoples without a collective historical event to refer to invent one in order to define their presence in their inherited country.'[137] Joss constructs the multinational past that inscribes his homeland in his music. His piecing together of himself is done through the narrative he 'blows', and the enabling form is a jazz music that is perfect for encapsulating the story of a 'stranger in a strange land', as it was developed in the US to tell the story of diasporan Africans. It is only natural for a black man in Scotland to use it to tell his own specific and similar story of exile. The tortured histories of slavery and of empire create such fractured personalities as Moody's, but jazz music allows the Scottish-African musician to resolve the contradictions of his multifarious identities through this African American art form, as Kay explains:

> When music moves you, it strips you bare, beyond being a boy or girl, black or white, gay or straight, old or young. The music contains so many

contradictions, and it doesn't have rigid boundaries, so it is very freeing. In *Trumpet*, jazz becomes a beautiful way of exploring identity, expressing that process of losing yourself, finding yourself, forgetting yourself and remembering yourself, going backwards and forwards.[138]

Joss is engaged in a form of self-invention through improvisation. Performing his own specific African-Scottish story, but surrounding it with a wider story of diaspora, allows him to claim a wider brotherhood. He explains this to Colman, describing how 'you make up your own bloodline … make it up and trace it back. Design your own family tree.'[139] In the context of a fractured diaspora, such willed invention is essential in order to reconstruct a genealogy that underpins identity. There is a self-awareness about Joss's invention that he reveals in talking to Millie about his hit 'Fantasy Africa'. Millie narrates:

We never actually got to go to Africa. Joss had built up such a strong imaginary landscape within himself that he said it would affect his music to go to the real Africa. Every black person has a fantasy Africa, he'd say. Black British people, Black Americans, Black Caribbeans, they all have a fantasy Africa. It is all in the head.[140]

This landscape of the mind is a mythological Africa that links diasporan blacks across the Atlantic and is the reason that jazz music has such transatlantic resonance for Africans in Europe and the US. The music creates a memorial to the homeland and helps through this to build an identity from fractured roots and routes.

One of the paradoxes about the of reception of the novel is that its acknowledged transatlantic link to the story of US jazz pianist Billy Tipton means that connections to post-war UK jazz have been ignored by most critics. As George McKay argues in his seminal study *Circular Breathing: The Cultural Politics of Jazz in Britain*, UK jazz musicians' contribution to the musical form is dramatically undervalued in many US accounts. He quotes Andrew Simons, an expert on swing, who rightly castigates the elision of the contributions of later more free-form artists:

The post-war Caribbean immigration would later enrich the London jazz milieu with Joe Harriott, trumpeter Shake Keane, guitarist Ernest Raglin and others. But the pioneering black British swing artists set the stage for subsequent stars of more recent times. The black community's struggle for equality and justice is still lumbered with the historical irony that so many of their jazz ancestors are under-documented if not outright undocumented today.[141]

The musician most undermined by these elisions is the Jamaican-born saxophonist Joe Harriott. His marginal status in black British historical memory is attested to by the lack of a biographical entry in the canon-forming *Oxford Companion to Black British History* (2007).[142] This is despite Harriott, with his compadres Shake Keane and Coleridge Goode, being the most important British free-jazz musicians of the late 1950s and 1960s. Harriott arrived in the UK from Jamaica in 1951 at the age of 23, and as his style developed he drew plaudits from the music press for bringing 'a strikingly new sound to British jazz',[143] which included the development of a free-form mode that privileged spontaneity and collectivity. Linked to developments in free jazz in the US but not derivative of it, Harriott and his group were determined 'to go beyond the stale "chord-bound" approach even if it meant going out on a limb and incurring the hostility of some jazz critics and jazz fans.'[144] As Harriott himself boasted, in reaction to the perception that UK jazz musicians were inherently inferior to their US cousins, 'Parker? There's them over here can play some aces too.'[145] His later development, with John Mayer, of indo-jazz fusion in three amazingly innovative albums was an important precursor of the world music phenomenon of the late twentieth century. His career ended in an obscurity that means his stellar contributions are marginalised and all but forgotten in discussions of black British artistic prowess. However, as McKay reminds us, 'the tensed surprise of the "free form" music [of Harriott] remains a hemispheric achievement that no one else was thinking of, that took from America, to the Caribbean, to London in an experimental sonicity of the black Atlantic.'[146]

Kay's character Joss has very different African diasporan routes to Harriott; however, I would argue that Harriott's biography gives historical weight to the fictional tale of a brilliant black, improvising musician dominating the UK jazz scene with his innovative playing. Harriott's highly creative career showcases a forgotten history of stellar black British achievement in jazz that Kay's novel helps us to remember. However important this is, though, Kay does not end her novel with Moody's jazz routes but with his written memories of his African father, which he leaves for Colman after his death. In his notes, Joss describes his father as a stranger who is able to make himself at home in Scotland through the power of music:

> he missed his mother, his country, his mother-country. My father had a wonderful singing voice and could sing from memory just about any folk song I wanted. Every time he sang a Scottish folk song, he'd have a far away look on his face. *Heil Ya Ho boys, Let her go boys, Swing her head round, And all together.*[147]

The faraway look on his face occurs because the Scottish song gives him space to be nostalgic about his other home. His appropriation of it is figured by Kay as an inevitable by-product of the African diaspora, which mixed peoples together in new locations. As Gilroy describes, 'The history of the black Atlantic yields a course of lessons as to the instability and mutability of identities, which are always unfinished, always being remade.'[148] For instance, the folk song has the rhythm of a shanty, the origin of which is in the collision of Celtic folk songs with African American work songs in the ports of the Deep South, as discussed in Chapter 4. Jazz is not the first musical form to have transatlantic resonance, but only one in a tradition stretching back to the slave trade and onwards to contemporary African Atlantic cultures and rap music. As Gilroy has discussed, such music forms a new culture of triangulation, 'a new structure of cultural exchange ... built up across the imperial networks which once played host to the triangular trade of sugar, slaves and capital'.[149]

As Kay shows, Moody's father can be at home in Scotland partly because folk memories are transported across and between cultures by music. Seeming disparity can be coalesced through artistic invention as Paul Robeson, singing world folk songs in Scotland, Wales and Russia, so amply exemplified. Joss finally reaches for a symbol of continuity and circularity that aptly figures his identity as Scottish and from the African diaspora and describes it thus: 'My own father is back by the bed here singing. The present is just a loop stitch. *Heil Ya Ho boys, Let her go boys*... My father came off a boat right enough.'[150]

What Kay describes is a mobile African Atlantic world where African Americans function as modern heroes to the British, but as she also shows, there are African-descended heroes too, and some of these black heroes are in fact just about as British as Spam. The loop stitch circles, constructing links between Africa, the US and Scotland that allow Joss's true genealogy to underpin his constructed identity. Transformative mobility is crucially figured by the boat here, as Gilroy's work reminds us. However, it is music, both jazz and folk, that provides the soundtrack to such journeys and is played with memorial resonance once destinations are reached. It is music that seems to offer a performative outlet for questions of diasporan identity for European Africans as seen in Kay's fiction. The monuments are syncretic jazz tunes that speak to fractured identities which are most fully reconciled in the act of making improvised, multi-accented routes music on both sides of the Atlantic. It is this memorial tradition that both Kay and Morrison pay homage to in their brilliant employment of the jazz aesthetic in their novels.

Notes

1. K. W. Benston, 'Late Coltrane: a re-membering of Orpheus', in M. S. Harper and R. B. Stepto (eds), *Chant of Saints* (Chicago, IL: University of Illinois Press, 1979), pp. 413–424 (416).

2. J. Baldwin, 'Of the sorrow songs: the cross of redemption' (1979) in J. Campbell (ed.), *The Picador Book of Blues and Jazz* (London, Picador: 1996), pp. 324–331 (330).

3. P. Gilroy, 'Living memory: Toni Morrison talks to Paul Gilroy', *City Limits*, 31 March 1988, pp. 11–12 (11).

4. Roach, *Cities of the Dead*, p. 286.

5. J. Kay, *Trumpet* (London: Picador, 1998), p. 131.

6. T. Morrison, *The Bluest Eye* (London: Triad Granada, 1981), p. 147.

7. Roach, *Cities of the Dead*, p. 66.

8. F. Douglass, *Narrative of the Life of an American Slave, Written by Himself,* 1845, ed. H. A. Baker Jr. (Harmondsworth: Penguin, 1986).

9. W. E. B. Du Bois, *The Souls of Black Folk* (New York: Vintage, 1990).

10. A. Baraka and L. Neal (eds), *Black Fire* (New York: Morrow, 1968).

11. A. Baraka, *Home: Social Essays* (New York: Morrow, 1966), p. 113.

12. M. Jaggi, 'Race and all that jazz', *The Guardian* ('Review' section), 5 December 1998, p. 10.

13. G. T. Hull, '"What is it I think she's doing anyhow?"': a reading of Toni Cade Bambara's *The Salt Eaters*, in M. Pryse and H. J. Spillers (eds), *Conjuring: Black Women, Fiction and Literary Tradition* (Bloomington, IN: Indiana University Press, 1985) pp. 216–232 (221).

14. N. Shange, *See No Evil: Prefaces, Essays and Accounts 1976–1983* (San Fransisco, CA: Momo's Press, 1984), p. 28.

15. A. Walker, *In Search of Our Mothers' Gardens* (London: Women's Press, 1984), p. 264.

16. Jaggi, 'Race and all that jazz', p. 10.

17. T. Morrison, 'Rootedness: the ancestor as foundation', in M. Evans (ed.), *Black Women Writers 1950–1980* (London: Pluto, 1985), pp. 339–45 (342).

18. D. Heinze, *The Dilemma of 'Double Consciousness': Toni Morrison's Novels* (Athens, GA: University of Georgia Press, 1993), p. 15.

19. Gilroy, *The Black Atlantic*, p. 168.

20. G. Jones, *Liberating Voices: Oral Tradition in African American Literature* (Cambridge, MA: Harvard University Press, 1991), p. 92.

21. Eckstein, *Re-Membering the Black Atlantic*, p. 40.

22. M. Diawara, 'Conversation with Édouard Glissant aboard the Queen Mary II (August 2009)', in T. Barson and P. Gorschluter (eds), *Afro Modern: Journeys through the Black Atlantic* (Liverpool: Tate Publishing, 2010), pp. 58–63 (61).

23. Quoted in L. W. Levine, *Black Culture and Black Consciousness* (Oxford: Oxford University Press, 1977), p. 238.

24. S. Bechet, *Treat It Gentle* (London: Corgi, 1964), p. 103.

25. A. Taylor, *Notes and Tones* (London: Quartet, 1986), p. 183.

26. S. Crouch, *The All-American Skin Game: or, The Decoy of Race* (New York, NY: Pantheon Books), 1995, p. 16.

27. Benston, 'Late Coltrane', p. 414.

28. R. Blesh, *Shining Trumpets: A History of Jazz* (New York, NY: Da Capo, 1975), p. 325.

29. Christopher Small, *Music of the Common Tongue* (London: John Calder, 1987), p. 329.

30. Gilroy, *The Black Atlantic*, p. 36.

31. Small, *Music of the Common Tongue*, p. 240.
32. Small, *Music of the Common Tongue*, p. 227.
33. Crouch, *The All-American Skin Game*, p. 15.
34. P. F. Berliner, *Thinking in Jazz: The Infinite Art of Improvisation* (Chicago, IL: Chicago University Press, 1995), p. 434.
35. B. Priestly, *Mingus: A Critical Biography* (London: Quartet, 1982), p. 114.
36. I. Monson, 'Doubleness and jazz improvisation: irony, parody and ethnomusicology', *Critical Inquiry*, 20 (1994), pp. 283–313 (310).
37. A. Douglas, *Terrible Honesty: Mongrel Manhattan in the 1920s* (London: Macmillan, 1995), p. 336.
38. R. B. Stepto and M. S. Harper, 'Study and experience: an interview with Ralph Ellison', in M. S. Harper and R. B. Stepto (eds), *Chant of Saints* (Chicago, IL: University of Illinois Press, 1979), pp. 451–469 (459).
39. M. Wallace, *Invisibility Blues* (London: Verso, 1990), p. 250.
40. Levine, *Black Culture and Black Consciousness*, p. 101.
41. C. Hartman, *Jazz Text* (Princeton, NJ: Princeton University Press, 1991), p. 21.
42. Hartman, *Jazz Text*, p. 21.
43. M. M. Bakhtin, *The Dialogic Imagination* (Austin, TX: University of Texas Press, 1981), pp. 293–294.
44. W. Shakespeare, 'The Tempest', *The Comedies of William Shakespeare* (London: Dent, 1916), Act I, Scene ii, p. 16.
45. Bechet, *Treat It Gentle*, p. 12.
46. B. Ostendorf, *Black Literature in White America* (Totowa, NJ: Barnes and Noble, 1982), p. 96.
47. Bechet, *Treat It Gentle*, pp. 72–73.
48. Blesh, *Shining Trumpets*, p. 172.
49. M. Stearns, *The Story of Jazz* (Oxford: Oxford University Press, 1956), p. 61.
50. Roach, *Cities of the Dead*, pp. 14–15.
51. Roach, *Cities of the Dead*, p. 14.
52. Roach, *Cities of the Dead*, p. 14.
53. Whitehead, *Memory*, p. 133.
54. B. Sidran, *Black Talk* (New York, NY: Da Capo, 1981), p. 103.
55. B. W. Peretti, *The Creation of Jazz: Music, Race and Culture in Urbanizing America* (Urbana, IL: University of Illinois Press, 1992), p. 213.
56. J. Hunt, 'Blacks and the classics: a conversation with T. J. Anderson', *Black Perspective in Music 1* (1973), pp. 157–165 (164).
57. Quoted in G. H. Lenz, 'Black poetry and black music: history and tradition: Michael Harper and John Coltrane', in G. H. Lenz (ed.), *History and Tradition in Afro-American Culture* (Frankfurt: Campus, 1984), pp. 277–326 (302).
58. J. Kay, interview, *The Poetry Archive*, http://www.poetryarchive.org/poetryarchive/singleInterview.do?interviewId=6580 [accessed 12 March 2008].
59. Taylor, *Notes and Tones*, p. 156.
60. Quoted in J. S. Roberts, *Black Music of Two Worlds*, second edition (Florence, KY: Wadsworth, 1998), p. 192.
61. Blesh, *Shining Trumpets*, p. 79.
62. Levine, *Black Culture and Black Consciousness*, p. 200
63. G. Addison Jr, *The Black Aesthetic* (Garden City, NY: Anchor-Doubleday, 1971), p. 14.

64. C. Bigsby, 'Jazz queen', *The Independent on Sunday*, 26 April 1992, pp. 28–29 (29).
65. Bigsby, 'Jazz queen', p. 29.
66. G. Schuller, *Early Jazz* (Oxford: Oxford University Press, 1968), p. 89.
67. A. Rice, unpublished interview with Toni Morrison, 29 February 1988.
68. T. Gioia, *The Imperfect Art* (Oxford: Oxford University Press, 1988), pp. 60–61.
69. Crouch, *The All-American Skin Game*, p. 18.
70. Small, *Music of the Common Tongue*, p. 226
71. Benston, 'Late Coltrane', p. 415.
72. K. Grime, *Jazz at Ronnie Scott's* (London: Robert Hale, 1979), p. 188.
73. A. Baraka (aka L. Jones), *Blues People* (New York: Morrow, 1963), p. 198.
74. Rice, interview.
75. E. Dolphy, *Status* (New York: Prestige, 1979) and Billie Holiday, *God Bless the Child* (New York: CBS, 1974).
76. N. Hentoff, liner notes on Albert Ayler, 'Truth is Marching In', *Albert Ayler in Greenwich Village*, LP (New York: Jasmine, 1967).
77. Hentoff, liner notes on Ayler.
78. Eckstein, *Re-Membering the Black Atlantic*, p. 228.
79. I. Monson, *Saying Something: Jazz Improvisation and Interaction* (Chicago, IL: University of Chicago Press, 1997), p. 8.
80. P. Gilroy, *Small Acts: Thoughts on the Politics of Black Cultures* (London: Serpent's Tail, 1993), p. 37.
81. T. Morrison, *Sula* (London: Triad Grafton, 1980), p. 98.
82. Morrison, *Sula*, p. 99.
83. M. Roach, *We Insist! Freedom Now Suite* (Candid: New York, 1987) and Archie Shepp, *Poem for Malcolm* (New York: Affinity, 1983).
84. M. G. Henderson, 'Speaking in tongues: dialogics, dialectics and the black woman writer's literary traditions', in C. A. Wall (ed.), *Changing Our Own Words* (London: Routledge, 1990), pp. 18–37 (33).
85. Morrison, *Sula*, p. 32.
86. Morrison, *Sula*, p. 99.
87. Morrison, *Sula*, p. 99.
88. R. Grant, 'Absence into presence: the thematics of memory and "missing" subjects in Toni Morrison's *Sula*', in N. Y. McKay (ed.), *Critical Essays on Toni Morrison* (Boston, MA: G. K. Hall, 1988), pp. 90–103 (99).
89. Morrison, *Sula*, p. 120.
90. Morrison, *Sula*, p. 122.
91. Morrison, *Sula*, pp. 122–123.
92. E. Dolphy, *Last Date*, liner notes (New York: Mercury, 1964).
93. Benston, 'Late Coltrane', p. 421.
94. Gilroy, 'Living memory', p. 11.
95. A. Lorde, *Sister Outsider* (New York, NY: Thunder's Mouth Press, 1984), p. 120.
96. T. Morrison, *Playing in the Dark: Whiteness and the Literary Imagination* (Cambridge, MA: Harvard University Press, 1992), p. 7.
97. A. Y. Jimoh, *Spiritual Blues and Jazz People in African American Fiction* (Knoxville, TN: University of Tennessee Press), 2002, p. 29.
98. T. Morrison, *Jazz* (London: Chatto and Windus, 1992), p. 98.
99. Rice, interview.
100. Rice, interview.

101. C. Tate (ed.), *Black Women Writers at Work* (New York, NY: Continuum, 1983), p. 120.

102. S. Wilson, 'Jazz messenger: an interview with Toni Morrison', *The List* (June 1992), p. 12.

103. J. A. Snead, 'On repetition in black culture', *Black American Literature Forum*, 15 (1981), pp. 146–154 (150).

104. N. Y. McKay, 'An inteview with Toni Morrison', *Contemporary Literature*, 24 (1983), pp. 413–429 (429).

105. Morrison, *Jazz*, p. 60.

106. Morrison, *Jazz*, p. 64.

107. Morrison, *Jazz*, p. 135.

108. Morrison, *Jazz*, p. 137.

109. H. L. Gates Jr, *The Signifying Monkey: A Theory of Literary Criticism* (New York, NY: Oxford University Press, 1988), p. 105.

110. Morrison, *Jazz*, p. 210.

111. Morrison, *Jazz*, p. 113.

112. Morrison, *Jazz*, p. 192.

113. Morrison, *Jazz*, pp. 196–197.

114. Morrison, *Jazz*, p. 51.

115. P. Connerton, quoted in Roach, *Cities of the Dead*, p. 26.

116. A. Young, L. Kart and M. S. Harper, 'Jazz and letters: a colloquy', *Tri-Quarterly*, 68 (1987), pp. 118–159 (130).

117. Morrison, *Jazz*, pp. 226–227.

118. S. Saul, *Freedom Is, Freedom Ain't: Jazz and the Making of the Sixties* (Cambridge, MA: Harvard University Press, 2003), p. 25.

119. Morrison, *Jazz*, p. 228.

120. T. Mack, 'The US isn't great on race: are you Brits any better?', *Observer Magazine*, 20 February 2000, p. 2.

121. Mack, 'The US isn't great on race', p. 2.

122. Rice, *Radical Narratives of the Black Atlantic*.

123. D. Brewster, *The House that Sugar Built* (Wigtown: GC Books, 1999), pp. 3–4.

124. R. Dyer, 'Jackie Kay in conversation', *Wasafiri*, 29 (Spring 1999), p. 58.

125. I follow Kay in referring to Joss as 'he' in my discussion of the novel.

126. Kay, *Trumpet*, p. 11.

127. Kay, *Trumpet*, p. 28.

128. Kay, *Trumpet*, p. 29.

129. Kay, *Trumpet*, p. 27.

130. J. Kay, 'Silence is golden', *Time Out* (3 February 2002), p. 105.

131. L. Brooks, 'Don't tell me who I am', *The Guardian* (12 January 2002), p. 34.

132. Kay, *Trumpet*, p. 192.

133. Kay, interview, *The Poetry Archive*.

134. A. Burnside, 'Outside edge', *The Sunday Herald* (2 April 2000), p. 8.

135. Gilroy, *Black Atlantic*, p. xi.

136. Kay, *Trumpet*, p. 136.

137. Quoted in G. Younge, 'Congo boys of Cardiff,' *The Guardian* (1 June 2002), p. 16.

138. A. Stuart, 'Performing writes', *The Independent* (8 August 2000), p. 8.

139. Kay, *Trumpet*, p. 58.

140. Kay, *Trumpet*, p. 47.

141. G. McKay, *Circular Breathing: The Cultural Politics of Jazz in Britain* (Durham, NC: Duke University Press, 2005), p. 135.

142. D. Dabydeen, J. Gilmore and C. Jones, *Oxford Companion to Black British History* (Oxford: Oxford University Press, 2007).

143. McKay, *Circular Breathing*, p. 153.

144. C. Blackford quoted in McKay, *Circular Breathing*, p. 157.

145. A. Robertson, *Joe Harriott: Fire in His Soul* (Wendover, Bucks: Northway Publications, 2003), back cover.

146. McKay, *Circular Breathing*, pp. 162–163.

147. Kay, *Trumpet*, p. 275.

148. Gilroy, *The Black Atlantic*, p.xi.

149. P. Gilroy, *There Ain't No Black in the Union Jack: The Cultural Politics of Race and Nation* (London: Hutchison, 1987, p. 206).

150. Kay, *Trumpet*, p. 277.

6

'Fighting Nazism, Jim Crow and Colonialism too': Creating Radical Memorials in Honour of African Atlantic Struggles in the War against Fascism

As we see so many of our of World War II veterans coming to the twilight of their years, it is especially important for us to remember, to record and to remind ourselves of how much that generation did on all our behalves. President Barack Obama in Dresden, Germany after visiting the Buchenwald concentration camp on June 5, 2009[1]

It was the unique and spine-chilling experience of hearing the singing of black servicemen in 'fatigues' who were 'digging in' an American military base at Stoke-by-Clare in Suffolk which stimulated a lifetime passion [for the blues]. Paul Oliver[2]

The multi-layered trauma – economic and cultural as well as political and psychological – involved in accepting the loss of empire would therefore be compounded by a number of additional shocks. Among them are the painful obligations to work through the grim details of imperial and colonial history and to transform paralysing guilt into a more productive shame that could be conducive to the building of a multicultural nationality that is no longer phobic about the prospect of exposure to either strangers or otherness... Post-imperial melancholia ... is associated with the neotraditional pathology of what in the British setting ... [can be identified] as the morbidity of heritage. Paul Gilroy[3]

Earlier in this volume, I have discussed the political and fundraising difficulties that have arisen in trying to get memorials built to victims of the slave trade in the UK, and the indifference of the political elite to such a project. Under the patronage of HRH the Prince of Wales, the project to memorialise the sacrifice of five million black ex-servicemen ran much more smoothly, attracting money from the great and the good so that it was only three years from its inception in 1998 to the laying of the first stone. The moral of this comparison is clear: it is always far easier to celebrate imperial sacrifice than it is to atone for imperial crimes; however, the war memorial has other pertinent resonances, both those it wears with pride and those radical histories it lays bare, which may go against the nostalgic instinct of many of those who contributed financially to it. The *Memorial Gates* for the African, Caribbean and Indian veterans of the two world wars (Figure 22), unveiled by the queen on Constitution Hill in London in 2002, are in keeping with the British imperial tradition. Stark and white, in Portland stone, they carry the names of the continents and countries the veterans left and the campaigns they fought, in which many died. The inscription on one gate is to a 'Debt of Honour', which the erecting of these gates seeks to pay back. They are the very image of what Paul Gilroy calls the post-imperial melancholia that makes up the antediluvian landscapes of our ex-imperial cities. The gates talk to past sacrifice without fully articulating what meaning this has for the present, freezing the soldiers' actions into a UK-scripted narrative of past imperial grandeur. The only concession to African diasporan voices is Ben Okri's anodyne epigraph on one of the gates: 'Our future is greater than our past', which hardly qualifies as African philosophy. Although it speaks to the multicultural consequences of the servicemen and women's sacrifice for a changing UK cultural landscape, this script is thoroughly contradicted by the reactionary message of the gates themselves, nostalgia for an imperial past. bell hooks has talked of such reactionary nostalgia and the need in commemorating the past to move to a 'politicisation of memory that distinguishes nostalgia, that longing for something to be as it once was, a kind of useless act, from that remembering that serves to illuminate and transform the present.'[4]

In considering specifically the legacy of the Second World War for African soldiers in the diaspora, I want to show how the *Memorial Gates* indulge in this reactionary nostalgia, which is contradicted by voices from below that tell a more complex story of racial exclusion and discrimination, of transnational solidarity and new post-imperial formations that worked for an emerging post-colonial world. It is fitting that, at long last, at the heart of the imperial metropolis, there is recognition of the crucial contribution of black troops to the fight against fascism; however, the conservative iconography of the memorial, which implicates the veterans fully in a narrative of imperial sacrifice for the British monarchy, of successful wars and lost empires, cannot do justice to the actualities of those veterans' simultaneous struggles for a post-imperial humanity which was still being denied them as they fought Nazism. The war accelerated the death of the British Empire and contributed to the slow death of Jim Crow racism in the US, as much as it led to the end of Hitler's racist regime, and black troops fighting for all the allies were instrumental in these epochal changes. The narrow, nationalist narrative of the Memorial Gates elides the implications of the war for Africans with different armies who fought the Axis powers. This chapter will seek to make links between soldiers from Africa and the West Indies memorialised by the gates and will also track Senegalese *tirailleurs*, black soldiers in the British army and the 'choc'late soldiers' from the USA as they fought racism at home and abroad, through case studies of the figure of the Second World War black soldier in history, literature and popular culture. It will propose a counter-narrative of transnational anti-imperialism that sought to remake the post-war world as one truly fit for black heroes.

The racist treatment took many forms in different battle theatres; for instance, some West Indian troops found discrimination from the officer class. In particular, on a number of occasions in their dealings with their US allies, the British acquiesced to a colour bar that discriminated against their own troops. For instance, all of the 200 West Indians sent to serve in the Auxiliary Territorial Service in Washington in 1943 were white; black servicewomen were not recruited. As Ben Bousquet and Colin Douglas pithily respond: 'And so even in the face of an abominable racist enemy, Britain was simply unable to embrace anti-racist principles.'[5] The situation was even worse for African troops, as shown in the documentary *Afrikan Heroes Re-visited*, which features interviews with veterans of the East African regiments who had fought alongside the British against the Axis powers. These testimonies show that racial discrimination permeated their lives whilst they fought as part of the British army. Chandavengerwa, a soldier from Mashonaland in Zimbabwe, remembers how there was a colour bar in Burma: 'latrines for Africans, a mess for the Africans and a mess for the Europeans. We were members of the British Commonwealth but we never gained anything. They should be thankful for our contribution, but it appears they don't care what we did.'[6] These testimonies, taken recently, show how the ex-soldiers' resentment at their treatment in the war, and later as veterans, is in stark contrast to the narrative contained in the imperial monolith of the Memorial Gates. The 'Burma boys', as these African soldiers came to be known, were indispensable to the campaign on the eastern fringes of the British Empire, providing vital manpower when the British campaign was fully stretched. This is shown by the testimony of Andrew Gengazha from the 1st Battallion Royal African Rifles:

I got hurt as we were approaching India. I tried to throw a grenade, but it exploded just before me and I lost my eye. I was attended by the regimental doctor but still I stayed on the war front. Soldiers then could not afford to be bedridden and be spoon-fed for nothing. They gave us a meagre send-off [at the end of the war] – imagine, just ten pounds. These white men are tricksters, we fought so hard and many of us died for nothing. These white people are no good. I tried to apply for compensation to the British, but they kept telling me to wait right up until today.[7]

As we can see from these remarkable testimonies, many of the African soldiers were radicalised by the war, which developed or cemented growing anti-colonial ideologies in the face of racist treatment in the imperial polity. These were to have their full flowering in the immediate post-war period. Just as the white British troops returned from the front less deferential and desiring 'homes fit for heroes', so their African colleagues, resentful at poor treatment and meagre pay-offs and newly emboldened by their success as soldiers and the widening horizons of service abroad, demanded new political accommodations once they returned to their colonised homes. Ally Sykes from Tanzania describes this new feeling:

> Before we went outside the country we always felt the white man was superior to an African. But when we were there things changed. We'd been exposed to the world. If we were just as good, if not better than the white man, why should they rule us?[8]

As the narrative of *Afrikan Heroes* asserts, war service 'demystified Europeanism and all the values it embodied'.[9] Of course for some Africans this process had begun earlier either with service in the First World War or with migrations to imperial centres such as London in the interwar years. As the pan-Africanist T. Ras Makonnen, talking in retrospect about the period 1914–1939, described it, there is a crucial awakening in being exposed to life away from the colonised polity for Africans from all corners of the diaspora:

> But when you look at the results of those Africans who had been to England, you wouldn't be far wrong in saying that England had been the executioner of its own colonial empire. In the sense that she had allowed these blacks to feel the contrast between freedom in the metropolis and slavery in the colonies. Hence it became the old retort: 'What are you going to do with these boys back on the farm, once they have seen Paree [Paris]?'[10]

Makonnen's astute reading of the growth of anti-colonial sentiments amongst an exilic community, and their inability to be assimilated back into colonial life on their return to Africa, can be extended to many of the African troops on their return from fighting for the allies in the Second World War. Broadened horizons meant that the straitened circumstance of life as a colonised individual was not acceptable any more. If Britain was the 'executioner of its own colonial empire', this empire was ironically lost for good in the aftermath of fighting a Nazi regime with racism and a global colonising agenda at its core. This paradox was pointed out most astutely by Aimé Césaire, who describes how Nazism's crimes were only seen as such because they were committed against white people. He describes how 'before they were its victims, [the allies] … were its accomplices' in their barbarous imperial practices in India, Africa and the Americas. He continues:

> that they tolerated Nazism before it was inflicted on them, that they absolved it, shut their eyes to it, legitimised it, because until then, it had been applied only to non-European peoples; that they have cultivated that Nazism, that they are responsible for it, and that before engulfing the whole of Western civilisation in its reddened waters, it oozes, seeps, and trickles from every crack.[11]

Hannah Arendt is more specific, describing how Nazi Germany was erected by leaders who had cut their teeth in the colonial German empire in Africa. She describes how

> African colonial possessions became the most fertile soil for the flowering of what became the Nazi elite. Here [they] had seen with their own eyes how people could be converted into races and how … one might push one's own people into the position of the master race.[12]

Arendt and Césaire's comments came after the war. However, the linkage between Nazism and European colonialism was astutely discussed throughout the African diaspora during the war itself, as anti-colonial commentators highlighted the hypocrisy of colonial powers propagandising around a war for freedom against tyranny. The Caribbean radical George Padmore made the link between Nazism and colonialism:

> The fact that I spent three months in a Nazi prison does not blind me to the fact that in a capitalist world, as long as Britain and France reserve the right to rule over 500 million coloured peoples and exploit their labour in the interests of plutocracy, they cannot expect Germany to be satisfied. Empire and Peace are incompatible.[13]

Padmore's critique, in a 1939 volume of the key African American journal *Crisis*, was just the beginning of a debate over European colonialism and its links to racial oppression which at its worst resembled Nazism, and the debate continued throughout the war. It was reiterated by African American commentators such as Walter White, John Robert Badger, Paul Robeson and, most saliently for my discussion on cultural ramifications here, Langston Hughes. The Council on African Affairs, founded in 1937 and chaired by Paul Robeson, stated that 'our fight for Negro rights here is linked inseparably with the liberation movements of the people of the

Caribbean and Africa and of the colonial world in general.'[14] This fight extended beyond the Anglo-American sphere and was arguably at its most intense in the French empire, where the tensions of defeat contributed to disrespect for the mother country and anti-colonial feeling. For instance, in Martinique the scales fell from the eyes of previously loyalist colonial subjects, as Frantz Fanon describes:

> De Gaulle, in London, spoke of treason, of soldiers who surrendered their swords even before they had drawn them. All this contributed to convincing the West Indians that France, their France, had not lost the war but that traitors had sold it out... One then witnessed an extraordinary sight: West Indians refusing to take off their hats while the Marseillaise was being played.[15]

For the black soldiers who served in the French forces (the *tirailleurs*), the awakening was even more harsh as they were marginalised in the theatre of war by De Gaulle's decision to prioritise the participation of white troops in the victory phase of the war. As Gregory Mann asserts:

> The history of the *tirailleurs* in World War II is capped by bitterness rather than victory. In spite of their contributions, most *tirailleurs* would watch the closing months of the war from the sidelines after having been removed from the front for logistical and political reasons... By the liberation of Paris, this *blanchissement*, or whitening, of the French army was effectively complete.[16]

Moreover, like British African soldiers, the *tirailleurs* were discriminated against when they were demobilised, receiving derisory payments in comparison to white veterans. The tensions this caused came to a head in a mutiny at Camp de Thiaroye, Senegal in December 1944, which was ruthlessly suppressed, leading to the death of 35 *tirailleurs*. In his second volume of poetry *Hosties Noires* (1948), Leopold Sedar Senghor, co-founder along with Césaire of the influential Negritude movement, 'insists on seeing these French colonial soldiers as sacrificial figures on the altar of European political interests',[17] with the Thiaroye incident the most extreme version of this haughty imperial attitude. In his poem 'Prayer for Peace' he shows how France 'treats /The Senegalese like mercenaries, the Empire's black watchdogs.'[18] Senghor's poetic response to the mutiny was to blame colonialism and its ideologies for blunting France's traditionally radical idealism:

> Black prisoners, I should say French prisoners, is it true
> That France is no longer France?
> Is it true that the enemy has stolen her face?
> Is it true that bankers' hate has bought her arms of steel?[19]

Senghor links colonialism to the enemy Nazism, which seems to have infiltrated the home country, which is at the mercy of a blind materialism. This makes it unrecognisable as a mythical, radical France. Ousmane Sembene's brilliant film *Camp de Thiaroye* (1988), based on what most historians now term a massacre, is also at its most moving in the comparison it makes between the actions of the ruthless colonial authorities and the Nazis in whose holding camps some of the *tirailleurs* had been kept for four years, echoing the pointed comparisons of critics such as Césaire. Sembene establishes this comparison early in the film as the soldiers spend their first few hours in the holding camp, showing how the guarded watchtowers and barbed wire fences evoke memories of concentration camps where some were held. This is accompanied by dissonant music and a dissolving shot from the camp in the African scrubland to a concentration camp. The soldier Pays, who had been imprisoned in Buchenwald, is told, 'You are no longer in Buchenwald, it's over.' For Pays, however, 'driven insane by his experiences at the hands of the Nazis', the war's horrors are far from over and he provides a telling counter-narrative to colonial hegemonic ideas throughout the film by donning his trophy SS helmet whenever the French officers act like fascists. This iconography establishes symbolically the close link between colonial and Nazi oppression, operating through racial stratification. Despite the heroism of the *tirailleurs* in defending France, they were now treated as inferiors. In particular, some had died fighting the idea of racial purity without receiving the support of their French colonial masters, and the memory of these actions is a spur to their revolt against injustice. The heroic Captain Ntochorere is invoked:

> His last action as a French, but black, officer? At Buchenwald Captain Ntochorere, as black as coal, crossed the field and joined the white officers, for he was an officer. The German head of the camp ordered him to break away from white officers. Captain Ntochorere refused. On the spot he was shot in front of white officers. Yes, and none of them had the courage to protest, nor even whisper. A few infantrymen, risking their lives, buried Captain Ntochorere, in anonymity, without a flag.[20]

Buried 'without a flag', Ntochorere is literally abandoned by France. The burial of Ntochorere by his black brothers after his betrayal by his white fellow officers underlines the collaborationist activities of the latter and adds to the many experiences of betrayal that contribute to the profound disenchantment of these troops who 'fought the war … even slept and ate with corpses'.[21] It is not just the officer class that the *tirailleurs* have witnessed collaborating. After being accused of stripping corpses for booty during his war service, one of them answers by evoking the extremity of life in the death-camps:

Here you dare accuse us of stripping corpses. Do you know the real strippers of corpses? We infantrymen saw those who opened the mouths of corpses to take out gold or silver teeth. Those who mutilated corpses to take rings. Shall I tell you about the French collaborators of the Gestapo?[22]

After sights like these, the troops were not prepared to be treated as inferiors by such hypocrites. As one veteran commented to Myron Echenberg in 1973, 'We were not like the veterans of 1914–18. We were not prepared to be treated like sheep.'[23]

Sembene's film ends with the bleak shot of the watchtowers of Buchenwald/Thiaroye, establishing the close relationship between Nazi oppression and colonial mastery. As Charles Forsdick contends, the film is a memorial that stands in for the lack of a physical memorial in Senegal to those massacred. In making the film, Sembene acts 'as guardian of the community's memory against the influence of lingering imperial structures and the passage of time'.[24]

The anti-colonial fight had implications throughout the black diaspora. As Peggy M. Von Eschen has asserted, 'By the last years of the Second World War, internationalist anti-colonial discourse was critical in shaping black American politics and the meaning of racial identities and solidarities.'[25] Nowhere was this more apparent than in the poetry and prose of Langston Hughes, whose linkage of colonialism, Nazism and the Jim Crow South enabled an internationalist vision to be brought to bear in the hitherto domestic realm of US racism. He encapsulated this vision of an octopus-like racist empire under fire from the participation of black troops in the war, describing how they 'will eventually shake the British Empire to the dust. That will shake Dixie's teeth loose too and crack the joints of Jim Crow South Africa.'[26] In his 1942 poem for the Associated Negro Press, 'Governor Fires Dean', Hughes responds to yet another attack by the segregationist governor of Georgia, Eugene Talmadge, on integrated education by comparing his racism to that so virulently playing itself out in Germany:

Ain't it funny how some white folk
Have the strangest way
Of acting just like Hitler
In the USA?[27]

Hughes's wartime collection, *Jim Crow's Last Stand* (1943), continually emphasised this link between domestic racism and Nazism, and he partic-ipated culturally in the African American political movement 'Double V', led by the union leader A. Phillip Randolph, which campaigned for military victory for democratic forces abroad and victory against economic and political discrimination at home. As early as December 1941, just after the attack on Pearl Harbor, Randolph was articulating the importance of this dual fight, in an article in the *New York Age*:

> If we fail to fight to make the democratic process work in America, while we fight to beat down Japan and Hitler, we will be traitors to democracy and liberty and to the liberation of the Negro people.[28]

Double V campaigned for desegregation of defence plants, which it achieved in 1943, and an end to segregated armed forces (which would have to wait until after the war), and saw black participation in the war as being dependent on full democracy being achieved both at home and abroad. Hughes was an enthusiastic supporter of this position, and in his journalism argued that the fight for civil rights should not be suspended because of the war:

> If now is not the time, then there never was a time. Now is when all the conquered nations of Europe are asking for freedom. Now is when the Jews are asking for it. Now is when America is fighting to keep it… How anybody can expect American Negroes not to catch the freedom fever, too, is beyond me – unless they think we are deaf, dumb, stupid and blind.[29]

This 1943 article from the *Chicago Defender* was read widely by troops in the segregated US army, as can be attested by numerous letters of support from black soldiers. The more general campaign for Double V had much purchase amongst troops, down to the humblest private, as can be seen from oral testimony like that of Private Leon Bass of the 183rd Engineer Corps, who reported on his mobilisation:

> They had a big discussion about why we were fighting the war. This officer from Georgia came in and said, 'We want to discuss why we fight – what do you think of why you fight?' And I said, 'Sir, we're fighting to make this world safe for democracy and for all the rights and privileges of Americans', but at the same time I'm not privy to those, I'm denied those opportunities, so I say we're fighting two forces, one at home and one abroad.[30]

Bass's testimony, together with that of many other veterans, shows that Hughes's prose and poetry reflected the views of many of the black soldiers serving in segregated units at home and abroad. The poems in *Jim Crow's Last Stand* are propagandist and polemical, gathered together in an inexpensive pamphlet intended to be sold cheaply to serving soldiers and other black audiences on the home front. At their best, the poems pithily and eloquently encapsulate the message of the Double V campaign. For example, 'Beaumont to Detroit: 1943' links the riots in Northern cities and the Jim Crow segregation in the South and in the army to the international fight against fascism. A note from a weary African American to 'America', the poem asks:

> Now your policemen
> Let your mobs run free
> I reckon you don't care
> Nothing about me.
>
> You tell me that hitler
> Is a mighty bad man
> I guess he took lessons
> From the ku klux klan...
>
> ...You jim crowed me
> Before hitler rose to power –
> And you're still jim crowing me
> Right now, this very hour.[31]

If this poem seeks to show Hitlerism at work in US racism, elsewhere in the collection Hughes links the fight against colonial oppression with that against the Jim Crow South, showing the paradoxes at work in the global fight for democracy. In 'How About It, Dixie?' he discusses President Roosevelt's much vaunted 'four freedoms', which he sees being restricted to white Americans:

> Show me that you mean
> Democracy, please –
> Cause from Bombay to Georgia
> I'm beat to the knees
>
> You can't lock up Gandhi
> Club Roland Hayes,
> Then make fine speeches
> About Freedom's ways.
>
> Looks like by now
> Folks ought to know
> It's hard to beat Hitler
> Protecting Jim Crow.[32]

The internationalising of Hughes's argument through the image of the fight for Indian independence links the struggle for human rights in the South with anti-colonial conflicts worldwide. The war, with its rhetoric of freedom and democracy, was an opportunity for African American activists and writers to hold the US government and its allies to account for its failures at home and abroad. Hughes's constant juxtaposition of Hitler and Jim Crow allies the nation's external bogeyman with its internal *bête noir*, undermining its claims to world democratic leadership. Hughes also illuminates how the cancer of Jim Crow segregation followed the US army on its travels around the world. In 'The Black Man Speaks' the narrator describes how:

> Down South you make me ride
> In a Jim Crow car.
> From Los Angeles to London
> You spread your color bar.
>
> Jim Crow Army
> And navy too –
> Is Jim Crow freedom the best
> I can expect from you?[33]

The allusion to the effect of US racial mores in Britain shows how Hughes is keen to publicise to the widest audience possible the way a segregated army is a liability in fighting a Nazi enemy. Nowhere was this more apparent than in Britain, where the deployment of Uncle Sam's segregated armed forces in 1942 created a range of social issues that undermined smooth relationships between the allies. Joseph Julian's report in *The Nation* in December 1942 describes how 'it is particularly shocking to observe the Jim Crow Bacillus being injected into England'.[34]

The contemporary novelist Caryl Phillips is interested in the arrival of these racist social conventions, and the final section of his novel *Crossing the River* examines the arrival of black US troops in a small white Yorkshire community during the Second World War; Phillips is fascinated too by the welcome given to black US troops by many Britons, whose generally humane treatment of these fighters for democracy was in such marked contrast to the segregation and racial prejudice they faced at home and continued to face from officialdom in the European battle theatre. In an interview with Alan Taylor, Phillips remarks:

> Can you imagine yourself as an eighteen-year-old black kid from Alabama and you suddenly find yourself in East Anglia where nobody is calling you nigger? You think to yourself: 'Well wait a minute.' It completely turns your whole world picture. It goes whoop and you think: 'I thought the world was black and white.' But when you get these little old ladies inviting you in for cheese and biscuits and what have you, you wonder what is going on. Then you get the pub landlord putting signs in the window saying we'll serve American soldiers as long as they're coloured. Black people were treated with a certain degree of decency and civility.[35]

This experience in Norfolk was repeated in many other locations as the white

British in general reacted tetchily to white US attempts to impose a colour line, and treated black US troops as equals. Oral memories from African American veterans and British civilians collected for the documentary *Choc'late Soldiers from the USA* (2008) provide graphic evidence of these radical social relations. For instance, Gillian Vesey, a resident of Bamber Bridge in Lancashire, reports how as a young barmaid she stood up for African American soldiers against attempts by white GIs to impose Jim Crow practices in her public house. She describes how, 'the American white soldiers always wanted serving before the coloured ones but I used to tell them to wait their turn, you know, because it wasn't their turn.'[36] British ideas of fair play chafed against the imposition of foreign racial practices that sought to make second-class citizens of African American troops. Another white British pub landlady replied to white Americans who had remonstrated with her because she served 'coloureds': 'Their money is as good as yours, and we like their company.'[37] British troops too commented positively on this new black presence. Graeme Smith, in his landmark study *When Jim Crow met John Bull: Black American Soldiers in World War II Britain*, quotes from a letter opened by censors:

> Our coloured friends are real gentlemen, well behaved and well spoken … a credit to their unit. British troops get on well with them, we can't help it. They don't boast and flash their money about or make themselves unpopular, we mix quite freely which does seem to surprise them rather … we don't have a colour distinction.[38]

There is much testimony too from African American troops that supports these accounts. For example, Sergeant Wilfred Strange of the 69th Infantry Division describes how several months of excellent race relations in the town of Uttoxeter were sullied by the subsequent arrival of white US airmen who resented the British acceptance of the African Americans into their social realm. As often in Britain, the issue at stake was access to the public houses in town. Strange relates how:

> The white soldiers wanted to take over the pub we used to go to and wanted to run us out, but the British civilians defended us and said no, if anyone's going to leave, the white troops are going to leave, we love the black soldiers.[39]

In a wide range of testimonies, African American troops at the time and veterans in their reminiscences have described a welcoming British public, which stood in stark contrast to the hostility and racism they encountered from their white comrades-in-arms. This can be summed up by a black US GI who told Joseph Julian, 'The English treat us fine – it's in the camp and around where we get all the trouble and riots.'[40] George Orwell captured the spirit of the British reaction best when he contrasted attitudes of the British to white and black GIs:

> There is a widespread anti-American feeling among the working class, thanks to the presence of the American soldiers and I believe, very bitter anti-British feeling among the soldiers themselves... If you ask people why they dislike Americans you get first of all the answer that they are 'always boasting' and then come upon a more solid grievance... An American private soldier gets ten shillings a day and all found, which means that the whole American Army is financially in the middle class and fairly high up in it... The general consensus of opinion is that the only American soldiers with decent manners are negroes.[41]

Between 1942 and D-Day in 1944, the numbers of non-white troops based in Britain rose from 7,000 to over 130,000, and although this put strain on the relations between the white British and the African American troops, they generally continued to be convivial. They are probably best summed up by stories about black Americans that 'probably had their origins in truth but assumed the status of popular myths'.[42] The most widely told was from a West Country farmer who, when asked about the visitors, replied, 'I love the Americans but I don't like these white ones they've brought with them.'[43] As this anecdote illustrates, the greatest strains seemed to come with the presence of white US troops and officers (particularly Southerners) who could not stomach the conviviality between the white British and the African Americans. As Maggi M. Morehouse, who gathered many first-hand testimonies of black troops, attests, 'Generally the only time black soldiers ran into blatant discrimination was when they encountered white American soldiers.'[44] The NAACP president Walter White, in his discussion of African American troops in Britain, concurred, highlighting many examples of the racism of white soldiers and the conviviality of relations between African Americans and British civilians. One anecdote from a black soldier combines the two:

> A distinguished British family invited a group of American soldiers to their home for dinner and dancing. Everything moved smoothly during dinner, but when one of the Negro soldiers danced with one of the English women, he had been assaulted by a Southern white soldier. A free-for-all followed in which the British took the side of the Negroes. And there was the story of the pub keeper who had posted a sign over his entrance reading 'THE PLACE FOR THE EXCLUSIVE USE OF ENGLISHMEN AND AMERICAN NEGRO SOLDIERS.'[45]

White's testimony from black soldiers is backed up again and again by the historical record. In racial incidents that developed into riots in Cosham near

Portsmouth and Bamber Bridge near Preston in 1943, it was white British bystanders who generally supported African American troops against the racist US military police. For instance, at Bamber Bridge, a white British soldier asked the military police who had come to arrest black soldiers out without passes and in the wrong uniform, 'Why do you want to arrest them? They're not doing anything or bothering anybody.'[46] Emboldened by such expressions of support, the black troops fought back, with a black sergeant telling the military police at the Cosham incident, 'We ain't no slaves, this is England.'[47]

Phillips was interested in resurrecting this almost forgotten history of African Americans in Britain because it illustrates how white British fascination with African American troops, despite its sometimes condescending nature, was key to the questioning of a racialised ideology, one of the most pernicious legacies left by the British empire. His own and other black British writers' fascination is linked to the timing of this 'invasion' as a prelude to the *Windrush*-era migration that would happen after the war. By dwelling on the surprising nature of general white welcome for the black presence, Phillips can complicate a narrative that claims that the British were uniquely susceptible to a racism that was unwelcoming to blacks; after all, they had just reacted in a generally favourable light to the billeting of a large number of black troops on their shores. The presence of African American troops was not always greeted with pleasure by the native white population, but progressive whites who were engaged in a life-or-death struggle with fascism were shown to be willing to question received racialised opinions about the abilities and capacities of non-whites.

An exemplary case of this liberal process at work is shown in Phillip's novel. The section 'Somewhere in England' tells the story of a white British woman, Joyce, who escapes a loveless marriage with a bigoted black-marketeer through an intense relationship with an African American soldier, Travis. Joyce tells the story in a series of flashbacks, which reveal that the arrival of these exotic strangers had a profound effect on the narrow, constricted working-class British worldview of the war years. Phillip's decision to use the white Yorkshirewoman as the narrative voice for this section of his novel adds a piquancy as he empathises with her position as oppressed female, discovering her voice through his own native tongue. Finding the truth through her voice simultaneously foregrounds his own Yorkshire heritage. As he says himself, 'Joyce speaks a Yorkshire dialect I grew up speaking. But it's probably the most painful thing I have ever written.'[48] In emphasising his Yorkshire past, Phillips moves away from an essentialising discourse to emphasise his hybrid identity as both regional Englishman and black Englishman. The complexity of his position here undermines glib generalisations about Phillips as simply a black British writer; he has other loyalties and allegiances, including those towards African Americans, which add to the melange of identities Phillips mediates.

Phillips uses Joyce's narrative voice to contrast her response to the arrival of the 'coloured' troops with that of a typical white US officer, who comes to the shop she runs and tries to explain the potential difficulties of dealing with such men. He says, 'A lot of these boys are not used to us treating them as equals, so don't be alarmed by their response.'[49] His description of them as 'not very educated boys' needing 'time to adjust to your customs and ways'[50] is typical of white US officers' attempts at liaison, as detailed in official documents about the stationing of African Americans in the war. For instance, in a War Office briefing by the US military in August 1942, it was asserted that 'British civilians needed to be educated out of their hospitableness towards black Americans.'[51] Such attempts to guide the white British civilian response to African American troops were legion, and were made by both the US military and by certain sections of the British establishment worried about miscegenation. Thus Phillips shows that, despite official attempts to police and contain white British fascination with the African American troops, Joyce refuses to kowtow to such pressure. He has her questioning each of this officer's seemingly irrefutable statements, thus highlighting the fact that the white British response to the 'coloured' troops was far more enlightened than the narrow segregationist attitudes of the US military. Joyce mocks the hubris of the officer 'lazily blowing out smoke' from his cigarette[52] and determines to make up her own mind about the troops. Joyce's attitude was shared by many British women, as shown by the First Lady, Eleanor Roosevelt, who received many letters from US soldiers in Europe, and commented that, 'the young Southerners were very indignant to find that the Negro soldiers were not looked upon with terror by the girls in England, Ireland and Scotland'.[53] In common with many British women, Joyce's first close encounter with the 'coloureds' was to happen at a dance. She narrates how two soldiers invite her whilst in her shop:

> And then they asked me to a dance they are having on Saturday. Asked me politely. Well, I can't dance, I told them. You'll learn, said the tall one. He smiled. We've got our own band ma'am, said the other one. You hear us play, you can't help but dance.[54]

At the dance, Joyce is the one who makes the first move to dance with the soldiers and is complimented by Travis, her dance partner, as being different from the others, 'not act[ing] like them in some ways'.[55] An outsider in her own community, Joyce is immediately more receptive to the marginalised African Americans, and Phillips, as author, is empathetic with her because of his own outsider status in contemporary Britain. Joyce is emboldened by contact with these African Americans to begin to assert her independence and to move away from the narrow provincial mores of her home village. Not used to being treated as an equal herself in the sexist culture of wartime Britain, she is transformed by contact with these soldiers (and Travis in particular) to a position where she questions the dictates of patriarchal society, including the sham of her marriage. As Les Back describes, 'the war had suspended some aspect of male power. In this context women were exploring quite new forms of autonomy in all matters from spending power to sex.'[56] Phillips reflects the cultural and social change black soldiers wrought on small-town English culture. This was attested to by both the indigenous population and the black troops. For instance, an anonymous commentator from Wiltshire noted that the blacks were 'better dancers. Some of them took over the band during the evening and we had some real swing and jitterbugging.'[57] A former black GI, Cleother Hathcock, remembers:

> At that time the Jitterbug was in and the blacks would get a buggin' and the English just loved that. We would go into a dance hall and just take over the place because everybody wanted to learn how to do that American dance, the Jitterbug. They went wild over that.[58]

The importance of popular culture and particularly music as an enabler of interracial exchange is foregrounded in such arenas and through such cultural forms, which the authorities find very hard to police. Black GI units rapidly formed swing bands (such as the band of the 923rd Regiment of the Aviation Engineers, The 923 Reveillers) to play at such dances and brought the latest tunes from Count Basie and Duke Ellington to be 'rendered in the heart of the English countryside'.[59] However, vernacular modes like jazz and its accompanying dance were seen as threatening by white cultural policeman on both sides of the Atlantic, as they had a potency that was partly a result of their liminality and marginality, and were able to cross geographical and cultural boundaries with ease. Paul Gilroy's description of such modes as 'insubordinate racial countercultures'[60] is apposite here, as it foregrounds the radical nature of such interventions in apparently monocultural societies like wartime Britain. US swing bands, playing music like the jitterbug with its physicality and eroticism, meant that British women were captured in a kind of erotic fascination that Phillips illustrates through Joyce's excitement at the exotic mores of these African American troops. He shows this in his descriptions of Travis's everyday differences: his Lucky Strikes, candy and, most sensually, his distinctive hair: 'His hair is well-combed, with a sort of razor parting on the left. It's short like thin black wool, but he puts some oil on it because it shines in the light. Quite bright actually.'[61]

Phillips describes Travis through Joyce's eyes; however, the author's own fascination with the exoticism of the African American comes through in this and other descriptions of the black US troops. The smart, rich and suave African Americans are as interesting to the Yorkshireman, the author, as they are to his character. Joyce's fascination with Travis encourages her to ask him out for a walk. Yet the outcome of this mixed-race assignation has a decidedly American denouement when he is beaten up by the US military police in a racist attack because of his 'uppity' behaviour in walking out with a white woman. The potential for new kinds of relationships away from the segregationist US is undermined by the racist nature of the US forces. This attitude, common amongst the white troops and particularly amongst Southerners, is seen at its most raw in private correspondence read by postal censors. For instance, a white lieutenant complained in a letter home,

> One thing I noticed here and which I don't like is the fact that the English don't draw any color line… The English must be pretty ignorant. I can't see how a white girl could associate with a negro.[62]

And a white sergeant wrote home in September 1942:

> One thing that would make you sick at your stomach tho' is the niggers over here tell the English they are North American Indians … so the English girls go with them. Every time so far that we have seen a nigger with a white girl we have run him away. I would like to shoot the whole bunch of them.[63]

There is much first-hand testimony in correspondence from African American troops too who were at the receiving end of the racism and ensuing violence. One of the most poignant is a letter from an anonymous black soldier to Eleanor Roosevelt in November 1944:

> We were told that there was no serigation [sic] in England, it isn't from the people, they are fine, only from our officers. We are receiving blurring rumours of reports they put out. We are forbidden any recreation that might cause us to mix as a whole with the people. We are a negro unit, I do hope you can help us in some way.[64]

Phillips draws on evidence of racism such as this and incidents like those at Bamber Bridge and Cosham to show the iniquity of US race relations and their effect, even in Britain. As he details, many British people railed against this racism, especially in the context of a war against the pernicious evils of Nazism. As one British soldier wrote,

> During the summer of 1942 there was that Army order about keeping aloof from coloured troops to avoid the risk of rows with white troops. That I'm glad to say, was very unfavourably received by the troops… It savoured of

Hitlerism. 'Just like Hitler and the Jews' was one typical reaction to the order, I remember.[65]

As can be seen from a response like this, ordinary soldiers as well as cultural workers such as Langston Hughes were making unflattering comparisons between the behaviour of senior army officials (both British and US) and that of the enemy. Phillips highlights the effects of such racism, and the opposition to it, through the military's attempts to influence Joyce against the black soldiers. Through this he shows that British good feelings towards, and ultimate fascination with, African Americans during the war continued, despite official attempts to police and temper the relationship by the British and US governments and military.

Eventually Travis is sent to Italy to fight directly against fascism. Here, the way a white imperial media marginalised black troops is highlighted by Joyce's comment that the newsreels 'never showed the coloureds'.[66] Joyce and Travis marry when Joyce is pregnant, but there is a constant refrain, 'We couldn't live together in America, it wouldn't be allowed.'[67] Before they can even try, Travis is killed in Italy, leaving Joyce widowed. She decides to give up her son, Greer, for adoption. This was by far the most common action of the British mothers of the thousand or so mixed-race babies from the immediate post-war period, as detailed in Smith's exhaustive survey.[68] Phillips, rather than over-romanticising his character, has Joyce commit this awful act of abandonment that complicates her heroic status. Her choice, though, is in keeping with that of the majority of the actual white mothers of 'brown babies' in the immediate post-war period.

The narrative is completed when Greer locates Joyce and visits her in 1963. Now a housewife with a new family she struggles to give the moment the right resonance: 'I took a deep breath and turned to face him. I almost said make yourself at home, but I didn't. At least I avoided that.'[69] Joyce struggles to make Greer feel truly at home but fails in the end. However, it is not with the relationship to her son that Phillips completes his tale, but with Joyce as a crucial player in his diasporan tale being designated as 'my daughter' by the African father who links the four sections of *Crossing the River*. As Phillips himself says, 'it seemed emotionally correct. She grew up without a dad, and what binds her to the others is that lack.'[70] What Phillips points to here is an emotional attachment that transcends racial difference. As a Yorkshirewoman she exhibits a crucial aspect of Phillips's own hybrid identity and exemplifies Phillips's tendency to a non-essentialised rendering of black Britishness. The way Joyce reaches out beyond her narrow background allows her to empathise with a diasporan people, fatherless like herself.

But Phillips also has Joyce exemplifying the many British people whose welcome to African American troops undermined the racist white British solidarity that would have been needful in order for segregation to work in a British context. Phillips also shows how the arrival of the Jim Crow army meant new perspectives for white British people whose horizons had up until then been limited by the restrictions of a class-ridden imperialist culture of Spam sandwiches, anodyne tea parties and warm beer. The wartime period, in which ordinary white British people seemed to welcome diasporan Africans, seems an almost lost utopian moment of racial harmony in comparison to the racist face Britons all too often showed Caribbean migrants over the next fifty years. Phillips revels in this moment but realises it was created by the strange historical nuances of the war.

A specific incident of fascination with the African American troops is related by Graham Smith, who details a telling anecdote from a report in the *Sunday Pictorial* of August 1945 that shows how the presence of African American troops had changed sexual and racial mores in Britain. It relates to an event in Bristol at the end of the war:

> Hundreds of screaming girls aged 17 to 25 besieged the barracks where black soldiers were preparing to go back to the US, singing a Bing Crosby hit, 'Don't Fence Me In'. Barriers were broken down and later the gates of the railway station were rushed. 'To Hell with the US Army color bars! We want our colored sweethearts' was the cry while one rain-soaked 18-year-old said, 'We intend to give our sweeties a good send off. And what's more, we intend going to America after them.'[71]

This news report shows how Phillips's description of Joyce's liberation from restrictive British mores through her relationship with an African American soldier is representative of many such encounters during the war years, attesting to a white British fascination with African Americans that had the consequence of liberalising British society. This liberalisation was not universally welcomed and created problems for the returning British husbands and fiancés from the front, who found a more emancipated female population. This is commented on by Les Back through a 1946 Stil cartoon, 'Tommy Comes Home', showing a dance floor full of 'airborne Lindy-hopping women' surrounded by their 'newly demobbed English partners stood rigid, stuck to the floor and unable to follow their steps' and with the tag-line 'What happened to you Myrtle – you never danced liked that before I went away.' These newly emancipated women, 'sexually knowing and fully initiated in American popular culture and style',[72] chafed against a British culture that wanted to keep women as housewives and mothers. The incident at Bristol and the cartoon have their own particularly pertinent soundtracks that accompany the white British women's performative direct action which is prescient of the rock-and-roll hysteria of the mid-1950s. This could be seen as an example of Gilroy's previously mentioned 'insubordinate racial countercultures' that interpolates these white British women as actors in a wider drama of hybridisation and the mixing of cultures that the arrival of African American troops into Britain brought about. Radical change is caused to actors from all sides of the drama.

Andrea Levy's more recent novel *Small Island* (2004) also discusses similar racial and gender issues and developments in the Second World War, but includes West Indians as central actors in the drama along with African Americans and white Britons. Her sprawling novel does not have the stripped-down economy of Phillips's *Crossing the River* and resembles an overwrought historical saga with rather too convoluted a plot, but it is useful to discuss it here because it was a very successful, multiple prize-winning (Orange, Whitbread and Commonwealth Writers' Prizes were awarded) and widely read work, as well as being the first major novel by a black British author to have race and the Second World War as its central theme. The novel will hopefully enable a discussion of the crucial role of Caribbean fighters in the war and their relationship to the racial issues brought about by the presence of the much larger number of African American troops in Britain.

During the war, over 10,000 British West Indians volunteered to fight for the mother country, and they joined the 15,000 black sailors in the British merchant navy and the 520 workers in munitions factories and over 800 forestry workers from Belize who helped the British war effort. In particular, in the wake of the catastrophic losses suffered by aircrew in the Battle of Britain (1940), the Royal Air Force started to recruit with vigour in the Caribbean. Ironically, the RAF had historically been the most racist of the British armed forces, restricting 'entry into the RAF to men of pure European descent',[73] a policy which was still operating at the outset of war in 1939 and throughout the first half of 1940 to forestall the danger of intimate contact in the cramped confines of military aircraft, as 'the presence of a colored man in such a crew would detract from efficiency'.[74] These Caribbean RAF recruits, amongst the first to break this colour bar, are central characters in Levy's novel. As with Phillips's narrative, Levy's focus on the war years is a deliberate broadening out of a hitherto limited black British historiography which had all too often had as its starting point the arrival of the ship *Empire Windrush*, with its hundreds of British Caribbean migrants, at Tilbury Docks in 1948. Like Phillips, Levy wants to emphasise how race relations were constructed in Britain during the war years as much as in the mass migrations that followed. The most important characters for a discussion of the novel in these terms are Queenie Bligh and Gilbert Johnson. The former is a white rural-born British woman whose life is transformed by her interaction with Caribbean servicemen, whilst Gilbert is a Jamaican RAF driver for whom the war is a life-changing experience and whose very presence, along with that of his Caribbean colleagues, challenges ideas about race both for the British civilians and for the US troops billeted among them. Gilbert had wanted to be an aircraftman, but has his hopes thwarted by the residual racism in the RAF that promoted light-skinned and college-educated West Indian men to the officer class and left dark-skinned recruits in the lower ranks; although there was no Jim Crow segregation in the British services, such petty discrimination over promotions was pervasive. As Alan Wilmot, a Jamaican who served in both the Royal Navy and the RAF, discussed,

> The British scene was different [from the US] – there was no official racial discrimination in the services, but seniority promotion for a black serviceman was rare, even though you were qualified to do the job. Excuses for non-promotion were always there, so you were simply allowed to carry on in the ranks, regardless of your ability. They didn't want black personnel in charge of white servicemen.
> But we were treated very well by white civilians because they were aware that you had left your safe country to face danger and help them in their time of need.[75]

In common with many Caribbean volunteers, Gilbert's first encounter with Jim Crow was during transit into the British army in holding camps in Virginia. The recruits are inducted into the camp by an American officer who

> was telling us that we West Indians, being subjects of His Majesty King George VI, had for the time being, superior black skin. We were allowed to live with white soldiers, while the inferior American negro was not. I was perplexed. No, we were all perplexed.[76]

Levy uses this incident to foreshadow Gilbert's experience of Jim Crow practices when he gets to Britain. This strange encounter with Southern mores was common to many West Indian servicemen, and Levy's use of it here authenticates Gilbert's experiences as he journeys to Britain via the US. For instance, the RAF veteran Vivian Blake discussed his experience at Fort Patrick Henry in Virginia in 1944 for a recent local oral history project in Gloucester:

> When we got there it was a very large station and we found there were different sections for blacks and whites and blacks weren't supposed to be able to join certain regiments like paratroopers. We were regarded as 'honorary whites' because we were British and we were billeted with the whites. I remember a white American officer reminding his men, 'These ain't Uncle Sam's niggers, these are King George's niggers.'[77]

As we can see from this testimony, white officers merely put up with the anomaly, doing little to disguise their racist mindset. Gilbert and his fellow West Indians' perplexity at the operation of Jim Crow was unfortunately not to be restricted to their sojourn in the US, as these racial practices crossed the Atlantic with disturbing ramifications for all black soldiers, as Langston Hughes so eloquently asserted. When he is sent as a driver to a US base near Grimsby, Gilbert comes face-to-face with a naked racism that shocks him out of a complacency induced by the general warm welcome he had received from his white fellow combatants and British civilians. The US officer is apoplectic that the 'fucking Limeys' have sent him a 'nigger', and rants so loudly that Gilbert in an adjoining room hears every word. Gilbert reflects on how his experiences of welcome in Britain had allowed him to bury the memory of the racism in Virginia and made him unprepared for this Jim Crow encounter:

> Was it the square-bashing at Filey, the trade-training in Blackpool, the posting to the airbase in Lincolnshire that made me forget? Perhaps it was my crew – white men every one – Charlie, Bill, Raymond, Arnold. Or the white women in the town – Enid, Rose, that other one with the roving eye. Was it the comely Annie from the Swan? Or was I now so used to England that it just escaped my mind? Of course if a coloured man finds himself on an American base surrounded entirely by white people, then, man!, he is in the wrong place. How could I forget?[78]

Still smarting with anger, Gilbert picks up two black American GIs hitch-hiking to a rendezvous with two English women in Lincoln. Levy uses this meeting to highlight difference between the unworldly black Americans and their Caribbean fellow combatant. The black Americans are portrayed as limited and uneducated in comparison to Gilbert. This stereotyping makes fun of the African Americans' unworldly innocence, geographical ignorance and slow-wittedness at exactly the historical moment that a committed internationalism, fostered by the very successful Double V campaign, permeated African American culture. Hence Levy, in accurately portraying a Caribbean tale of adventurous sojourns to fight the fascist enemy, does so at the expense of the African American troops she so casually stereotypes. The historical record tells a different story of West Indian servicemen supporting African American troops in their encounters with Jim Crow. Alan Wilmot outlines how important it was for him to show racial solidarity with black GIs:

> The black American GIs were a different story. We got along very well indeed – we British black servicemen were their protectors. At times, they were attacked by groups of white GIs, especially if they were in the

company of white girls. If they attempted to defend themselves against the white GIs, police were always at hand to arrest the black ones for the stockade, so we would go to their rescue and try to prevent them being arrested. Because the US GI police had no jurisdiction over British servicemen, we could defend them (and ourselves) until the British police arrived on the scene, along with the ambulance for the wounded.[79]

This oral memory of racial solidarity in the face of Jim Crow racism and the violence that upheld it shows a specific West Indian response to racial dynamics in Britain during the war. As usual, it is the presence of white women with the black soldiers that angers the white GIs and sends them into a violent frenzy; the arrival of the racist military police merely makes the situation worse and the danger greater for the African Americans. Wilmot's memory of acting in solidarity with black GIs in racial incidents chimes with those of some British civilians and troops, but the West Indians in doing so took part in a racial insubordination that helped to undermine the power of segregation by using their British citizenship as a weapon against the power of Jim Crow.

Solidarity between African American troops and West Indians was not universal, however, and it reached its nadir in Trinidad in 1942 when the introduction of a segregated unit, the black 99th Anti-Aircraft Artillery Unit, led to serious violent incidents between the domestic population and the troops.[80] Earl Lovelace's novel *The Wine of Astonishment* (1982) highlights the impact of the US troops on Trinidadians and the resentments caused, through the narration of local Baptists horrified at the 'invasion':

> That year the great war against Japan and the Germans was still fighting. The American soldiers who came down to Trinidad to protect us from invasion was still in Bonasse, drinking Cockspur Rum and filling up the women, driving their jeeps and screeching their brakes like madmen all over the place, waking Christian people up all hours of the night to hear bottles crash and women scream and guns shoot off and make Bee curse the day that these heathen people land in this colony with money in their pockets and guns on their waist to have mother and daughter whoring down the place and big men touts behind the Yankee dollar.[81]

The foreigners with far superior financial resources and the glamour of their US uniforms soon found the local women so 'obliging' that local calypsonians would lament, 'I was living with my decent and contented wife/Until the soldiers came and broke up my life.'[82] Another calypso noted a rise in prostitution which followed the US arrival, with 'Both mother and daughter/Working for the Yankee dollar.'[83] Here it seemed the Americanness of the troops trumped their blackness, and their colonial attitude to the locals meant that racial solidarity was at a premium. Objections to the black unit led to their removal from the island in 1943 and should warn us against projecting from British examples of trans-racial solidarity into other theatres where economic differences between troops and civilians led to resentments that undermined intra-race relations. These soldiers were disgracefully Jim Crowed, but this did not undermine their chauvinist attitudes to the island folk they encountered as they exhibited conspicuous consumption and ethnocentrism that enraged the locals.

To return to the domestic British front, Levy's novel does highlight crucial aspects of race in wartime as its narrative unfolds, most importantly in the depiction of the friendship of Gilbert Joseph and Queenie Bligh. Throughout the novel, Queenie's humanitarian response to West Indian servicemen is used to show a British working class acceptance of blacks as fellow-fighters in a war against fascism. Like Joyce in *Crossing the River*, she reacts first to black servicemen as exilic people needing home comforts. Her hospitality, like Joyce's, is complicated by the presence of white US troops who resent her inter-racial mixing. Some of the most astute writing in *Small Island* comes with the description of the tensions caused by Queenie's innocent cultivation of friendship with Gilbert. Having decided to eat together in a café, Gilbert muses on the intervention of an ugly racial politics into a typical British context:

> I had just finished seating Queenie into a chair and was half-way into my own when they became apparent to me. Three White American GIs. As I took my seat, Queenie, joking loudly to me said, 'You're a gentleman, Airman.' She slipped off her cardigan, placing it on the back of the chair. The three GIs noticed us, as I knew they would. One nudged the other's arm, nodding towards our table while another stared directly at me with a blinkless gaze that did not falter. Queenie, with her back to them had no reason to feel their curiosity… I, knowing fear can animate a face, returned to them an expressionless stare.[84]

The irony of Queenie designating Gilbert a 'gentleman' at the exact moment he is being assigned a thoroughly different and unequivocally lesser status by the watching GIs is a brilliant juxtaposition and highlights the attempted workings of Jim Crow segregationist mores in a non-US context. The highly-charged atmosphere is created by gesture and gaze, so that each seemingly innocent action is magnified. For instance, Queenie's disrobing has an altogether charged meaning for the GIs as she is exposing flesh in front of a black man. Queenie is oblivious to the highly charged atmosphere, because she has her back to the GIs; however, her ignorance could be seen to be symbolic of a generalised white British innocence about the working of racism that the cauldron of war and the larger black presence was bringing to the fore. The juxtaposition of this genteel British scene and extreme racial tensions enables Levy to document the way West Indian troops were put at tremendous risk by the presence of a segregated US army in their midst. Gilbert articulates this violent enmity from his supposed allies in the war against fascism as he sits in the café; having discussed how the Nazis were the army hated most by the British Tommies, he continues:

> from that first uneasy hospitality at the American base in Virginia to this cocky hatred that was charging across the room to yell in the face of a coloured man whose audacity was to sit with a white woman. I was learning to despise the white American GI above all other. They were the army that hated me most! Out of place in the genteel atmosphere of this dreary tea-shop, these three aggrieved GIs twitched with hostile excitement, like snipers clearing their aim at a sitting target. Surrounded by grey-haired old ladies – cups twinkling like bells as uncertain hands placed them on saucers, the clip of cutlery on floral plates, a gentle gurgle of pouring tea, a little slurping, a hushed conversation – these poor GIs were in murderous mood watching a nigger sitting with his head still high. If the defeat of hatred is the purpose of war, then come let us face it: I and all the other coloured servicemen were fighting this war on another front.[85]

Gilbert's final thought chimes with the Double V campaign, showing how the pervasiveness of Jim Crow makes racial solidarity across national borders essential to survival for all black troops in the allied forces. Gilbert manages to extract himself and Queenie from the café before he is physically attacked. However, having met up with her father-in-law, they are unluckier in their next venue, a movie theatre. Here the usherette tries to sit them in the balcony with Jim-Crowed black American troops. Gilbert, with the support of Queenie, refuses, and repeats his assertions throughout the conversation:

> 'I am not an American, I am with the British RAF.'

> 'This is England … This is not America. We do not do this in America. I will sit anywhere I please.'

> 'Madam, there is no Jim Crow in this country.'

> 'Segregation, madam, there is no segregation in this country. I will sit wherever I like in this picture house. And those coloured men at the back should have been allowed to sit wherever they so please. This is England, not Alabama.'[86]

Gilbert juxtaposes this racism with the Nazism that the allies are meant to be opposing, describing how 'we are fighting the persecution of the Jew, yet even in my RAF blue my coloured skin can permit anyone to treat me as less than a man.'[87] A full-scale riot erupts as Gilbert and Queenie's refusal to be segregated sparks the African Americans into revolting against this Jim Crow facility. The presence of segregated movie theatres in certain towns in Britain came hand in hand with designated black and white areas in those towns dominated by white Americans. No less a luminary than Joe Louis, the black heavyweight champion of the world, reported on a segregated cinema in Salisbury, Wiltshire which he visited on a propaganda tour in 1944. As he recollected,

> The ticket taker told us we'd have to sit in a special section. Shit! This wasn't America, this was England… The theatre manager … knew who I was and apologised all over the place. Said he had instructions from the army. So I called my friend Lieutenant General John Lee and told them they had no business messing up another country's custom with American Jim Crow.[88]

Louis thought his complaint had ended such segregation, but it continued after his visit. The riot in the fictional movie theatre and the surrounding streets has a tragic denouement when Queenie's father-in-law Arthur Bligh is shot dead in the crossfire. Gilbert comments: 'Arthur Bligh had become another casualty of war – but come tell me someone … which war?'[89] Of course the reader is able to answer the rhetorical question armed with the context that Levy's novelisation of the long arm of Jim Crow segregation has provided. The 'race war' is one that played itself out as an accompaniment to the war against fascism and it had its own casualties, including innocent bystanders like Arthur Bligh. The historical record is replete with examples of West Indians servicemen who, like the fictional Gilbert, refused to bow down to the imposition of Jim Crow. For instance, Baron Baker, a Jamaican RAF policeman, describes how

> Our first major racial problem was with the American soldiers. In a pub in Gloucester, we were told by American GIs that 'back home niggers aren't allowed in our bars'. This was in early 1944. There was no problem with this pub before the Americans came. On a Saturday night some of our chaps went into town and they were badly beaten by these Americans. So we fought the American soldiers and won.[90]

That an RAF policeman should involve himself in defending his fellow Caribbean servicemen shows the extremity of the situation caused by the segregation that white GIs attempted to impose. But Baker went further, agitating for a solution that would mean his British citizenship, and that of his fellows, would trump their black skin colour. His intervention is full of the transnational rhetoric of Double V, imploring his commanding officer to think about his responsibilities to those fighting Britain's wars:

> I said to my Commanding Officer, 'We came here to fight a war for you, and so you can't kick us about.' So both the American and English commanders got together and realised something had to be done. They made certain places out of bounds to the Americans. I told them, 'We are King George VI's soldiers not Roosevelt's black boys'. We made it clear that if they put anywhere out of bounds to us we would fight them like hell.[91]

From testimony like this it can be seen that the war emboldened black troops in the various allied armies to demand their democratic rights on the home front at the same time as fighting a war for democracy. This is articulated best within a US context by GIs who returned and became involved in the struggle against segregation. Wilford Strange expresses this sentiment most eloquently:

> I think the impact these soldiers had by volunteering was the initiation of the civil rights movement, 'cos these soldiers were never going back to be discriminated against again, none of us were.[92]

Black troops' oppression was most starkly impressed on them when they came face-to-face with extreme forms of racism either from their own officers or the excesses of the enemy. For the Guyanese Cy Grant, an RAF officer and prisoner of war, the conflict had a profound effect. Experiencing the comradeship of his white crew members, he testifies to the importance of the war for forging inter-racial harmony. However, his capture after a bombing raid over Holland in July 1943 meant that his race became again his defining feature. After a week in solitary confinement, his picture was taken and appeared in the German newspaper with the caption, 'A member of the Royal Air Force of indeterminate race.' His officer status was seen by the Nazis as proof positive of 'how degenerate the RAF had become'.[93] As a British POW, he was lucky to escape the worst of Nazi racism whilst in the prison camp; however, even here he was not immune to the racist barbs of his fellows: 'An American airman called me a nigger! He was from the deep South… and just could not understand that I was an officer in the British Royal Air Force.'[94] Grant's liberation from the camp is attended by a racial memory that separates him from his white compatriots and links him to the historical oppression of his people. As he is transported in a boxcar to freedom, he describes how

> We lay on our sides, jammed like sardines hard against one another in two rows, facing each other with feet interlocking. The atmosphere was

stifling and it was impossible to sleep. This seemed a great hardship, until I recalled the purgatory endured by slaves, my forebears, of the Middle Passage, a journey of some six thousand miles. What was one night cramped like sardines in a cold boxcar, compared to weeks drowning in despair, violence, vomit and excreta in the holds of a slave ship?[95]

This historical transnational perspective can be linked to the way Sembene, Césaire, Padmore et al make the link between Nazism and the history of colonial race relations in their art or theoretical writings. Grant here uses his own captivity and liberation to talk back to, and gain perspective from, a historical racism founded on the slave trade. Many troops from the African diaspora had similar moments of enlightenment, as we have seen throughout this chapter. Those who encountered the Nazi death camps were often the most moved to new understandings of their place as soldiers in a segregated army and black men in a racist world. For instance, Leon Bass comments:

It was only when I went into the concentration camp at Buchenwald in Germany did I see that there was something I really had to fight for. I now knew that the racism that I had experienced all my life, especially in the military, that racism had been carried to the ultimate right there, at Buchenwald. So I had a new outlook, my blinders came off you see, the tunnel vision was gone, dissipated and I understood that all of us can suffer and I saw that with all the different people that were placed in the concentration camp by the racist Germans.[96]

Bass, in common with the poet Langston Hughes, understands the continuum of racism from the Jim Crow military to the Nazi regime, allowing him to have a wider, less egocentric perspective, seeing racism as far more than a personal or even merely US issue. This perspective was articulated by many soldiers throughout the African diaspora, whose war experiences helped to radicalise them in ways that meant pre-war racial realities were blown away for ever. In Europe, Africa and the Americas, as the black troops returned from combat, many of them were not willing to resume relations as though nothing had changed.[97]

In a sense, this is the worst aspect of the Memorial Gates that opened this discussion. It places black British and African combatants for the allied cause in an imperial freeze-frame that cannot speak to the future-world that many troops saw as the most important legacy of the war. There is only one thing worse than the absence of a memorial and that is one so inappropriate that it promotes ideologies that undermine the very sacrifices made by those who served, those they commemorate. In Bass's spirit of transnational and cross-racial solidarity, Scots poet Hamish Henderson's elegy 'End of a Campaign', describing the dead on both sides in the African campaign in which he fought, shows movingly the inadequacy of imperial narratives to explicate the horrors of war:

> There were our own, there were the others.
> Their deaths were like their lives, human and animal.
> There were no gods and precious few heroes.
> What they regretted when they died had nothing to do
>   with race and leader, realm indivisible,
> laboured Augustan speeches or vague imperial heritage.
> (They saw through that guff before the axe fell.)[98]

As Henderson describes, there are alternative visions, not hidebound to imperial ideologies and post-imperial apologies, and some of them are contained in the novels, memoirs and films discussed in this chapter, which provide alternative memorial texts about the impact of the Second World War for African diasporan troops and their descendants.

A work that effectively memorialises such servicemen, and would be a more fitting memorial to them, was constructed by the Jamaican-raised, US-based sculptor Michael Richards (1963–2001). Richards, who died in the World Trade Center attacks on 11 September 2001, was obsessed by the symbolism of flying and created sculptures based on the experiences of the Tuskegee airmen, whose legendary exploits in the Second World War meant they were awarded more than 150 Distinguished Flying Crosses, but who were 'racially segregated second-class citizens when back on US soil, even if they were heroes in the skies'.[99] His bronze *Tar Baby vs St Sebastian* (1999) (Figure 23) portrays a life-sized, uniformed airman, eyes uplifted to the skies, with model planes impregnating his body. As Jorge Daniel Veneciano comments:

> Each of his works engages the notion of flight in at least two important senses, as a form of flight away from what is repressive, and as a form of flight toward what is redeeming.[100]

In this sense, the airman in the sculpture is representative of the black servicemen whose service for the allies so often led them through danger and against prejudice to new understandings. Like the tar baby of African American folklore, he has got too close to a dangerous situation and is horribly ensnared and eventually martyred like St Sebastian, who was killed by arrows for protecting the captured Christians he was supposed to imprison. In the sculpture, the planes pierce the body of the airman as if taunting his desire for flight as escape from the racism that pervades his home space. Richards himself commented that fliers were:

Only being free, really free, when they were in the air. They serve as symbols of failed transcendence and loss of faith, escaping the pull of gravity, but always forced back to the ground. Lost navigators, always seeking home.[101]

His sculpture, free from the limitations of martial nationalism and replete with the pain of racial exclusion, assuredly conveys the transcendental power of freedom expressed through these men's heroic flights. As such it is surely a most fitting memorial to the multiple heroic experiences of all those African diasporan fighters of the Second World War who fought a double war for democracy at home and abroad.

Notes

1. Quoted in 'The civil rights struggle, African American GIs and Germany, digital archive, oral history collection and research project' (leaflet), Vassar College, German Historical Institute, Washington, DC and Heidelberg Center for American Studies, http://aacvr-germany.org/AACVR.ORG/images/stories/flyer_aacvr.pdf [accessed 22 July 2009].

2. P. Oliver, 'Taking the measure of the blues', in N. Wynn (ed.), *Cross the River Blues: African American Music in Europe* (Jackson, MI: University Press of Mississippi, 2008), p. 24.

3. Gilroy, *After Empire*, p. 108–109.

4. b. hooks, *Yearning: Race, Gender and Cultural Politics* (London: Turnaround, 1991), p. 147.

5. B. Bousquet and C. Douglas, *West Indian Women at War* (London: Lawrence and Wishart, 1991), p. 13.

6. *Afrikan Heroes Re-visited: The Forgotten Heroes of Commonwealth*, dir. R. Chikukwa (Imperial War Museum North: Manchester, 2006).

7. *Afrikan Heroes Re-visited*

8. *Afrikan Heroes Re-visited*

9. *Afrikan Heroes Re-visited*

10. Quoted in B. H. Edwards, *The Practice of Diaspora: Literature, Translation and the Rise of Black Internationalism* (London: Harvard University Press, 2003), p. 241.

11. A. Césaire, *Discourse on Colonialism* (New York, NY: Monthly Review Press, 1972), p. 14.

12. Quoted in P. Gilroy, *Between Camps: Nations, Cultures and the Allure of Race* (London: Penguin, 2000), p. 54.

13. Quoted in P. M. Von Eschen, *Race Against Empire: Black Americans and Anticolonialism, 1937–1957* (Ithaca, NY: Cornell University Press, 1997), p. 42.

14. Von Eschen, *Race Against Empire*, p. 20.

15. F. Fanon, *Toward the African Revolution: Political Essays*, trans. Haakon Chevalier (New York, NY: Grove Press, 1967), p. 23.

16. G. Mann, *Native Sons: West African Veterans and France in the Twentieth Century* (Durham, NC: Duke University Press, 2006), pp. 19–20.

17. M. Dixon, 'Introduction', *The Collected Poetry of Leopold Sedar Senghor* (Charlottesville, VA: University of Virginia Press, 1998), p.xxxii.

18. Dixon, p. 71.

19. Dixon, p. 68.

20. O. Sembene (dir.), *Camp de Thiaroye* (1988).

21. Sembene, *Camp de Thiaroye*.

22. Sembene, *Camp de Thiaroye*.

23. M. Echenberg, *Colonial Conscripts: The Tirailleurs Senegalais in French West Africa, 1857–1960* (Portsmouth: Heinemann, 1991), p. 124.

24. C. Forsdick, '"Ceci n'est pas un conte, mais une histoire de chair et de sang": representing the colonial massacre in francophone literature and culture', in L. Milne (ed.), *Postcolonial Violence and Identity in Francophone Africa and the Antilles* (New York, NY: Peter Lang, 2007), pp.31–57, p.50.

25. Von Eschen, *Race Against Empire*, p. 2.

26. Von Eschen, *Race Against Empire*, p.34.

27. Quoted in B.V. Mullen's *Popular Fronts: Chicago and African American Cultural Politics, 1935–46* (Champaign, IL: University of Illinois Press, 1999), p. 61.

28. Quoted in L. Potter, W. Miles and N. Rosenblaum, *Liberators: Fighting on Two Fronts in World War II* (New York, NY: Harcourt Brace Jovanovich, 1992), p.52.

29. *Chicago Defender*, 30 January 1943, quoted in A. Rampersad, *The Life of Langston Hughes Volume II: 1941–1967 I Dream a World* (Oxford: Oxford University Press, 2002), p. 67.

30. N. Izon and G. Cook (dirs), *Choc'late Soldiers from the USA* (Hesh Productions, 2008).

31. A. Rampersad (ed.), *The Collected Poems of Langston Hughes* (New York, NY: Vintage, 1995), p. 281.

32. Rampersad, *The Collected Poems of Langston Hughes*, p. 291.

33. Rampersad, *The Collected Poems of Langston Hughes*, pp. 288–289.

34. J. Julian, 'Jim Crow goes abroad', *The Nation* (5 December 1942), p. 610.

35. A. Taylor, 'Two-way traffic,' *Scotland on Sunday* (30 May 1993), Section 2, p. 2.

36. Izon and Cook, *Choc'late Soldiers from the USA*.

37. Julian, 'Jim Crow goes abroad', p. 611.

38. G. Smith, *When Jim Crow Met John Bull: Black American Soldiers in WWII Britain* (London: IB Tauris, 1987), p. 117.

39. Izon and Cook, *Choc'late Soldiers from the USA*.

40. Julian, 'Jim Crow goes abroad', p. 612.

41. P. Lewis, *A People's War* (London: Thames Methuen, 1986), pp. 205–206.

42. Smith, *When Jim Crow Met John Bull*, p. 118.

43. Smith, *When Jim Crow Met John Bull*, pp. 118–119.

44. M. M. Morehouse, *Fighting the Jim Crow Army: Black Men and Women Remember WWII* (Lanham, MD: Rowman and Littlefield, 2000), p. 200.

45. Quoted in L. Back, 'Syncopated synergy: dance, embodiment and the call of the jitterbug', in V. Ware and L. Back (eds), *Out of Whiteness: Color, Politics and Culture* (Chicago, IL and London: University of Chicago Press, 2002), pp. 169–195 (185).

46. K. Werrell, 'The mutiny at Bamber Bridge', *After the Battle* (1978), p. 1.

47. D. Reynolds, *Rich Relation: The American Occupation of Britain 1942–1945* (London: Harper Collins, 1996), p.305.

48. M. Jaggi, 'Spectral triangle', *The Guardian* (5 May 1993), p. 4.

49. C. Phillips, *Crossing the River* (London: Picador, 1994), p. 145.

50. Phillips, *Crossing the River*, p. 145.

51. Smith, *When Jim Crow Met John Bull*, p. 55.

52. Phillips, *Crossing the River*, p. 145.

53. A. M. Osur, *Blacks in the Army Air Forces During World War II* (Washington, DC: Office of Air Forces' History, 1977), pp. 98–99.

54. Phillips, *Crossing the River*, p. 149.

55. Phillips, *Crossing the River*, p. 163.

56. Back, 'Syncopated synergy', p. 182.

57. Smith, *When Jim Crow Met John Bull*, p. 124.

58. Morehouse, *Fighting the Jim Crow Army*, p. 199.

59. Back, 'Syncopated synergy', p. 183.

60. Gilroy, *The Black Atlantic*, p. 200.

61. Phillips, *Crossing the River*, p. 167.

62. Osur, *Blacks in the Army Air Forces*, p. 98.

63. Smith, *When Jim Crow Met John Bull*, p. 133.

64. Smith, *When Jim Crow Met John Bull*, p. 165.

65. Smith, *When Jim Crow Met John Bull*, p. 61

66. Phillips, *Crossing the River*, p. 223.

67. Phillips, *Crossing the River*, p. 225.

68. Smith, *When Jim Crow Met John Bull*, pp. 180–220.

69. Phillips, *Crossing the River*, p. 232.

70. Jaggi, 'Spectral triangle,' p. 4.

71. Smith, *When Jim Crow Met John Bull*, p. 204.

72. Back, 'Syncopated synergy', p. 194.

73. R. Lambo, 'Achtung! The black prince: West Africans in the Royal Air Force, 1939–46' in David Killingray (ed.), *Africans in Britain* (London: Frank Cass, 1993), p. 145.

74. Internal RAF memo quoted in Lambo, 'Achtung! The black prince', p. 149.

75. A. Wilmot, 'Making a difference – experiences of a black British serviceman', oral memoir on 'WW2 People's War', BBC, http://www.bbc.co.uk/ww2peopleswar/stories/96/a1921196.shtml [accessed 14 July, 2008].

76. A. Levy, *Small Island* (London: Headline, 2004), p. 131.

77. V. Blake, 'Birthday fib gets Jamaican schoolboy into the RAF', oral memoir on 'WW2 People's War', BBC, http://www.bbc.co.uk/ww2peopleswar/stories/41/a3754541.shtml [accessed 14 July 2008].

78. Levy, *Small Island*, p. 153.

79. Wilmot, 'Making a difference'.

80. See A. Palmer, 'The politics of race and war: black American soldiers in the Carribean theater during the Second World War', *Military Affairs* 47 (April 1983), pp. 59–62.

81. E. Lovelace, *The Wine of Astonishment* (London: Heinemann, 1982), p. 18.

82. Palmer, 'The politics of race and war', p. 59.

83. Palmer, 'The politics of race and war', p. 61.

84. Levy, *Small Island*, p. 176.

85. Levy, *Small Island*, p. 177.

86. Levy, *Small Island*, p. 184–185.

87. Levy, *Small Island*, p. 186.

88. Smith, *Jim Crow*, p. 109.

89. Levy, *Small Island*, p. 193.

90. Bousquet and Douglas, *West Indian Women at War*, p. 77.

91. Bousquet and Douglas, *West Indian Women at War*, p. 77.

92. Quoted in Cook and Izon, *Choc'late Soldiers from the USA*.

93. C. Grant, *A Member of the RAF of Indeterminate Race: WW2 Experiences of a Former RAF Navigator and POW* (Bognor Regis: Woodfield Publishing, 2006), pp. x–xi. Grant had an inspiring life after the war too: a singer, actor and writer, he became the first black artist to appear regularly on British TV, dying aged 90 in 2010.

94. Grant, *A Member of the RAF of Indeterminate Race*, p. 64.

95. Grant, *A Member of the RAF of Indeterminate Race*, p. 84.

96. Quoted in Cook and Izon, *Choc'late Soldiers from the USA*.

97. This chapter discusses the radicalism awakened in many troops and shown in a variety of sources; however, there are commentators who disagree about what they perceive as an over-romanticised view, particularly when it is applied to French West African veterans. See especially Mann's *Native Sons*.

98. H. Henderson, *Elegies for the Dead in Cyrenaica* (Edinburgh: Polygon, 1990), p. 17.

99. A. Dannant, 'Obituary of Michael Richards', *The Independent*, 24 September 2001, p. 6.

100. Quoted in Dannant, 'Obituary of Michael Richards', p. 6.

101. Quoted in Dannant, 'Obituary of Michael Richards', p. 6.

7

Accounting for the Bodies and Revealing Ghostly Presences: Utopian and Dystopian Imaginations of the African Atlantic in the work of Ellen Gallagher, Godfried Donkor and Lubaina Himid

This boat is your womb, a matrix and yet it expels you. This boat pregnant with as many dead as living under the sentence of death. *Édouard Glissant*[1]

...the time of modernity, which piles up from an exceptional historical catastrophe. And that catastrophe is the catastrophe of the Atlantic abyss. *Ian Baucom*[2]

...the lingering past, the luminous presence of the seemingly invisible... the water and what is down there, you have seen the ghostly matter: the lost beloveds and the force that made them disposable. *Avery Gordon*[3]

How to account for the Africans transported out of the continent as part of the transatlantic slave trade? It is remarkable how germane this single question was to everyone involved, those who profited and those who were victims of the trade, investors in Europe and those trading in human bodies in Africa, Africans forcibly transported to the Americas and those remaining on the continent of their birth. The question remains pertinent to historians, cultural commentators and artists trying to make sense of the trade's legacies, which continue into the twenty-first century. Of course to use the word 'account' immediately brings us face-to-face with the dual meaning of the word: a tale that needs to be told and retold so that it can be fully narrated, and a transaction that needs to be comprehensively deconstructed so all its fiscal manifestations are made transparent. Marcus Rediker, in *The Slave Ship: A Human History*, articulates this duality at the heart of the 'peculiar' trade:

> It is as if the use of ledgers, almanacs, balance sheets, graphs and tables – the merchants' comforting methods – has rendered abstract,

and thereby dehumanised, a reality that must, for moral and political reasons, be understood concretely. An ethnography of the slave ship helps to demonstrate not only the cruel truth of what one group of people (or several) was willing to do to others for money – or better, capital – but also how they managed in crucial respects to hide the reality and consequences of their actions from themselves and from posterity. Numbers can occlude pervasive torture and terror, but European, African and American societies still live with their consequences, the multiple legacies of race, class and slavery. The slaver is a ghost ship sailing on the edge of modern consciousness.[4]

Note how Rediker stresses the interlinked nature of accounting (financial) and also accounting (narrating). He describes how the former is a 'comfort blanket', seeming, by closing the account, to make abstract a horrific reality and prevent it from being fully narrated. This failure to properly account in humanistic terms for the horrors perpetrated means that even now in the twenty-first century the capitalist economies of Western Europe and North America that grew hugely on the profits of the trade are haunted by what Ian Baucom, in another recent magisterial monograph, has called *Specters of the Atlantic* (2005). Baucom shows how, in the period after the founding of the Bank of England in 1694, the complex financial machinations needed to deal with an irregular and unpredictable trade in living commodities across large geographical areas and timeframes led to a 'financial revolution' based on loans, debt, credit and insurance. Vital to the working of such a system was the transformation of the slave cargo from human subjects into floating bills of exchange. The ships might be bursting with an African cargo speeding to plantation destinations, but in both these places, and full-sail in mid-Atlantic, their accounts were conjured with and played out in the trading houses of European and North American financial centres. Baucom explains:

> The slaves were thus treated not only as a type of commodity but as a type of interest-bearing money. They functioned in this system simulta-neously as commodities for sale and as the reserve deposits of a loosely organised, decentred, but vast trans-Atlantic banking system: deposits made at the moment of sale and instantly reconverted into short-term bonds. This is at once obscene and vital to understanding the full capital logic of the slave trade, to coming to terms with what it meant for this trade to have found a way to treat human beings not only as if they were a type of commodity but as a flexible, negotiable, transactable form of money.[5]

In such a system, the most realistic account of the enslaved African's position in the system would be as a bank note 'promising to pay the bearer on demand the sum of...'. As floating money, the Africans were of value alive or even, if relevant insurance was bought, when they died. Such accounts completed the narration for the merchants who closed the deal on these enslaved bodies. Many Africans, meanwhile, developed an understanding of this primary narrative of the economics of the slave trade, so that the cowrie shells that were used as a currency within the trade took on horrific connotations. For if they were from the sea, then surely their provenance symbolised much more than mere currency. As Africans began to account for the brutal trans-shipment of millions from the continent, these cowries told their own deep subterranean stories:

> The shells, so it is said, came from the off-lying waters where they fed on the cadavers of the less desirable slaves thrown into the sea as their food. The bodies, or sometimes dismembered limbs, when pulled ashore were covered with attached cowries. Though macabre, this tradition, as allegory, is right on the mark – slaves certainly did in an economic sense 'feed' the shell trade.[6]

This account, like that of the European financiers, deals with the economics of the slave trade, but brings the bodies used and abused in that trade back to the centre of the narrative. Its macabre tracking of the fleshy limbs shows the need to make visible what the paper trails of the European accounting methods seek to obfuscate: that the vast profits made by the transatlantic slave trade were literally made at the expense of these legions of black bodies. Such oral narratives are mindful of financial accounting whilst constructing an imaginative explication that also mourns those lost in the sea. As W. T. Mitchell theorises, the very act of storytelling is ever mindful of accounting:

> *Narration as enumeration.* We need to be mindful of the whole panoply of figures that link narration to counting, recounting, 'giving an account' (in French a *conte*), 'telling' and 'tallying' a numerical total, and the relation between 'stories' and 'storage'. Description in particular is often figured as the textual site of greatest wealth, an unbounded cornucopia of rich detail, rendered in the rhetoric of 'copiousness'.[7]

Giving flesh to the counted bodies is vital to all genres and artistic accounts of the middle passage. The imagination that plumbs the depths to have shells feeding off cadavers is one that has deep resonances for African Atlantic visual artists who are attempting to interpret the slave trade for our times. The millions of black bodies used in labour have been represented and re-represented so that our imaginations of torture and exploitation, of banality and superhuman courage have almost been sated. Dionne Brand talks to this hyper-representation of the black body over the last five centuries since enslaved Africans were first taken from West Africa:

> The body is the place of captivity. The black body is situated as a sign of particular cultural and political meanings in the diaspora. All of these meanings return to the Door of No Return – as if those leaping bodies, those prostrate bodies, those bodies made to dance and then to work, those bodies curling under the singing of whips, those bodies cursed, those bodies valued, those bodies remain curved in these attitudes. They remain fixed in the ether of history. They leap onto the backs of the contemporary – they cleave not only to the collective and acquired memories of their descendants but also to the collective and acquired memories of the other. We all enter those bodies.[8]

So for good and ill these bodies have already entered our imaginations as degraded and aestheticised, as commodified and caricatured, so that it appears there is nothing new to say and no way to redeem these bodies from the limitations of the historical record or the visual archive. However, in the subterranean depths lurk other hitherto marginalised accounts whose surplus value we are only now beginning to fully explore. In these depths several African Atlantic artists work with and against the grain of written and other archival records to create new work that challenges our visual map of slavery and its consequences. Stuart Hall highlights the importance of such visionaries who bring us face to face with a new visual grammar of the black Atlantic:

> Some of the invisibilities … came to constitute the very absent objects against which much of the practice of more recent diasporic artists was directed. Their project was to challenge certain erasures and marginalities inscribed in the visual field itself, to try to establish a certain 'presence' within the frame, to come 'into the field of vision'. If there are 'legacies', then they are likely to be broken and de-centred ones, distended or condensed across time, space and context, ruptured by a turbulent history and the traumas of migration.[9]

Hall's description of the praxis of diasporic artists forging new work in the face of the majority culture's work of marginalisation is pertinent to a whole range of African Atlantic artists, but in this chapter I want to concentrate on three exemplary artists and their works, which most effectually 'account' for the historic legacy of transatlantic slavery as they 'refuse to be constrained by national boundaries, emphasising instead a lateral, diasporic, transnational perspective'.[10] They are from three distinct backgrounds in the circum-Atlantic: the Cape Verdean/Irish/American painter Ellen Gallagher, the Ghanaian-born, British-based Godfried

Donkor, and the Zanzibar-born, British-raised and -educated Lubaina Himid.

It is pertinent to start with the most primal image and with what could even be seen as a virtual submarine birthing of the black Atlantic. Gallagher's monumental canvas *Bird in Hand* (2006) (Figure 24) is a phantasmagorical depiction of a mythical seascape that re-imagines the shadowy depths of Atlantic seas not as burial ground for African victims of a slave trade that relegated their bodies to commodities, but as birthplace of new African Atlantic agents of modernity. In sum, it is a memorial to those who survived the middle passage, and to those who did not. Her piratical peg-legged figure has developed new modes of being in the Atlantic depths, entwined and hybridised amidst seaweed and crustacean forms and sporting a jelly-fish-shaped Afro of Herculean proportions. He stares out from the canvas, lord of his oceanic depths. Karen Alexander describes the portrait well:

> A beautiful portrait that has cosmic and supernatural overtones. 'Peg Leg' looks out, only part-human, with one leg at the surface and the other taking root in the earth. His presence encapsulates all black possibility, curiosity, adventure and ambition. Like a magnificent wreck on the seabed, he emerges hungry to draw everything to him, reaching out to every island, continent and sea: to touch base with forgotten ghosts of the diaspora. His enormous Afro appears to be undergoing a borg-like regeneration, as his magnetic presence sucks in the whole of black history.[11]

This multi-directional portrayal of an individual is science fiction fantasy that reaches backwards to re-envision Africans' middle passage experience and attempts to grasp redemptory meaning from that hellish space of death and destruction. It attempts to give flesh to those 'forgotten ghosts' whilst linking them backwards and forwards chronologically and geographically.

The mythological conceit that underpins the image has a long and complex history in African Atlantic thought, and Gallagher draws on its totality. She feeds off traditional mythology, like that of the tale of the cowrie shells, but refuses to be hidebound by its depressing economic logic. The imagined body here is not merely anatomical, but has deeper resonances which are brought to life through the intervention of this most skilled of African Atlantic artists: 'The body is a form of memory ... non-linear, heterogeneous, resistant and, above all, lived.'[12] She exults in the fact that hundreds of thousands of Africans escaped being swallowed up by a monstrous system, either through committing suicide by drowning or by being drowned as a consequence of the transatlantic slave trade, and so went on to live utopian counter-cultural afterlives, which she memorialises through her artwork.

Such ideas reached their apotheosis in the concept of Drexciya, developed by the Detroit-techno protagonist James Stinson and his compatriots, whose musical output envisaged a watery Atlantis-like utopia populated by African slave descendants. The sleeve notes to the 1997 album *The Quest* plot this history:

> Could it be possible to breathe underwater? A foetus in its mother's womb is certainly alive in an aquatic environment. During the greatest holocaust the world has ever known, pregnant America-bound African slaves were thrown overboard by the thousands during labour for being sick and disruptive cargo. Is it possible that they could have given birth at sea to babies that never needed air? Are Drexciyans water-breathing aquatically mutated descendents of those unfortunate victims of human greed? Recent experiments have shown a premature human infant saved from certain death by breathing liquid oxygen through its underdeveloped lungs.[13]

Stinson and his collaborators create musical imaginations of Drexciya that illuminate a complex civilisation of underwater transportation and communication with electronic music that sounds out the submarine depths of the ocean created by these survivors of the middle passage. This mythical civilisation had been created, not by the drowned Africans themselves, but interestingly by a very specifically described sub-section of that population: the embryos of the pregnant women who had committed suicide or been murdered in the middle passage. These 'water-breathing' descendants of Africans 'had ejected themselves from the womb, adapted gills and built a civilisation beneath the Atlantic, an Aquatopia ... known as Drexciya'.[14] Pregnant enslaved Africans were seen by slaveholders as valuable 'property that reproduces itself': the very imagination that emancipates these spectral beings from the belly of the economic system of slavery to float free in a new world of possibility articulates a deep desire in African Atlantic thought to envisage a utopian space that accounts for the bodies thrown overboard as more than mere numbers. To account for the embryos obviously adds to a tally of victims beyond those on the listings of the slave ships themselves: all, born and unborn, are accounted for and in their afterlife they cheat the slave system of their forced labour and create an aquatopia where they are emancipated and free-swimming. In this science fiction fantasy, radical possibilities are imagined, as Paul Gilroy articulates in discussing the power of futurologists such as the musician Sun Ra, whose utopian work, in refusing to be bound by earthly limitations, is a direct precursor of Drexciya and Gallagher's watery oeuvre:

> The assertion of radical alterity by blacks and the associated invocation of forces beyond this world have become integral to a post-traditional critique of ... raciology and raciality. Barred from ordinary humanity and offered the equally unsatisfactory roles of semi-deity, janitor or pet,

artists seek, like Sun Ra, another mode of recognition in the most alien identity they can imagine. The momentum they acquire in moving from the infrahuman to the superhuman finally carries them beyond the human altogether.[15]

For Gallagher the momentum takes her directly to the ocean floor. But Gallagher is not merely interested in creating a visual version of a musical form based on a science fantasy reaction to the middle passage, however stunning that is. Her vision is a multi-layered one that speaks back multifariously, to histories of the growth of urban life in centres like Harlem, to the creation of black cultures in the diaspora and to free black agency on the sea during slavery. In thinking of the legacy of the middle passage for the creation of African diasporan cultures in the Caribbean, Édouard Glissant describes how the subterranean horrors of slave transportation helped to create new cultural forms across the ocean:

> Experience of the abyss lies inside and outside the abyss. The torment of those who never escaped it: straight from the belly of the slave ship into the violet belly of the ocean depths they went. But their ordeal did not die; it quickened into this continuous/discontinuous thing: the panic of the new land, the haunting of the former land, finally the alliance with the imposed land, suffered and redeemed. *The unconscious memory of the abyss served as the alluvium for their metamorphoses.*[16]

Glissant traces new cultural forms to the 'violet belly of the ocean depths' and it is this subterranean world that Gallagher imagines in *Bird in Hand* as she mines for hidden histories amidst the mud of the ocean floor. The development of these Africans into New World peoples is described by Glissant as coming from their *'memory of the abyss'*, and Gallagher transmogrifies this hitherto alien space into a utopian aquatic world where African subjects have developed the ability to live, breathe and make culture. Her subjects make a life in the midst of a harsh environment by hybridising and becoming half sea-creatures. Her Peg Leg sailor's neck consists of fleshy sea-creature-like tendrils, and his wooden leg is wrapped in larger limb-like roots. Hybridity allows him to exist in this alien world, just as displaced Africans accommodated to European modes in order to survive. There is a species mutability here that speaks back to Enlightenment racial science, which had stigmatised the African race as being mutated with apes. Only now, far from such mutability being problematic, it is seen as salvational as it allows the African to exist in utopian worlds away from European exploitation. Peg Leg's elaborate costume of heavily-brocaded lace points to his stylistic adaptation to circum-Atlantic piratical dress-codes, whilst its similarity to coral shows Gallagher's desire to have even his most acculturated tastes adapted to the oceanic environment where he has developed his freedom. His freedom, though, is imagined in the light of the struggles which have gone on before in the slave ship and those that will follow in a racialised world. The canvas talks back to the slave ship mainly through re-imagining its instruments of torture. Marcus Rediker has spoken of how

> the ship was worst for the enslaved, for whom it appeared as a collection of 'instruments of woe' – shackles, manacles, neck rings, locks, chains, the cat-o'-nine tails, the speculum oris. The lower deck was a floating cave, the hatchway a belching monstrous mouth. The carceral ship ate people alive.[17]

The conceit of Drexciya, which Gallagher adapts here, refuses to let the middle passage experience discipline, and then wholly consume its victims. What Gallagher does is to transmogrify these instruments of torture into slippery tendrils that attach to the body: no longer manacled to the side of the ship and to his fellows by chains, the emancipated being is walking the ocean floor with the tendrils of sea-creatures and sea plants wrapped around his ankles, fully alive, a new creature who has survived the hell-ship. The chains have transformed into benign tendrils that enable him to live an emancipated life. Gallagher has created imaginatively what Glissant theorised in his *Caribbean Discourse*:

> Submarine roots: that is floating free, not fixed in one position in some primordial spot, but extending in all directions in our world through its network of branches.[18]

Her diasporan figure is the emancipating imaginary that envisions how culture is retained and transformed by oceanic travellers populating worlds with new hybridised cultures. Gallagher's work shows the folly of attempting to 'erase or transcend the sedimented power relations in which we lived then and live now'.[19] Her work disturbs the sediment, bringing forth from its buried depths the bastard children of the horrific slave trade who expose the hidden story of lives sacrificed to the accountancy gods and reveal an imaginative retrieval of their transcendent beauty. The sea is the arena for the transformation, but its reverberations are felt in linked African Atlantic cultures whose interactions are, as Glissant reminds us, routed ('floating free … extending in all directions') as well as rooted in African cultures. The slave ship was a factory to create worker 'drones' for the plantation economies; however, it was not successful. As Rediker reminds us,

> each ship contained within it a process of cultural stripping from above and an oppositional process of cultural creation from below. In the shadow

of death, the millions who made the great Atlantic passage in a slave ship forged new forms of life – new language, new means of expression, new resistance and a new sense of community. Herein lay the maritime origins of cultures that were at once African American and pan-African, creative and hence indestructible.[20]

This cultural creation from below can be traced through music and dance, with its ur-form being what Geneviève Fabre has called the 'slave-ship dance', the first of the many syncretic forms made out of the interaction between European forms and African style, 'an epic drama that announces the emergence of the New World Negro'.[21] It can also be traced in the biographies of Africans who survived the horrors of the middle passage and forged lives in the maelstrom of the circum-Atlantic. Some escaped their enslaved existence to form viable African and multi-racial communities (land-based maroon or seaborne piratical) whose hitherto hidden narratives of counter-cultural rebellion have been revealed in studies such as Linebaugh and Rediker's *The Many-Headed Hydra: Sailors, Slaves, Commoners and the Hidden History of the Revolutionary Atlantic*. Linebaugh and Rediker describe these sea-borne communities:

> The pirate ship was motley – multinational, multicultural and multiracial ... a 'banditti of all nations'. Some slaves and free blacks found aboard the pirate ship freedom, something that, outside of the maroon communities, was in short supply in the pirate's main theatre of operations, the Caribbean and the American South. Indeed pirate ships themselves might be considered maroon communities, in which rebels used the high seas as others used the mountains and the jungles.[22]

As well as envisioning the utopian world of Drexciya, Gallagher's Peg Leg pays tribute to these historical figures whose radical alterity and disruptive revolutionary actions in a marine confederation Rediker and Linebaugh have called a 'self-organised ... hydrarchy',[23] and who helped to undermine the slave power's iron grip on the early eighteenth century circum-Atlantic. In addition to paying tribute to these mercurial and liminal figures, the positioning of the Peg Leg figure, staring straight out at the viewer, is reminiscent of the John Thomas Smith's portraits of 'vagabondia',[24] made on the streets of London and originally published in 1815. These black figures, crippled and pensioned off from the army or navy in the Revolutionary or French Wars, remain some of the very few images of free working class blacks that have survived. As Linebaugh and Rediker assert,

> The figure of the starving, often lame sailor in the seaport town became a permanent feature of European civilisation, even as the motley crew became a permanent feature of modern navies.[25]

Gallagher's Peg Leg could be based, at least in part, on one of these figures, for example the famous Billy Waters (c.1778–1823), who busked with a violin and whose right leg, like Peg Leg's, had been amputated at the knee. His distinctive hat with feathers speaks to his diasporic origins in Africa and/ or the Caribbean and provides a headdress template for Gallagher's fully fledged Afro. Probably the most famous of the depictions in Smith's book, and another that is an obvious source for Peg Leg, is of Joseph Johnson, a man with a ship on his head, which he used as a unique begging prop, as manipulating it 'by a bow of thanks, or a supplicating inclination to a drawing-room window, [he] give[s] the appearance of sea motion'.[26] The ship talked to Johnson's marine career in the British navy. Begging in London, Johnson kinaesthetically imagined his routed maritime world. In *Bird in Hand*, Gallagher imaginatively emancipates such crippled figures from the confined spaces of London streets and sets them free in oceanic worlds where they are masters of their own destinies, not mastered by economic and racial servitude. Crippled on land and using sticks or prosthetic limbs, they are emancipated in their aquatopia. It is this very multi-layered nature of the depiction of Peg Leg, speaking back to a variety of historical black figures from throughout the circum-Atlantic, that gives the painting its power as an image. Gallagher conjures these various characters through her depiction of Peg Leg at home in the ocean as a means to reawaken forgotten histories and refigure the narrative of the African Atlantic with the agency of the enslaved Africans and working class free blacks as central. In such a narration she awakens what the sociologist Avery Gordon describes as historical 'ghosts':

> The ghost is not simply a dead or missing person, but a social figure, and investigating it can lead to that dense site where history and subjectivity make social life. The ghost or apparition is one form by which something lost, or barely visible, or seemingly not there to our supposedly well-trained eyes, makes itself known or apparent to us, in its own way of course.[27]

Gallagher's fertile imagination reawakens these ghosts, showing us realities we were unaware of before her translucent vision made them available to us. Her special skill though is to do so in a context that glories and revels in black style and excess at the same time as it narrates the history of black struggle. Nowhere is this more evident than in the glorious excess of Peg Leg's Afro hairstyle. Like Joseph Johnson's ship swaying to and fro, envisaging worlds beyond the streets that signify poverty, it is an excessive signifier of freedom, the freedom to be black and different. As Shane and Graham White discover in looking at slave style, woolly hair, worn long and bushy, an arrangement that emphasised and even flaunted its distinctive texture, may have been an affirmation of difference and even defiance, an attempt to revalorise a biological characteristic that white racism had sought to devalue.[28]

Peg Leg stands defiant, his glorious hair a signifier of his emancipation from a plantation economy which would have seen it as an impediment to his ability to work and would have seen the time taken to groom it as valuable labour time gone to waste. Moreover, it contrasts with a visual economy which valued the straight hair of whites and disdained black hair as woolly and animal-like. We know Peg Leg is an emancipated figure by his Afro's excess and his joy in it. Shane and Graham White discuss how slaves through dance refigured the black body away from the limitations of the slave economy:

> By aestheticising the black body, by putting its vitality, suppleness and sensuality defiantly and joyously on display ... [they] repudiated slavery's evaluation of the slave body as brute physical labour, and constructed, for a time, a world of difference, sharply at variance with that which blacks were normally compelled to inhabit.[29]

Gallagher's stylisation of her piratical central figure is her visual response to such dancing and its 'aestheticising of the black body'. She shows him emancipated from the slave ship and plantation regimes, wherein his body is commodified and reduced to pure labour value, and sets him free to roam the ocean floor, seeing to his own needs and reflecting his aesthetic *jouissance*, signalled by an Afro whose protean energy makes it seem kinetic and mobile, alive and dancing. The kinaesthetic nature of black culture is reflected in Gallagher's depiction of the seemingly swirling Afro, which reflects the importance of dance and music in the creating of African-influenced cultural forms in the diaspora. The Afro's meaning in Gallagher's dynamic portrayal is not limited to its slave trade-era valences, but speaks also to its transcendent political significance in African Atlantic cultures. As Kobena Mercer has discussed in a seminal article on the political importance of black hairstyling, 'the Afro symbolised a reconstitutive link with Africa as part of a counter-hegemonic process helping to define a diaspora people, not as Negro, but as Afro-American.'[30] The Afro and its near neighbour, dreadlocks, were far more than stylistic affectations:

> Both these hairstyles were never just natural, waiting to be found: they were stylistically *cultivated* and politically *constructed* in a particular historical moment as part of a strategic contestation of white dominance and the cultural power of whiteness.[31]

Thus, although Gallagher's Afro is multi-accentual and should not be reduced to a signature of any one chronological time, its development as symbol of revolutionary fervour during the black power era of the late 1960s and the 1970s is a key element she wants to invoke to ally her Peg Leg figure with movements for cultural change across chronologies. Robin Kelley has discussed the Afro's importance:

> More than dashikis, platform shoes, black berets and leather jackets, the Afro has clearly been the most powerful symbol of black power-style politics. Although hair had long been a site of contestation within black communities and between African Americans and the dominant culture, the Afro, unlike any other style, put the issue of hair squarely on the agenda.[32]

Peg Leg's Afro, however, is not merely a revolutionary symbol stretching back to slave style and forward to the black power revolutionaries; it tells other histories too, which complicate Gallagher's depiction but in the end make it all the more powerful. Gallagher is aware that her marine imagination has a slippery chronology that enables it to work on many different levels. Recently she described how she creates an ethereality through her Aquatopian portrayals:

> This realm is so abstract, there's a kind of ability for it to be both of a certain time and not to be captured by that time, so it's both specific and it's a kind of bodily present that is immaterial.[33]

These multiple chronologies and viewpoints are shown by the histories enmeshed in the Afro itself, which bear witness to African diasporan modernity and its clash in advanced capitalist economies with racist representations and practices. As the leaflet for the Tate Liverpool exhibition of 2007 explains, in *Bird in the Hand*, 'the minutiae of detail and magnitude of the canvas invite a reading both close to the canvas and from afar ... a fluctuation in scale between the miniature and the enormous.'[34] The Afro-futuristic fantasy of freedom in the water celebrated by the distanced view of the canvas is challenged by the close-up view of the composition of the canvas. Collaged and woven into the Afro are cuttings from mid-twentieth century 'race' magazines that illuminate complex interactions with racist, capitalist US realities such as hair-straightening solutions or skin-whitening products. As the leaflet describes, 'the realisation of their negative connotations stimulates an uncomfortable jolt.'[35] This discomfort does not allow the viewer an over-easy access to *Bird in the Hand* as a simply redemptory work, but shows that the representation of African diasporan figures is always constrained by contact with wider societal constructions which at times seek to confine African Atlantic figures to racial representations and 'normativity' that are often limiting. Gallagher, however, refuses to be limited by these burdens from the past, preferring to see in them the building blocks for a revisionist and satirical perspective at once menacing and playful. In this she follows Mercer, who articulates the radical ambivalence of

> distinct patterns of style across a range of cultural practices ... which are politically intelligible as creative responses to the experience of oppression and dispossession. Black hairstyling may thus be evaluated as a popular art form articulating a variety of artistic solutions to a range of problems created by ideologies of race and racism.[36]

In Gallagher we see this radical stylistic response in the constructed world of the beauty adverts, which is written onto the Afro with individual words and letters cut out to build a kaleidoscopic and multifarious commentary on disaporan African lives and what was made of them in the mid-twentieth century. She picks up on Kobena Mercer's radical ambivalence through phrases such as 'Miracle Whip, Skin Hitened, Greaseless, Straightened, Health Support Girdle, Waist Clincher, Coloring, Slim Teen and Adjustable Waist' and teases them out to emphasise the commodified world that black bodies still inhabited, long after the transatlantic slave trade had literally put a value on their bodies, and the way that diasporan Africans make lives amidst this commodification. As Karen Alexander observes, these bodies are 'appropriated and recontextualised into delicate arrangements, surfacing like a hidden code to a repository of colonial memory.'[37] As the Afro gives a long view of hundreds of years of struggle for cultural autonomy, so the close-up view of the advertisements shows the terms of the engagement and the price paid. It is diasporan black bodies in struggle in the post-slavery world that Gallagher inserts all over the Afro:

> Disembodied heads, eyes and hairpieces appear like bubbles or nodes, caught up in or clinging to different 'strands' of memory, history or representation ... in Gallagher's fantasy of black survival and evolution.[38]

This multi-faceted fantasy includes, as well as black faces, detached black hands under the magnifying glass, as though at the mercy of scientific experimentation. The faces build up a kaleidoscopic image of African diasporan characters of all kinds surviving, whilst the hands show the realities of their bodies being always under the scopophilic gaze of European Enlightenment and post-Enlightenment polities, and having to continually be vigilant in a culture dominated by beauty standards constructed by Anglo-Americans. To the right of Peg Leg's face, the words 'Stays Dyed Forever' are collaged next to a hair-straightened woman's disembodied head. The homophone 'died' is conjured here as Peg Leg and the other inhabitants of this aquatopia have refused to 'stay died forever'. These aquatic ghosts, though, do more than hark back to the middle passage; they sweep up with them the wonders and detritus of the African Atlantic diaspora, as Gallagher constructs a science fantasy which juxtaposes African, Atlantic and US cultural artefacts as still-living organisms that reflect the multiplicity of black Atlantic biographies and refuse to 'stay died forever'. Jackie Kay discusses the way the Afro encompasses this multiple history, folding into itself the multifarious experiences of a diasporan people. Peg Leg is

> part tree, part root. His head is a huge Afro made up of other heads, his head seems to contain all the dead. The Afro is made up of tiny bits of post-war images from the magazines *Ebony* and *Sepia*, which morph into what look like a shoal of jellyfish or plankton forms. Beneath him are roots which suggest that the dead have roots in the living – they continue somehow and are not forgotten. He is entangled, his body could be the body of a tree, perhaps the one his ancestors were tied to when they were whipped.[39]

Kay outlines the way Gallagher makes memorial art from an historical struggle, achieving this through foregrounding black style's encounter with post-war modernity. For it is black style that has in part enabled black resistance and survival, as Kaiser et al. eloquently assert:

> African Americans have not imitated European American style. Instead they have drawn upon a rich history of aesthetic creativity and innovation from West African cultures. Forced to adopt Euro-American dress, they have, throughout their history, articulated their own diasporic forms of improvisation that appropriates European-American style to create an aesthetic of resistance. This practice has manifested itself in numerous ways, but by borrowing from white, European dress to create a more expressive model of fashionability, the idea of style as resistance – both spiritual and political, but no less beautiful – has permeated African American self-representation.[40]

'Style as resistance' is emphasised in *Bird in Hand* by the submarine regions it inhabits, which garners for the canvas an otherworldiness where these two seemingly contradictory terms are as comfortable in the hybridised fantasy world as Peg Leg himself. Gallagher's dynamic vision is akin to Glissant's idea of a routed and submarine construction of culture, which can be extended beyond the Caribbean to the entire Americas, and her Peg Leg staring out from the canvas is surely the most dynamic visual representation of this utopian vision of survival:

Subterranean convergence [in] diverse histories of the [black Atlantic] ... relieves us of the linear, hierarchical vision of a single History that would run its unique course. It is not this History that has roared round the edge of the [ocean], but actually a question of the subterranean convergence of our histories... The unity is Submarine. To my mind this expression can only evoke all those Africans weighed down with ball and chain and thrown overboard whenever a slave ship was pursued by enemy vessels and felt too weak to put up a fight. *They sowed in the depths the seeds of an invisible presence...* We are the roots of a cross-cultural relationship. [41]

Gallagher's vision of Drexciya glories in visioning for us what has come from those 'seeds of an invisible presence': that the surviving cultures are routed, at least in part, through the subterranean black Atlantic, and through middle passage and diasporic experiences that create cultures on the move. Gallagher's insistence on relating multiple histories that range from those Africans thrown overboard during the slave trade, through free black sailors, to style kings and queens in metropolitan New York in the 1940s and 1950s, showing their inter-relatedness and their stylistic and heroic hybridity, refuses a narrow essentialist vision to revel in the survival of African Atlantic cultures despite the deathly accounting of the slave trade and the horrific commodification of racialised representation in the modern circum-Atlantic. Peg Leg serenely stares back at his viewers, supremely confident in an aquatic world which has had to adapt to him as much as he has adapted to it. He is the heroic, ghostly presence of the black Atlantic par excellence:

In these exceptional moments of crisis, of time 'out of joint', ghosts signal our inheritance of the past and the necessity to act responsibly to change the future. They disrupt our sense of the linear progressive nature of history that passes naturally and easily from the past to the present to the future. The fixed and discrete quality of these time periods explodes as spectres move back and forward and events that were experienced in the past are experienced again for the first time. The idea of origins as the teleological beginning no longer holds as time spirals through an ocean of memory. Events do not belong solely in the past; they belong to the present and future as well. Ghostly traces signify a fragmented idea of time that can repeat itself or be new centuries later.[42]

Following Young's finely tuned exploration of the ghostly, we understand the Janus-faced nature of Peg Leg, a ghost of both past and future time, bringing forth buried history whilst positing an Afro-utopia that makes memorial reparation for all those bodies lost in the Atlantic. Gallagher creates what Édouard Glissant has called a prophetic vision of the past....[in which] the past must not only be recomposed objectively (or even subjectively) by the historian. It must also be dreamt prophetically by the people, the communities and the culture whose people has been occulted.[43]

Glissant's invocation here of the prophetic nature of African Atlantic creative works illuminates the special quality of Gallagher's work, which refuses to be bound by slavery's melancholic weight and conjures fantastic futures from the wreckage of the past. In this sense, the ghostly presence imagined by Gallagher through her visual rendering of Drexciya does the cultural work of redemption in much the same way as Giorgio Agamben envisaged the 'remnant' working in salvational terms in Jewish history. He describes how, 'in the end the remnant appears as a redemptive machine allowing for the salvation of the very whole whose division and loss it had signified.'[44] Gallagher's epic canvas inscribes a history of slavery and racism, of resistance and triumphant survival in the maelstrom of transatlantic slavery. It is a memorial for victims and survivors. Central to her vision, her piratical hero gloriously survives, his monumental Afro mobile and swaying in the ocean currents, envisioning as yet undiscovered imaginaries.

The Atlantic ocean and its historical excesses are also the obsession of the Ghanaian-born, Brixton-based Godfried Donkor, who is interested in accounting for the black bodies that were transported during slavery and their historical representation. He critiques the limitations of these representations and their insidious power through a large body of collaged work, which reached its apotheosis in a wonderful triptych in response to Thomas Stothard's infamous pro-slavery print *The Voyage of the Sable Venus*, which Bryan Edwards had used as a key illustration in his history of the West Indies.[45] Stothard's imaginary, in a grotesque counterfactual of the horrors of the slave trade, includes a bevy of sweet cherubs smoothing the *Sable Venus*'s passage across the Atlantic. As Dionne Brand has discussed, such grotesqueries were legion in the contemporary fine art and cartography of the late eighteenth century. In this iconography,

> there are angels, or cherubs, mouths pursed, blowing the trade winds west on the Atlantic. You must remember there is one point of the middle passage. People are to be lost here, drowned here; people are to be sold, backs and hearts broken; those cherubs, their sweet lips pursed, blow a rough trade. Only an artist could render an angel here.[46]

Godfried Donkor interprets this 'rough trade' in his *Triptych: The Birth of Venus* (2005), (Figure 24)[47] his response to Stothard's image. He answers its excess with collaged depictions of bodies indulging in sexual pleasures, reflecting the pornography of slavery with his own borrowings from pornographic imagery. His collaged version exemplifies what Kobena Mercer and Isaac Julien have described as 'colonial fantasy':

> a rigid set of racial rules and identities which rehearse scenarios of desire in a way which traces the cultural legacies of slavery, empire and imperialism. This circuit for the structuring of sexual representation is still in existence.[48]

The weight of colonial and racial representation still bears down in Donkor's twenty-first century *Venus*. The three images of the *Triptych* are designed to overwhelm the viewer with an excess of repeated sexualised images, in much the same way that Stothard created his *Sable Venus* as an excessive cornucopia of sexual possibility that the exploitation of slavery made possible. As in Stothard's image, flesh in Donkor's images is the primary narrative; however, he shows us the reality of the exploitation and forced relationships that slavery gave rise to. His naming of his piece *The Birth of Venus* inscribes this as a seminal image in the making of relationships between races and sexes in the Atlantic world. Close examination of the sun's rays in his collage shows Donkor using pages from the *Financial Times*. In an interview with me he discussed the use of this particular newspaper:

> I think it began with an artistic intention which subsequently became a motif. I started using *Financial Times* again around about the early 1990s purely for the aesthetics of it and I decided to choose the financial papers because that was an area where I had uniformities, so I could have the numbers and I didn't have to deal with articles getting in the way, or images or story lines or headlines getting in the way. So I could just have the numbers playing, and I also quite like the fact that I use, because of my work, numbers and figures – they are kind of somehow related so I was playing with those, the kind of artistic element there.[49]

Donkor's mainly pragmatic explanation for choosing the *Financial Times* should not blind us to its multifaceted iconography, which is suffused with cultural and political meaning. The pink colouring of the paper makes its own comment on flesh; however, his use of the newspaper here also highlights the commodification of this flesh through the workings of commerce. The financial figures can be seen imprinted on the paper, illustrating how both late eighteenth-century mercantile capitalism and contemporary global markets hide their exploitation behind financial returns. Ian Baucom in *Specters of the Atlantic* discusses this historical development and places the development of new forms of capital accumulation as exactly contemporary with the rise of the system of transatlantic chattel slavery, describing how in this process, 'capital sets itself free from the material constraints of production and distribution and revels in its pure capacity to breed money from money – as if by a sublime trick of the imagination.'[50] Through a system of credit that spurred the development of a complex and highly profitable trade, slaves came to be treated 'not only as a type of commodity, but as a type of interest-bearing money'.[51] This 'colonisation of human subjectivity by finance capital'[52] is revealed by Donkor's juxtapositions, and his use of pornography shows the link between such monetary capital and the erotic capital which was the consequence of the sexual exploitation of female slaves, which through sexual reproduction led to the growth of yet more capital through the enhancement of the slave population. Donkor shows how the 'cultural construction of race has always been fuelled by the corrupt conjunction of … hybridized sexual and economic discourses'.[53] He foregrounds the wealth that flows from this juxtaposition of flesh and labour that the original *Sable Venus* had merely hinted at. To an extent at least, he puts back into the image the blood and sweat Stothard had left out. He reveals the reality that Baucom so eloquently describes and shows how the Stothard image, though revelatory in itself, can reveal even more through his illuminating reinterpretation.

In *Financial Times* (2007),[54] his installation at Hackney Museum, London, Donkor used the unique nature of the newspaper to make work that continues to comment on flesh, labour and capital accumulation. In the installation it was the latter that was overwhelming, as the viewer was brought face to face with the market pages of the newspaper in a blitzkrieg of company names and figures that assaulted the eyes on all sides of the gallery space, 'disseminating the minutiae that is the world's fiscal data by way of monotonous streaming print'.[55] This conscious foregrounding of figures talks to the commodification of black human beings by slavery and post-slavery labour regimes, and the stream of numbers 'betray their own history: the trade of goods, be they consumable or animate; or shifting borders predicated on the rise of fortune in one nation and the loss of it in another … a history of Empire through code.'[56] Donkor shows this history at its most blatant through the flags of the imperial power of the UK and the US, entirely composed out of the *Financial Times*. National entities, he is saying, are important as the globalised realities that colonial/imperial nations created and they continue to dominate through the workings of modern, transnational capitalism, but the capital flows exemplified by the pages of the *FT* transcend these national borders so that the UK and the US are in hoc ultimately to the money gods. As Ian Baucom observes of Britain's earlier dominance

> Britain's global hegemony … to the middle of the nineteenth century was an oceanic hegemony, its capitalism a transmarine capitalism and its speculative culture once secured, as the jingo cadences have it, by

the assurance that 'Britannia rules the waves'. Ruling the waves, Britain derived its rules of sovereignty from its maritime hegemony, not just its naval dominance of the Atlantic, Mediterranean and Indian Oceans, but from the rules of commerce that made of those oceans the primary territories of capital accumulation. Absent the flow of commodities crisscrossing the trade routes of the marine expanses, and Britain could not have maintained its hegemony.[57]

Capital accumulation and the flow of commodities are aptly demonstrated in Donkor's flags by the flow of figures and trading companies of which they are composed. The flags though are the metropolitan narrative frame that contains a more hidden accountancy Donkor also wants to engage with. This story is of the people caught up by this whirlwind of numbers and how they were accounted for, literally and figuratively. 'Slavery', Donkor contends, 'was based on speculation and the imagination, however macabre it may be and however … terrifying',[58] and it is this juxtaposition of financial speculation and imaginative representation that Donkor riffs on in his multi-faceted installation.

'Crafting wallpaper made from *FT* pulp',[59] Donkor has at the centre of his installation six portraits of African diasporan women. Surrounded by the figures of the *FT* wallpaper beneath the heading '*FT* Managed Funds Service', these women are in various colonial settings exemplifying their importance to the profits made in those milieu and the everyday nature of the use of their bodies for labour and reproduction in imperial economies. This is amplified by the way the figures from the *FT* seep from being merely borders and invade the illustrations of the women, encircling and ultimately commodifying them. As Courtney Martin notes, 'the women become monetary units on which the installation's economy is backed.'[60] But this is not the only way they are numerically defined, for they are assigned spurious raciological types – Quadroon, Quintroon and Octoroon – by which their worth, that is, the amount of white blood they have in them, is designated. This emphasises the doubled nature of their exploitation, as mere numbers in a globalised capitalist economy and as inferior racialised types in definitions established by those exploiters as a means of enshrining the primacy of whiteness in colonial slave systems. Young describes the way non-white colonial subjects are formed in such modernising economies, and emphasises

> the centrality of diasporic Africans to the building of modernity. Black bodies were the indispensable coerced mechanisms of labour, the Other against whom the whiteness of the imperial subject was formed. Diaspora Africans are both inside and constitutive of modernity and outside and negated by modernity: both haunted and haunting.[61]

This duality is shown here by the way the women are contained in the pages of the *Financial Times* and yet are positioned as alien and different. Young's delineation of such characters as 'haunted and haunting' highlights the liminality of colonial subjects that Donkor illuminates here. Donkor's juxtaposition of the mathematics of finance and the fractional accounting of race is a deliberate political statement that Western globalised capital has invariably been race-partisan, accompanying its capitalist exploitation with racial taxonomies and regimes of violence that have established the ongoing rules of colonial and post-colonial economies and established white racial supremacy. Young describes the way that black bodies are routinely commodified in slave economies, literally made 'ghostly'; she observes how

the violence of the sale ... refashioned [slave] bodies into instruments of labour. Ghastly apparitions of violence testify to the largely untold history of acts whereby the body and spirit of the African were broken to create the commodity. Theorising the ghost uncouples the link between enslavement and an essential blackness, foregrounding the violence that rendered complex persons into market-alienable flesh that could be worked, wounded, brought and sold. The haunted nature of the slave as commodity assumes vast political importance as it enables us to speak about the effective imprints of violence, injury, and grief that continue to permeate the worlds we live in.[62]

Donkor shows how his characters became 'market alienable flesh' not only through violence, but also through the working of international capital. Their historical presence, years before the *Financial Times*'s first issue in the 1880s and thousands of miles from the city of the birth of international capital, haunts the pages of modern Western capitalism. Donkor makes their presence felt in order to demystify the workings of capitalism and show its historic crimes. As Celeste-Marie Bernier, in an astute article on the installation, contends,

He politicises the seeming neutrality of Western statistics not only to expose ambiguous relationships between 'speculation' and the 'imagination', but also to suggest how these figures can mislead and erase the underlying realities of the slave trade. Financial data, he suggests, can only ever illuminate a small part of an otherwise vast skein of marginalised histories.[63]

Bernier accurately delineates Donkor's purpose in foregrounding the blandness of the financial in order to re-tell the stories that underlie it. In Donkor's skilled rendering of this in *Financial Times*, his female figures spectrally rise up out of the salmon-pink pages to attempt a different, more human accounting and memorialising of what the figures mean (or as Lubaina Himid would have it, a literal 'naming the money'). 'Broken to create the commodity', Donkor's female figures refuse to be reduced to the market figures or racial designations that the financial pages or their colonial masters want to make of them, but tell a parallel story of the survival of humanity despite commodification. Bernier later discusses how the portraits of the women deliberately signify on stereotypical representations of black female figures, creating new hybridised accounts of black identity that play on representations from the majority Anglo-American culture:

> All six female figures communicate aesthetic autonomy in their elaborate and individualised choice of dress, jewellery and hairstyles. Standing in front of colonial mansions, wearing crucifixes and sporting fans, they have much more in common with the Southern belle of plantation mythology than they do with stereotypes of the 'mammy' or 'jezebel'.[64]

Their self-presentations struggle through the reductive racial taxonomies and mathematical formulae that surround them to make the point that despite racial violence and stereotyping, they can make individual lives that have meaning. Donkor's choice of techniques to illustrate their agency, despite the horrors of slavery, commodification and racism, is appropriate. As Arlene R. Keizer asserts, 'the refigurative properties and collage techniques of improvisation in African [Atlantic] culture make it an apt metaphor for human agency-in-resistance in general.'[65] Donkor uses the traditional material of the financial pages to get inside the belly of the beast and reveal the iniquities of capitalism. His collaging of the *Financial Times* 'facilitates effective resistance to hegemonic ideologies'.[66] Gillian Tawadros, in discussing other black artists, describes how they use 'collage and bricolage ... to contest the apparently seamless linear and unifying logic of Western visual culture'.[67] Likewise, Donkor uses collage here to critique the status quo both now and in the past.

As Donkor has shown in a series of other works that juxtapose contemporary Caribbean models and pugilists with slave ships and/or pages from the *Financial Times* to make similar ideological points, the issues of the commodification and fetishisation of black bodies is as relevant in the contemporary post-colonial/postmodern world as it was in the eighteenth century. To quote Baucom, paraphrasing Walter Benjamin, 'as time passes the past does not wane but intensifies; as history repeats itself it repeats in neither attenuated nor farcical form by "redeeming" the what-has-been, "awakening" it into a fuller, more intense form.'[68] Donkor's historical revisionings work so well because they illuminate the cyclical nature of a historical process which is reflected in the way the iconography of racial representation still haunts us over two hundred years later. What better way to show this than through a reworking of the iconography of financial capitalism at its most nakedly transparent: the numbers to which it tries to reduce all human enterprise. Donkor's triumph is to use this method of the collage to account for the bodies and to reveal ghostly presences even in the most dystopian and commodified of images, the body reduced to numbers. He makes of these familiar images memorials that work to reawaken human agency in the midst of a racially based commodification.

If Donkor shows us how the body reduced to numbers can be redeemed and remembered through his dynamic collage technique, Lubaina Himid creates artworks that account for those African peoples' stories which have been lost in Eurocentric retellings of the history of the Atlantic world. Himid continues to remind her audiences of the indebtedness of their identities to a middle passage history and to the legacies of slavery, empire, colonialism and post-colonialism that we still inhabit today. Her *Naming the Money* (2004) (Figure 26),[69] an installation piece that was spread over five rooms at the Hatton Gallery in Newcastle, comprises a hundred colourful, life-size, cut-out figures and is an exemplary illustration of the complexity of the diasporan lives she has done so much to save from the detritus of history. This is illustrated at its most banal and shocking in the texts on the back of each cut-out figure, written on accounting paper. As Stephanie Smallwood reminds us, such economical narratives are often the only evidence we have of individuals who were traded in the transatlantic slave system:

> The ledgers' double-entry pages and the neat grid of the invoice gave purposeful shape to the story they told. Through their graphic simplicity and economy, invoices and ledgers effaced the personal histories that fuelled the slaving economy. Containing only what could fit within the clean lines of their columns and rows, they reduced an enormous system of traffic in human commodities to a concise chronicle of quantitative 'facts' ... erasing from view the politics that underlay the neat account keeping.[70]

The accounting paper in the installation bears witness to this tortured history as a memorial trace of the slave system as trade and plantation economy; for, as Hortense Spillers succinctly reminds us, in slavery the 'cultural subject is concealed beneath the debris of the itemised account'.[71] As slavery commodified these individuals, listing them with fine cottons, wines or hats on board ship or with the beasts of burden and household goods on shore, so the memorial artist's job is to remember this horror and to show its human cost, to put the 'politics' back into view. Brand highlights the banality of this corrupting institution when she describes a plantation's annual record:

I look down each list, I try to imagine someone writing these lists. Would they have written them down at the beginning of the crop, at the end of the crop, or would they have kept a running record? Would they have had a cup of tea before going to the job or would they have stopped in the middle, gone home to have an afternoon nap, and returned thinking what a nuisance paperwork was? Or would this person have written the names quite happily with a flourish in the wrist, congratulating himself or herself on the good condition and quantity of the livestock?[72]

Himid too puts back the politics back, but she does it through the individual texts she writes on each of her figures' accounting paper. These often poetic fragments (placed importantly alongside fragments of cloth that signal the trade that enmeshes them all) signify the doughty survival of the remembered lives of these people despite the privation of their new manifestation as cogs in the machine of the slave economy or Western global capitalism. The original idea for *Naming the Money* had come from magnificent paintings of three African slave servants given as presents by the king of Spain to the king of France, which Himid had seen in La Rochelle in the 1980s. In her interview with me, Himid described another impetus for the work:

> The group of a hundred people are made up of ten groups of ten, so there are ten ceramicists, ten viola da gamba players, ten drummers, ten dancing masters. So each of those people has a story about who they really are, what their real name is, what their given-name is, what it's convenient to call them. Everybody knows about the Bangladeshi man, whose name is one thing but everyone calls him Tony. So there are all kinds of analogies there. Everybody knows about the Albanian refugee who was a doctor in his homeland and is now sweeping the streets of Glasgow. So there are all kinds of stories conjured up.[73]

This linking to a postmodern twentieth-century fortress Europe as well as to the life of a nineteenth century servant, then back to the world of the slave who has a whole new life in a different place which doesn't reflect his previous existence, is an important aspect of the work. Himid's multi-chronology is similar to that of Donkor and Gallagher as she seeks to show the long reach of the history of the transatlantic slave trade and its continuing resonances for economic and social relations today; existing beyond the merely historic realm, the work comments on contemporary forms of enslavement. Himid explains:

> I'm not sure that was what the intention was when I began it. I think it was quite specifically about the slave/servant and that, visually, is what it looks like – these are black slave/servants and the names that they have are African names, West African, East African, Muslim names, but more

and more the work came to have more contemporary resonances. What I carry with me became more important. It was supposed to be about history ... [but] that history isn't yesterday in some convenient package over there, it's all the time now, it's a sort of continuum. So accidentally taking in all these other kinds of issues and other kinds of people, that wasn't the intention. I had a specific set of circumstances in mind but the piece eventually encompasses all kind of different eras and different kinds of people.[74]

Hence the historical specificity of the work is complicated by the implications it engenders. The work surely also talks to the exploitation of people like the cockle pickers who died on Morecambe Bay in February 2004 as much as it talks to the long-distanced past. Himid had started her work before the tragedy, but has talked of its resonances for such a disaster.[75] These people, transported halfway across the world by people traffickers and then set to work by gangmasters for a pittance in the dangerous bay, had different other lives before poverty forced them into their deadly work. As Himid and I discussed, such lives, spanning the centuries, are 'human beings to be bartered and used like checkers on a checkerboard'.[76] As she told me, she wanted to commemorate the 'throwaway people' of the middle passage, to essay

what it meant to be a people who were neither one thing nor the other, however horrendous being either of those things was, either slaves or colonised – or thrown overboard off a ship, for if you're thrown overboard off a ship, then you didn't exist any more at all. So I was trying to find a way, as an artist, in a world of art: how do you talk about something that can be seen and be thought of as not being there? Inside the invisible, if you like.[77]

Himid here is talking of a people whose very existence was predicated on being on the threshold, of living a liminal existence between worlds. This obviously has resonances for Gallagher's *Bird in Hand*, where those thrown overboard make new worlds beneath the sea and are re-imagined, or, using Himid's terminology, are made visible again; however, Himid's visual imagination pushes her beyond the canvas to express this liminality in different ways. Her methodology for expressing her characters' duality was not to restrict them merely to the visual frame or even to frame them two-dimensionally, but in this instance to gloriously set them free into a gallery space as three-dimensional, almost kinetic, figures who interact together and moreover have their ulterior lives expressed through a different genre, the written texts that accompany them and the soundscape that surrounds them. Getting 'inside the invisible' involves maximising the expressive possibilities, as the slave characters are shown to have lives way beyond the limitations their slave status imposes in actuality and (traditionally at least) imaginatively. It involves 'accounting' for them beyond the ledger or, as it were, allowing them the space so that they can account for themselves by narrating their own stories, which bring them back from the margins of history. Himid's *Naming the Money* foregrounds other routes to knowledge about slaves and their descendants, a people for whom traditional empirically-based history has been an inadequate paradigm. Avery Gordon's envisioning of ghostly presences is a theoretical paradigm that chimes with Himid's artistic praxis here:

> What kind of case is a case of a ghost? It is a case of haunting, a story about what happens when we admit the ghost – that special instance of the merging of the visible and the invisible, the dead and the living, the past and the present – into the making of worldly relations and into the making of our accounts of the world. It is a case of the difference it makes to start with the marginal, with what we normally exclude or banish, or, more commonly, with what we never even notice.[78]

Gordon's use of the language of visibility links this quotation directly to Himid's description of her own desire to portray the world 'inside the invisible' and to her desire to work across chronologies to present the lives of those many of us 'never even notice'. Himid's working praxis does more, however; setting her characters free in the gallery space is also about making the spectator engage with them more dynamically than with long lines of canvas paintings on the wall. Himid here deliberately uses her 'theatrical legacy' (her first degree was in theatre design), 'bringing things into the real, rather than having them as illusionary' so that the audience is more fully engaged. She describes the process as 'making these pieces as if you were the actors in the theatre, so that the audience are the actors, or your work moves in among the audience's life'.[79] Himid thus breaks down the barrier between audience and artwork so that the experience of being in the gallery begins to resemble more an 'African masquerade' or 'a masked ball ... something that belongs to everyone and that everyone is part of. It's a performance, it's a ritual.'[80] In this way it summons the ghostly presences of these historical figures, taking them from the bland regime of the accountants' ledgers and making them three-dimensional, colourful presences narrating their multifarious stories fully lived out despite the privations of slavery, commodification and capitalist exploitation. Stuart Hall vividly describes the kinaesthetic energy of the installation:

> freestanding in space, her figures – doing, making or playing things, walking or posing and dancing – are astonishingly lively and mobile in

stance, posture, movement and attitude. They have lost all lingering sense of servitude or deference. In the artist's original installation, they seem to be moving and conversing among themselves, vividly convivial, in a vibrant scene, a fancy-dress party, a stage, a market.[81]

Such a performative artistic mode seems to take its kinetic energy from the black musical tradition, and surely it is theoretical constructs culled from this that describe most aptly the kind of praxis Himid engages in here. Thus we could invoke Christopher Small's term 'musicking'[82] to describe a process that black improvising musicians engage in; here the important element in the music is not the final form but the making of it in the present or, as Samuel Floyd Jr described it:

> aesthetic deliberation about African American music requires a perceptual and conceptual shift from the idea of music as an object to music as an event, from music – as a frozen, sonic ideal – to music as making.[83]

This exactly describes Himid's process and the interactions which make up her work. Its 'mobility and social momentum' means that it is far from conventionalised art presented as a *fait accompli* to a passive audience, but interacts in a meaningful way with that audience. In this way Himid herself questions the definition of her work as 'contemporary art' and explicates how it works in an aesthetic much more attuned to improvisatory black music than to the fine art tradition:

> It's not so much that I am not an artist, it's that this maybe is not art, which is a slightly different thing. I'm undoubtedly an artist – if not then we're in a dangerous place – but I think I'm making work that you're supposed to do something with, or that you're supposed to interact with and then do something about it. It's not entirely for a contemplative relationship, not that I think there's anything wrong with that contemplative relationship. It's not really supposed to confirm a viewer's expectations either, but whoever you are, whatever kind of viewer you are, there's always been a need for me to make you do something. You bring your history, your story to the work and then we move amongst each other with it. I don't think that's what contemporary art is meant to do.[84]

Her work then is more staged than displayed, thus disrupting traditional genre ideas so that the work exists between and amidst different genres: writing, drama, fine art, the masque, improvised music, the carnival procession. The move is primarily from art as object to art as process in order to make a more effective memorial; or, as Leroi Jones (Amiri Baraka) had it, moving 'from Noun to Verb'.[85] Such improvisatory practices could be said to be 'transgressive narratives that affirm [black Atlantic] culture in the face of colonisation and slavery'.[86] The obvious ideological consequences of this improvisatory focus require a movement from a passive to an active audience that Himid's praxis promotes. Like improvised musicking, *Naming the Money* could be said (following Daniel Fischlin and Ajay Heble's schema) to

> celebrate human contact by reinvigorating our understanding of the possibilities of social interaction. Central to this understanding is a commitment to listen to the voices of those around us, and moreover to be able to do so with trust, humility, generosity and a genuine spirit of openness.[87]

This ethical dimension is central to Himid's purpose of bringing her characters with all their historical baggage centre-stage to interact with an audience willing to listen and contribute and, yes, to bring their baggage too or, to foreground another African American musicking praxis, to engender a call-and-response mode. Movement too is important, as the audience is enabled to interact with the cut-outs whose own imaginative movements have been creatively engendered by Himid. As the poetic texts express the duality of the lives of these slave/servants, so the audience is encouraged to see multiplicity in these character's lives, which have so often only been defined by their function. They are all far more than their defined role as dog-trainer, musician, toy-maker, shoe-maker, etc. The texts that are attached to the cut-outs are all five lines long and follow similar syntactic patterns. One of the major themes is memory (sometimes obviously, sometimes implied, sometimes shown as a difficulty) as it connects the life led in the north, in Europe, with that left behind in the south, in Africa:

My name is Akron
They call me Henry
I used to play at weddings
Now I play at funerals
But I have the memory

My name is Ahmed
They call me Henry
I used to play the music of my people
Now I play to forget them
But I love the notes

My name is Ramadhan
They call me Jack
I used to decide distances
Now I count trees
But I have my memories[88]

These poetic fragments give voice to Himid's characters and work alongside the accompanying soundscape to create a multi-accentual performance, insisting on their full humanity despite their chattel status. As Stuart Hall has discussed, 'the double-naming process is fundamental to the conception of the piece',[89] showing the characters' African names and the English ones given to them by their masters or slave owners, and the way they have to negotiate between these realities to create identities in the contested maelstrom of enslaved societies. The double-naming brings forth the economic motif at the heart of the work; the European names the Africans are given show that they are owned and accounted for. Himid told me how the name of the installation changed to reflect this:

> It was going to be called *Gifts for Kings*. It was just going to be called *Money* and then that seemed rather crude. It is a fact that this is about money, this is about who is used as money, and who is used by the monied to make more money. But it seemed too crude really and I suppose *Naming the Money* seemed the action I was doing. So it was still a crude thing to name it. It was called *Kuffi*, but now you name the money *Sam* because now you own it and it's yours to exchange, it's a commodity now. And the name also has some of the connotations, I hoped, of that great phrase, 'Show me the money'.[90]

The crude economicism of slavery is conjured here in a way that resonates with Stephanie Smallwood's discussion of 'the transformation of African captives into Atlantic commodities'[91] by the workings of the transatlantic slave trade or indeed with Stephen M. Best's discussion of the power of commodification in constructing slave identity. He describes how 'slavery as a system of exchange has perhaps progressed so far as to be linked inextricably to its object of exchange.'[92] *Naming the Money* artistically imagines such a world, but shows the way that these figures try to break out of accountancy to imaginatively account for their lives. However, Himid, like Best, is aware that 'Slavery threatens to leave in perpetuity its unique scandal of value. The slave has become a money form.'[93] Himid's agenda is not to allow this commodification to dominate the historical record and imaginative landscape by fully accounting for these lives beyond their reduction to money. Himid shows how the human displacement initiated by the transatlantic slave trade is accompanied by what Best, following Eric Cheyfitz, calls a 'translation ... [a] coercive reversal that is all rhetoric', which seeks to hide the illicit and forced transportation by inventing a new name. Cheyfitz shows how seamlessly the 'rhetoric' of the name change is connected to its enchaining implications:

> The skilled translator, or rhetorician, like the skilled overseer with a slave,

must use force in transporting a word from its proper, or 'natural' place, but conceals that force, or tries to, under the semblance of the word's willingness to give up its property in itself.[94]

The proper nouns or Christian names that name the slave in their new environs mirror the way the slaves/servants are forced to 'give up their property in themselves'. Himid's work is designed to show the dehumanisation of this renaming and to use the imaginative, alchemical tools of colour, music and poetry to rescue the characters from this fate. These tools help to provide effective and wonderful memorials to these African Atlantic lives. As Himid explains, what seemed to be an accounting, almost a literal monetary tallying, changes to a recording of lives in danger of being lost to the historical record. What had seemed at first to be an indictment metamorphoses into a celebration:

> I thought I was talking to a firm of accountants in order to help them get the books straight, to get them to record the contribution, in figures, that we from somewhere else make to this place, this wealth, but I was wrong to try to do this.
>
> What happened was that gradually I realised that a hundred people were talking to me as if I was a records clerk, telling me to write a sort of registry of names as proof they existed as individual named people with real lives and real identities. I did as I was told.
>
> Perhaps I am a records clerk employed by a firm of accountants.[95]

Himid's description of her praxis here uses symbols familiar to those used in the documentation of the slave system and the later organisation of so-called free labour, with its accent on a brutal economism and a lowest common denominator recording of the bare facts and figures of such people's existence. She shows, however, that the making of art out of these bland economic and indexical facts undermines the ruthless diminution of these people, allowing them to speak their full, rich and varied existences with their multi-accentual improvisational valences in the staging of her work. Money, 'disguised and glamorised' through capitalist praxis, is here laid bare, effectively named and shamed, so that the human traces it covers over – literally buries – are brought thrillingly to life in the imaginative spectacle of her work. The piece moves the description of these slaves and slave descendants from the narrowness of the accountants' ledgers to their full glory in the artistic account. What Himid revels in here is presence; despite the elision of such African people's lives, and despite the racialised history of Europe, she insists that Africans have been crucial agents in its development. Her work memorialises this presence in the face of a throwaway and amnesiac world.

Himid's *Naming the Money* is a work of historical reconstruction that revels in a dancing, joyous, multifarious African presence in Europe. Although the work has never been shown in its entirety again, the bicentennial of the abolition of the slave trade in 2007 opened up the possibility of an edited version of the exhibition. Commissioned by the Victoria and Albert Museum for the exhibition 'Uncomfortable Truths', several groups of the cut-out characters were arranged in strategic places in the building, commenting obliquely on the tainted nature of some objects displayed there. However, the figures are compromised; the texts were on virtually unreadable brass plaques rather than on accounting paper, diluting their political meaning.[96] Recently, Himid wistfully commented on this diminution of her installation, that the cut-out people would be 'ambling through the British galleries in threes and fours as you'd come across them in a painting, not like in *Naming the Money* where they own the place'.[97]

It is, of course, a supreme irony that in the very year the ending of the slave trade was celebrated in the UK, a black artist was forced to compromise her vision in order to be able to show her work at all. 'Owning the place' is still very much a pipe-dream, not only for the characters in Himid's installations, but also for the creative artist, Himid herself.

The horrors of slavery are such that it is often felt to be an inappropriate topic for anything more than a relation of the bare and awful facts. Forged in the cauldron of a violent and dehumanising historical process, African Atlantic culture's variegated means of expressing horror would be elided and forgotten in such a limiting vision. Joseph Roach expresses the importance of rendering the multifarious narrative of colonialism and slavery in all its complex horror when thinking of the creation of circum-Atlantic modernity:

> While a great deal of the unspeakable violence instrumental to this creation may have been officially forgotten, circum-Atlantic memory retains its consequences, one of which is that the unspeakable cannot be rendered forever inexpressible: the most persistent mode of forgetting is memory imperfectly deferred.[98]

African Atlantic artistic performance at its best works against 'official ... forgetting' and does not allow the 'unspeakable' to be sidelined and, as Himid would term it, effectively 'invisibilised'. Roach's catalogue of performances (including jazz funerals with their second lines, as discussed in Chapter 5) that refuse the limitation of vision that the tyranny of notions of the 'inexpressible' brings forth are mirrored in the visual arts by works such as those of Gallagher, Donkor and Himid, which refuse to be bound by notions of inexpressibility. Paul Ricoeur, in more philosophical mode, has warned too of the limitation of such a vision:

It is an illusion to believe that factual statements can satisfy the idea of the unrepresentable, as though facts could through the virtue of their literal representation be disassociated from their representation in the form of events in a history; events, history, plot all go together on the plane of figuration.[99]

The multi-layering that Ricoeur talks of here to essay the 'unrepresentable' is discussed in terms of a different kind of narrative history. Himid attempts a visual representation of this horrific past, which uses a similar dialogical technique to interrogate the objects that surround her interventionist work. In undertaking such work, Himid is one of many African Atlantic artists to make artwork from what has been termed the 'unrepresentable' pain of the experience of slavery. In talking about writers such as Toni Morrison, Paul Gilroy alerts us to the

vital work of enquiring into terrors that exhaust the resources of language amidst the debris of a catastrophe which prohibits the existence of [her] art at the same time as demanding its continuance.[100]

For Himid, representing slavery visually is just as problematic and is an issue she has grappled with throughout her career. Ricoeur, in talking about the 'vulnerability of memory which results from the relation between the absence of the thing remembered and its presence in the mode of representation',[101] highlights the fundamental paradox of artworks that grapple with hidden/bypassed/elided/traumatic histories. In representing the event, the artist is in danger of making commonplace and representable events whose very power lies in their essential unrepresentablity. In talking about 'limit events' such as the Holocaust and slavery, Dominick LaCapra describes this problematic:

Here the facts may go beyond one's powers of imagination and may even seem incredible... The seemingly unimaginable nature of the limit event is also a reason why fictional or artistic treatment of such events may seem unsatisfying or lacking. This excess of event or fact over imaginative power – this beggaring of the imagination (which has been disconcertingly prevalent in the recent past) – poses a great challenge for artistic representation or treatment.[102]

LaCapra's astute observation on the difficulties of creating aesthetically valid art in such traumatic contexts effectively calls on artists and their audiences to foreground an empathy with a traumatic history that will enable work that speaks to, of and from that place. Gallagher, Donkor and Himid use very different techniques and artistic agendas, but all succeed in making work that brilliantly accounts for the ghostly presence of slavery. Avery Gordon describes how ghosts are never innocent: the unhallowed dead of the modern project drag in the pathos of their loss and the violence of the force that made them, their sheets and chains... Following ghosts is about making a contact that changes you and refashions the social relations in which you are located. It is about putting life back in where only a vague memory or a bare trace was visible to those who bothered to look ... ghost stories, stories that not only repair representational mistakes, but also strive to understand the conditions under which a memory was reproduced in the first place, toward a counter-memory of the future.[103]

Gallagher, Donkor and Himid 'repair representational mistakes' by using the very archive of slavery and its varied representations to evoke the lives the horrific institution had so often elided, and this is finally what links such disparate artists, apart from their shared African Atlantic backgrounds and subject matter. They acknowledge the 'sheets and chains' their subjects bring with them and make from the 'bare trace[s]' left by the historical record artistic celebrations and imaginings that help to fashion anew the visual imagination of slavery and its aftermath. They create memorial works that help to build contemporary identities that reflect these 'ghost' stories (their historical reincarnations and their horrific legacies) without being hamstrung by them; they are effectively creating 'a counter-memory of the future' in their depiction of 'ghosts' rising up from the 'itemised account', envisioning guerrilla memorials that talk back to the past as a strategic gesture to create new conceptual realities in the present and for the future.

Notes

1. É. Glissant, *Poetics of Relation*, trans. Bestsy Wing (Ann Arbor, MI: University of Michigan Press, 1997), p. 6.
2. Baucom, *Specters of the Atlantic*, p. 320
3. A. Gordon, *Ghostly Matters: Haunting and the Sociological Imagination* (Minneapolis, MI: University of Minnesota Press, 1997), p. 205.
4. M. Rediker, *The Slave Ship: A Human History* (London: John Murray, 2007), pp. 12–13.
5. Baucom, *Specters of the Atlantic*, pp. 61–2
6. J. S. Hogendorn and M. Johnson, *The Shell Money of the Slave Trade* (Cambridge: Cambridge University Press, 1986), p. 156.
7. W. J. T. Mitchell, *Picture Theory* (Chicago, IL: University of Chicago Press, 1994), p. 195.
8. Brand, *A Map to the Door of No Return*, p. 35.
9. S. Hall, 'Afterword: the legacies of Anglo-Caribbean culture – a diaspora perspective', in T. Barringer, G. Forrester and B. Martinez-Ruiz (eds), *Art and Emancipation in Jamaica: Isaac Mendes Belisario and His Worlds* (New Haven, CT: Yale University Press, 2007), pp. 179–195 (184).
10. S. Hall quoted in Bailey, Baucom and Boyce, *Shades of Black*, p. 2.

11. K. Alexander, 'A challenge to history: Ellen Gallagher's Coral Cities', in E. Gallagher, *Coral Cities* (London: Tate, 2008), pp. 71–78 (76–77).

12. Young, *Haunting Capital*, p. 4.

13. Drexciya, *The Quest*, CD (Detroit: Submerge Records, 1997).

14. G. Tate, 'Are you free or are you a mystery?', in E. Gallagher, *Coral Cities* (London: Tate, 2008), pp. 16–29 (19).

15. Gilroy, *Between Camps*, p. 348.

16. Glissant, *Poetics of Relation*, p. 33.

17. Rediker, *The Slave Ship*, p. 154.

18. Glissant, *Caribbean Discourse*, p. 66.

19. Gordon, *Ghostly Matters*, p. 188.

20. Rediker, *The Slave Ship*, p. 265.

21. G. Fabre, 'The slave ship dance', in M. Diedrich, H. L. Gates Jr and C. Pedersen (eds), *Black Imagination and the Middle Passage* (Oxford: Oxford University Press, 1999), p. 42.

22. P. Linebaugh and M. Rediker, *The Many-Headed Hydra: Sailors, Slaves, Commoners and the Hidden History of the Revolutionary Atlantic* (London: Verso, 2000), pp. 164–167.

23. Linebaugh and Rediker, *The Many-Headed Hydra*, p. 145.

24. J. T. Smith, *Vagabondia or, Anecdotes of Mendicant Wanderers Through the Streets of London; With Portraits of the Most Remarkable* (London: Chatto and Windus, 1874).

25. Linebaugh and Rediker, *The Many-Headed Hydra*, p. 151.

26. Smith, *Vagabondia*, p. 33. I have discussed the life of Joseph Johnson at length in *Radical Narratives of the Black Atlantic* (London: Continuum, 2003), pp. 206–210.

27. Gordon, *Ghostly Matters*, p. 9.

28. G. White and S. White, *Stylin': African American Expressive Culture from its Beginnings to the Zoot Suit* (Ithaca, NY: Cornell University Press, 1999), p. 47.

29. White and White, *Stylin': African American Expressive Culture*, p. 84.

30. K. Mercer, 'Black hair/style politics', in K. Owusu (ed.), *Black British Culture and Society: A Text Reader* (London: Routledge, 2000), pp. 111–121 (117).

31. Mercer, 'Black hair/style politics', p. 117.

32. Quoted in S. Kaiser, L. Rabine, C. Hall and K. Ketchum, 'Beyond binaries: respecting the improvisation in African American style', in C. Tulloch (ed.) *Black Style* (London: V&A Publications, 2004), pp. 48–67 (58).

33. *Night Waves* feature on Ellen Gallagher (BBC Radio 3, broadcast 23 March 2009).

34. E. Gallagher, *Coral Cities* (Liverpool: Tate, 2008), n.p.

35. Gallagher, *Coral Cities*, n.p.

36. Mercer, 'Black hair/style politics', p. 112.

37. Alexander, 'A challenge to history', p. 73.

38. Alexander, 'A challenge to history', p. 72.

39. J. Kay, 'Souls of the sea', *The Guardian* (Review section), 28 April 2007, p. 13.

40. Kaiser et al., 'Beyond binaries', p. 52.

41. Glissant, *Caribbean Discourse*, p. 66 (my words in parantheses).

42. Young, *Haunting Capital*, p. 41.

43. Glissant, *Poetics of Relation*, pp. 86–87 (slightly adapted).

44. G. Agamben, *Remnants of Auschwitz: The Witness and the Archive*, trans. Daniel Heller Roazan (New York, NY: Zone Books, 1999), p. 163.

45. T. Stothard, *Voyage of the Sable Venus* (engraving) in B. Edwards, *History Civil and Commercial of the British Colonies in the West Indies* (London: John Stockdale, 3 vols, 1793–1801), n.p.

46. Brand, *A Map to the Door of No Return*, p. 200.

47. G. Donkor, *Triptych: The Birth of Venus*, (Manchester: Whitworth Art Gallery, 2005).

48. K. Mercer and I. Julien, 'True confessions', in T. Golden (ed.), *Black Male: Representations of Masculinity in Contemporary American Art* (New York, NY: Whitney Museum of American Art, 1994), pp. 191–200 (193).

49. A. Rice, interview with Godfried Donkor (2005), 'Commemorating abolition' website, www.uclan.ac.uk/abolition [accessed 12 July 2009].

50. Baucom, *Specters of the Atlantic*, p. 27.

51. Baucom, *Specters of the Atlantic*, p. 61.

52. Baucom, *Specters of the Atlantic*, p. 139.

53. R. Young, *Colonial Desire: Hybridity in Theory and Practice* (Routledge: London, 1995), p. 158.

54. G. Donkor, *Financial Times* (London: Hackney Museum, March 2007).

55. C. J. Martin, 'In financial time', in *Financial Times* catalogue (London: Hackney Museum, 2007), pp. 2–9 (2).

56. Martin, 'In financial time', p. 2.

57. Baucom, *Specters of the Atlantic*, p. 107.

58. C.-M. Bernier, '"Speculation and the imagination": history, storytelling and the body in Godfried Donkor's *Financial Times*', *Slavery and Abolition*, 29 (June 2008), pp. 203–217 (203).

59. Martin, 'In financial time', p. 7.

60. Martin, 'In financial time', p. 9.

61. Young, *Haunting Capital*, p. 47.

62. Young, *Haunting Capital*, p. 40.

63. Bernier, 'Speculation and the imagination', p. 205.

64. Bernier, 'Speculation and the imagination', p. 210.

65. Keizer, *Black Subjects*, p. 47.

66. Keizer, *Black Subjects*, p. 47.

67. G. Tawadros, 'The Sphinx contemplating Napoleon: black women artists in Britain', in K. Deepwell (ed.), *New Feminist Art Criticism* (Manchester: Manchester University Press, 1995) pp. 25–30 (26).

68. Baucom, *Specters of the Atlantic*, pp. 21–22.

69. Lubaina Himid, *Naming the Money* (Newcastle: Hatton Gallery, March 2004). Work from the exhibition can be viewed at http://www.lubainahimid.info/naming_the_money [accessed 1 July 2009].

70. S. E. Smallwood, *Saltwater Slavery: A Middle Passage from Africa to the American Diaspora* (Cambridge, MA: Harvard University Press, 2007), p. 98.

71. H. Spillers, 'Mama's Baby, Papa's Maybe: an American grammar', in A. Mitchell (ed.), *Within the Circle: An Anthology of African American Literary Criticism from the Harlem Renaissance to the Present* (Durham, NC: Duke University Press, 1994), pp. 454–481 (461).

72. Brand, *A Map to the Door of No Return*, pp. 203–204.

73. Rice, 'Exploring inside the invisible', p. 26.

74. Rice, 'Exploring inside the invisible', p. 26.

75. L. Himid, '*Naming the Money* and its resonances', personal email correspondence, 23 March 2004.

76. Rice, 'Exploring inside the invisible', p. 26.

77. Rice, 'Exploring inside the invisible', p. 24.

78. Gordon, *Ghostly Matters*, pp. 24–25.

79. Rice, 'Exploring inside the invisible', p. 20.

80. Rice, 'Exploring inside the invisible', p. 21.

81. Hall, 'Afterword: legacies of Anglo-Caribbean', p. 186.

82. Small, *Music of the Common Tongue*. This phrase is the signal expression in the book to describe African and African diasporan praxis in music.

83. S. A. Floyd Jr, *The Power of Black Music: Interpreting its History from Africa to the United States* (New York, NY: Oxford University Press, 1995), p. 232.

84. Rice, 'Exploring inside the invisible', p. 20.

85. Baraka, *Blues People*.

86. D. Fischlin and A. Heble (eds), *The Other Side of Nowhere* (Middletown, CT: Wesleyan University Press, 2004), p. 38.

87. Fischlin and Heble, *The Other Side of Nowhere*, p. 35.

88. L. Himid, *Naming the Money* (Newcastle upon Tyne: Hatton Gallery, University of Newcastle upon Tyne, 2004), pp. 11, 19 and 24.

89. Hall, 'Afterword: legacies of Anglo-Caribbean', p. 186.

90. Rice, 'Exploring inside the invisible', p. 24.

91. Smallwood, *Saltwater Slavery*, p. 36.

92. Best, *The Fugitive's Properties*, p. 1.

93. Best, *The Fugitive's Properties*, p. 2.

94. E. Cheyfitz, *The Poetics of Imperialism: Translation and Colonialism from The Tempest to Tarzan of the Apes* (Oxford: Oxford University Press), p. 37.

95. Himid, *Naming the Money*, p. 3.

96. The work was part of an exhibition, 'Uncomfortable Truths: The Shadow of Slave Trading on Contemporary Art and Design' (London: Victoria and Albert Museum, February–June 2007).

97. Himid, 'Gallery talk'.

98. Roach, *Cities of the Dead*, p. 4.

99. Ricoeur, *Memory, History and Forgetting*, p. 257.

100. Gilroy, *The Black Atlantic*, p. 218.

101. Ricoeur, *Memory, History, Forgetting*, pp. 57–58.

102. D. LaCapra, *History in Transit: Experience, Identity, Critical Theory* (Ithaca, NY: Cornell University Press, 2004), p. 133.

103. Gordon, *Ghostly Matters*, p. 22.

Bibliography

Adams, Jessica, *Wounds of Returning: Race, Memory and Property on the Postslavery Plantation* (Chapel Hill, NC: University of North Carolina Press, 2007).

Afrikan Heroes Re-visited: The Forgotten Heroes of Commonwealth, dir. Raphael Chikukwa (Manchester: Imperial War Museum North, 2006).

Agamben, Giorgio, *Remnants of Auschwitz: The Witness and the Archive*, trans. Daniel Heller Roazan (New York, NY: Zone Books, 1999).

Alexander, Karen, 'A challenge to history: Ellen Gallagher's Coral Cities', in *Coral Cities*, by Ellen Gallagher, exhibition catalogue (London: Tate Publishing, 2007), pp. 71–78.

Amazing Grace, dir. Michael Apted (Momentum Pictures, 2007).

Anon., 'Four Models of Freed Slaves' (Manchester: Whitworth Art Gallery, 1834–1836).

Anon., *Cotton pickers in the American South* (Bolton: Bolton Museum and Archives Service, 1895).

Back, Les, 'Syncopated synergy: dance, embodiment and the call of the jitterbug', in *Out of Whiteness: Color, Politics and Culture*, ed. Vron Ware and Les Back (Chicago, IL and London: University of Chicago Press, 2002), pp. 169–195.

Bailey, David A., Ian Baucom and Sonia Boyce, *Shades of Black: Assembling the 1980s Black Arts in Postwar Britain* (Durham, NC: Duke University Press).

Bakhtin, Mikhail M., *The Dialogic Imagination* (Austin, TX: University of Texas Press, 1981).

Baldwin, James, 'Of the sorrow songs: the cross of redemption', in *The Picador Book of Blues and Jazz*, ed. James Campbell (London: Picador, 1996), pp. 324–331.

Baraka, Amiri (a.k.a. Jones, Leroi), *Blues People* (New York, NY: Morrow, 1963).

Baraka, Amiri, *Home: Social Essays* (New York, NY: Morrow, 1966).

Baraka, Amiri and Larry Neal, eds, *Black Fire* (New York, NY: Morrow, 1968).

Barker, Ian, 'Slavery is part of what we are', letter to *Lancaster Guardian*, 14 January 2005, p. 6.

Baucom, Ian, *Specters of the Atlantic: Finance Capital, Slavery and the Philosophy of History* (Durham, NC: Duke University Press, 2005).

Bechet, Sidney, *Treat It Gentle* (London: Corgi, 1964).

Bell, Alan A., 'Sambo's Song' (Fleetwood: Tamlyn Music, 1973).

Bell, Alan A., written correspondence, 13 June 2008.

Bennett, Tony, 'Exhibition, difference and the logic of culture', in *Museum Frictions: Public Cultures/Global Transformations*, ed. Ivan Karp et al. (Durham, NC: University of North Carolina Press, 2006), pp. 46–69.

Benston, Kimberly W., 'Late Coltrane: a re-membering of Orpheus', in *Chant of Saints*, ed. Michael S. Harper and Robert B. Stepto (Chicago, IL: University of Illinois Press, 1979), pp. 413–424.

Berliner, Paul F., *Thinking in Jazz: The Infinite Art of Improvisation* (Chicago, IL: Chicago University Press, 1995).

Bernier, Celeste-Marie, '"Speculation and the imagination": history, storytelling and the body in Godfried Donkor's *Financial Times*', *Slavery and Abolition* 29 (June 2008), pp. 202–217.

Best, Stephen M., *The Fugitive's Properties: Law and the Politics of Possession* (Chicago, IL: The University of Chicago Press, 2004).

Bigsby, Christopher, 'Jazz queen', *The Independent on Sunday*, 26 April 1992, pp. 28–29.

Blackburn, Robin, *The Making of New World Slavery: From the Baroque to the Modern 1492–1800* (London: Verso, 1998).

Blackett, Richard J. M., *Divided Hearts: Britain and the American Civil War* (Baton Rouge, LA: Louisiana State University Press, 2001).

Blake, Vivian, 'Birthday fib gets Jamaican schoolboy into the RAF', oral memoir on 'WW2 People's War', BBC, http://www.bbc.co.uk/ww2peopleswar/stories/41/a3754541.shtml [accessed 14 July 2008].

Blesh, Rudi, *Shining Trumpets: A History of Jazz* (New York, NY: Da Capo, 1975).

Bolster, Jeffrey, *Black Jacks: African American Seamen in the Age of Sail* (Cambridge, MA: Harvard University Press, 1997).

Bousquet, Ben and Colin Douglas, *West Indian Women at War* (London: Lawrence and Wishart, 1991).

Brand, Dionne, *A Map to the Door of No Return: Notes to Belonging* (Toronto: Doubleday Canada, 2001).

Brewster, Donna, *The House that Sugar Built* (Wigtown: GC Books, 1999).

Brooks, Libby, 'Don't tell me who I am', *The Guardian*, 12 January 2002, p. 34.

Brown, Henry Box, *Narrative of the Life of Henry Box Brown* (1851), ed. Richard Newman (Oxford: Oxford University Press, 2002).

Bruner, Edward, 'Tourism in Ghana: the representation of slavery and the return of the black diaspora', *American Anthropologist* 98.2 (1996), pp. 290–304.

Buntinx, Gustavo and Ivan Karp, 'Tactical museologies', in *Museum Frictions: Public Cultures/Global Transformations*, ed. Ivan Karp et al. (Durham, NC: Duke University Press, 2006), pp. 207–218.

Burnside, Anna, 'Outside edge', *The Sunday Herald*, 2 April 2000, p. 8.

Camp de Thiaroye, dir. Ousmane Sembene (New York Video, 1988).

Campbell, James T., *Middle Passages: African American Journeys to Africa 1787–2005* (London: Penguin, 2006).

Carretta, Vincent, 'Olaudah Equiano or Gustavus Vassa? New light on an eighteenth century question of identity', *Slavery and Abolition* 20.3 (1999), pp. 96–105.

Carretta, Vincent, *Equiano, the African: Biography of a Self-Made Man* (Harmondsworth: Penguin, 2006).

Césaire, Aimé, *Discourse on Colonialism* (New York: Monthly Review Press, 1972).

Chater, K., 'From slavery to show business', *Ancestors* (December 2005), pp. 32–33.

Cheyfitz, Eric, *The Poetics of Imperialism: Translation and Colonialism from The Tempest to Tarzan of the Apes* (Oxford: Oxford University Press, 1991).

Chicago, Judy, *The Dinner Party*, exhibition leaflet (Edinburgh: no pub., August 1984).

Choc'late Soldiers from the USA, dir. Noel Izon and Gregory Cook (Washington, DC: Hesh Productions, 2008).

'The civil rights struggle, African-American GIs and Germany: digital archive, oral history collection and research project', leaflet (Washington, DC: Vassar College, German Historical Institute and Heidelberg Center for American Studies), http://aacvr-germany.org/AACVR.ORG/images/stories/flyer_aacvr.pdf [accessed 22 July 2009].

Collins, Paul, 'Lancaster faces up to its shameful past', *Lancaster Guardian*, 28 October 2005, p. 2.

Connarty, Jane, 'Mary Evans', in *Port City: On Mobility and Exchange*, ed. Tom Trevor et al. (Bristol: Arnolfini, 2007), pp. 92–99.

Crouch, Stanley, *The All-American Skin Game, or, The Decoy of Race* (New York, NY: Pantheon Books, 1995).

Cugoano, Quobna Ottobah, 'Thoughts and sentiments on the evil and wicked traffic of slavery and commerce of the human species...' (1787) in *Unchained Voices*, ed. Vincent Carretta (Lexington, KT: University Press of Kentucky, 1996), pp. 145–184.

Dabydeen, David, John Gilmore and Cecily Jones, *Oxford Companion to Black British History* (Oxford: Oxford University Press, 2007).

Dannant, Adrian, 'Obituary of Michael Richards', *The Independent*, 24 September 2001, p. 6.

Davis, David Brion, *Inhuman Bondage: The Rise and Fall of Slavery in the New World* (Oxford: Oxford University Press, 2006).

Debrunner, H. W., *Presence and Prestige: Africans in Europe: a History of Africans in Europe Before 1918* (Basel: Basel Afrika Bibliographien, 1979).

Diawara, Manthia, 'Conversation with Édouard Glissant aboard the Queen Mary II (August 2009)', in Tanya Barson and Peter Gorschluter (eds), *Afro Modern: Journeys through the Black Atlantic* (Liverpool: Tate Publishing, 2010), pp. 58–63 (61).

Dixon, Melvin, 'Introduction', in *The Collected Poetry of Leopold Sedar Senghor*, transl. Melvin Dixon (Charlottesville, VA: University of Virginia Press, 1998).

Dolphy, Eric, liner notes, *Last Date*, LP (New York: Mercury, 1964).

Donkor, Godfried, 'Dessert', *Vauxhall Pleasure Series*, collage (Manchester: Whitworth Art Gallery, 2001).

Donkor, Godfried, *Triptych related to Stothard's Voyage of the Sable Venus*, three collaged sheets (Manchester: Whitworth Art Gallery, 2005).

Donkor, Godfried, *Financial Times* (London: Hackney Museum, 2007).

Douglas, Ann, *Terrible Honesty: Mongrel Manhattan in the 1920s* (London: Macmillan, 1995).

Douglass, Frederick, *Narrative of the Life of an American Slave, Written by Himself*, 1845, ed. Houston A. Baker Jr (Harmondsworth: Penguin, 1986).

Douglass, Frederick, 'The Life and Times of Frederick Douglass' (1881), in *Autobiographies*, ed. Henry Louis Gates Jr (New York, NY: Library of America, 1994), pp. 453–1045.

Douglass, Frederick, 'My bondage and my freedom' (1855), in *Autobiographies*, ed. Henry Louis Gates Jr (New York, NY: Library of America, 1994), pp. 103–452.

Drescher, Seymour, 'Commemorating slavery and abolition in the United States of America', in *Facing up to the Past: Perspectives on the Commemoration of Slavery from Africa, the Americas and Europe*, ed. Gert Oostindie (Kingston, Jamaica: Ian Randle Publishers, 2001).

Drescher, Seymour, 'Public opinion and parliament in the abolition of the British slave trade', in *The British Slave Trade: Abolition, Parliament and People*, ed. Stephen Farrell, Melanie Unwin and James Walvin (Edinburgh: Edinburgh University Press, 2007), pp. 42–65.

Drexciya, *The Quest*, CD (Detroit: Submerge Records, 1997).

Du Bois, W. E. B., *Black Reconstruction* (Millwood, NY: Kraus-Thomson, 1935).

Du Bois, W. E. B., *The Souls of Black Folk*, first published 1903 (New York, NY: Vintage, 1990).

Dyer, Richard, 'Jackie Kay in conversation', *Wasafiri* 29 (Spring 1999), p. 58.

Echenberg, Myron, *Colonial Conscripts: The Tirailleurs Senegalais in French West Africa, 1857–1960* (Portsmouth: Heinemann, 1991).

Eckstein, Lars, *Re-Membering the Black Atlantic: On the Poetics and Politics of Literary Memory* (Amsterdam: Rodopi, 2006).

Edwards, Brent Hayes, *The Practice of Diaspora: Literature, Translation and the Rise of Black Internationalism* (London: Harvard University Press, 2003).

Edwards, Bryan, *History Civil and Commercial of the British Colonies in the West Indies*, 3 vols (London: John Stockdale, 1793–1801).

Eichstedt, Jennifer L. and Stephen Small, *Representations of Slavery: Race and Ideology in Southern Plantation Museums* (Washington, DC: Smithsonian Books, 2002).

Elder, Melinda, *The Slave Trade and the Economic Development of 18th Century Lancaster* (Keele: Ryburn Press, 1992).

Elder, Melinda, *Lancaster and the African Slave Trade* (Lancaster: Lancaster City Museums, 1994).

Entertainments bill, *Henry Box Brown Showing a Mirror of Africa and America at the Music Hall*, 12–17 December 1859, 665/4/367, Shropshire Archives.

Equiano, Olaudah, *The Interesting Narrative and Other Writings* (1789), ed. Vincent Carretta (Harmondsworth: Penguin, 1995).

Equiano, Olaudah, *The Interesting Narrative of the Life of Olaudah Equiano, or Gustavus Vassa, the African, Written by Himself* (1789) in *Unchained* Voices, ed. Vincent Carretta (Lexington, KY: University Press of Kentucky, 1996), pp. 185–318.

Eshun, Ekow, *Black Gold of the Sun: Searching for Home in African and Beyond* (New York, NY: Random House, 2005).

Evans, Mary (dir.), *Blighty, Guinea, Dixie* (Bristol: Port City, 2007).

Fabre, Geneviève, 'The slave ship dance', in *Black Imagination and the Middle Passage*, ed. Maria Diedrich, Henry Louis Gates Jr and Carl Pedersen (Oxford: Oxford University Press, 1999).

Fanon, Frantz, *Toward the African Revolution: Political Essays*, trans. Haakon Chevalier (New York, NY: Grove Press, 1967).

Fischlin, Daniel and Ajay Heble, eds, *The Other Side of Nowhere* (Middletown, CT: Wesleyan University Press, 2004).

Flowers, Sue and Lubaina Himid, *Abolished?*, exhibition catalogue (Lancaster: Lancashire Museums, 2007).

Floyd, Samuel A. Jr, *The Power of Black Music: Interpreting Its History from Africa to the United States* (New York, NY: Oxford University Press, 1995).

Forsdick, Charles, '"Ceci n'est pas un conte, mais une histoire de chair et de sang": representing the colonial massacre in Francophone literature and culture', in *Postcolonial Violence and Identity in Francophone Africa and the Antilles*, ed. Lorna Milne (New York, NY: Peter Lang, 2007), pp. 31–57.

Frazier, Lessie Jo, 'Subverted memories: countermourning as political action in Chile', in *Acts of Memory: Cultural Recall in the Present*, ed. Mieke Bal, Jonathan V. Crewe and Leo Spitzer (Hanover: Dartmouth College Press, 1998), pp. 105–119.

Gallagher, Ellen, *Coral Cities* (Liverpool: Tate, 2008).

Gates, Henry Louis Jr, *The Signifying Monkey: A Theory of Literary Criticism* (New York, NY: Oxford University Press, 1988).

Gayle, Addison Jr, *The Black Aesthetic* (Garden City, NY: Anchor-Doubleday, 1971).

Ghosts, dir. Nick Broomfield (Beyond Films, 2006).

Gilroy, Paul, *There Ain't No Black in the Union Jack: The Cultural Politics of Race and Nation* (London: Hutchison, 1987).

Gilroy, Paul, 'Living memory: Toni Morrison talks to Paul Gilroy', *City Limits*, 31 March 1988, pp. 11–12.

Gilroy, Paul, *The Black Atlantic: Modernity and Double-Consciousness* (London: Verso, 1993).

Gilroy, Paul, *Small Acts: Thoughts on the Politics of Black Cultures* (London: Serpent's Tail, 1993).

Gilroy, Paul, *Between Camps: Nations, Cultures and the Allure of Race* (London: Penguin, 2000).

Gilroy, Paul, *After Empire: Melancholia or Convivial Culture* (Abingdon: Routledge, 2004).

Gioia, Ted, *The Imperfect Art* (Oxford: Oxford University Press, 1988).

Glissant, Édouard, *Caribbean Discourse: Selected Essays*, trans. J. Michael Dash (Charlottesville, VA: University of Virginia Press, 1989).

Glissant, Édouard, *Poetics of Relation*, trans. Bestsy Wing (Ann Arbor, MI: University of Michigan Press, 1997).

Gordon, Avery, *Ghostly Matters: Haunting and the Sociological Imagination* (Minneapolis, MI: University of Minnesota Press, 1997).

Grant, Cy, *A Member of the RAF of Indeterminate Race: WW2 Experiences of a Former RAF Navigator and POW* (Bognor Regis: Woodfield Publishing, 2006).

Grant, Robert, 'Absence into presence: the thematics of memory and "missing" subjects in Toni Morrison's *Sula*', in *Critical Essays on Toni Morrison*, ed. Nellie Y. McKay (Boston, MA: GK Hall, 1988), pp. 90–103.

Grime, Kitty, *Jazz at Ronnie Scott's* (London: Robert Hale, 1979).

Hall, Stuart, 'Afterword: The legacies of Anglo-Caribbean Culture – a diaspora perspective', in *Art and Emancipation in Jamaica: Isaac Mendes Belisario and His Worlds*, ed. Tim Barringer, Gillian Forrester and Barbaro Martinez-Ruiz (New Haven, CT: Yale University Press, 2007), pp. 179–195.

Harris, Wilson, 'History, fable and myth in the Carribean and Guianas', in *Selected Essays of Wilson Harris: The Unfinished Genius of the Imagination*, ed. Andrew Bundy (London: Routledge, 1999), pp. 152–166.

Hartman, Charles, *Jazz Text* (Princeton, NJ: Princeton University Press, 1991).

Hearne, Thomas, *The Island of Montserrat from the Road before the Town*, watercolour and bodycolour over pen and ink on two joined sheets of laid paper (Manchester: Whitworth Art Gallery, 1775–1776).

Hearne, Thomas, *View of St. Christopher's: The Salt Pond, part of St. Christopher's and Nevis from the Shore at Basseterre*, watercolour and bodycolour over pen and ink on two joined sheets of laid paper (Manchester: Whitworth Art Gallery, 1775–1776).

Heinze, Denise, *The Dilemma of 'Double Consciousness': Toni Morrison's Novels* (Athens, GA: University of Georgia Press, 1993).

Henderson, Hamish, *Elegies for the Dead in Cyrenaica* (Edinburgh: Polygon, 1990).

Henderson, Mae G., 'Speaking in tongues: dialogics, dialectics and the black woman writer's literary traditions', in *Changing Our Own Words*, ed. Cheryl A. Wall (London: Routledge, 1990), pp. 18–37.

Hentoff, Nat, liner notes on Albert Ayler, 'Truth is Marching In', in *Albert Ayler in Greenwich Village*, LP (New York, NY: Jasmine, 1967).

Herbert, Philip, 'Saint Georges, le Chevalier de', in *The Oxford Companion to Black British History*, ed. David Dabydeen, John Gilmore and Cecily Jones (Oxford: Oxford University Press, 2007), pp. 426–427.

Hesse, Barnor, *Unsettled Multiculturalisms: Diasporas, Entanglements, Transruptions* (London: Zed Books, 2000).

Himid, Lubaina, '*Cotton.com* texts', manuscript (n.p., 2002).

Himid, Lubaina, 'Notes on *Cotton.com*', personal email correspondence, 12 September 2003.

Himid, Lubaina, 'Monument talk', Dukes Theatre, Lancaster, 15 November 2003.

Himid, Lubaina, *Naming the Money* (Newcastle: Hatton Gallery, University of Newcastle upon Tyne, 2004).

Himid, Lubaina, '*Naming the Money* and its resonances', personal email correspondence, 23 March 2004.

Himid, Lubaina, personal communication, 20 March 2004.

Himid, Lubaina, 'Gallery talk', Judges' Lodgings, Lancaster, 17 October 2006.

Himid, Lubaina, *Naming The Money*, http://www.lubainahimid.info/naming_the_money [accessed 1 July 2009].

Himid, Lubaina, 'What are monuments for? Art of the black diaspora, possible landmarks on the urban map', presentation given at the Collegium for African American Research Conference, Bremen, 26 March 2009.

Hochschild, Adam, *King Leopold's Ghost: A Story of Greed, Terror and Heroism in Colonial Africa* (London: Pan Macmillan, 1999).

Hogarth, *William, Marriage à la Mode, Plate 4: The Countess's Levée* (Manchester: Whitworth Art Gallery, 1745).

Hogendorn, Jan S. and Marion Johnson, *The Shell Money of the Slave Trade* (Cambridge: Cambridge University Press, 1986).

Hollett, David, *The Alabama Affair: The British Shipyards' Conspiracy in the American Civil War* (Bebington: Avid Publications, 1993).

hooks, bell, *Yearning: Race, Gender and Cultural Politics* (London: Turnaround, 1991).

Hugill, Stan, *Shanties from the Seven Seas: Shipboard Work-Songs and Songs Used as Work-Songs from the Great Days of Sail* (Mystic, CT: Mystic Seaport, 1994).

Hull, Gloria T., '"What is it I think she's doing anyhow?": a reading of Toni Cade Bambara's *The Salt Eaters*', in *Conjuring: Black Women, Fiction and Literary Tradition*, ed. Marjorie Pryse and Hortense J. Spillers (Bloomington, IN: Indiana University Press, 1985), pp. 216–232.

Hunt, Joseph, 'Blacks and the classics: a conversation with T. J. Anderson', *Black Perspective in Music* 1 (1973), pp. 157–165.

Hyber, Fabrice, *Le Cri, L'Écrit* (Paris: Luxembourg Gardens, 2007).

Jaggi, Maya, 'Race and all that jazz', *The Guardian*, 5 December 1998, p. 10.

Jaggi, Maya, 'Spectral triangle', *The Guardian*, 5 May 1993, p. 4.

Jimoh, A. Yemisi, *Spiritual Blues and Jazz People in African American Fiction* (Knoxville, TN: University of Tennessee Press, 2002).

Johnson, James, *The Life of the Late James Johnson, Coloured Evangelist: An Escaped Slave from the Southern States of America, 40 Years Resident in Oldham England* (Oldham: W. Galley, 1914).

Jones, Gayl, *Liberating Voices: Oral Tradition in African American Literature* (Cambridge, MA: Harvard University Press, 1991).

Julian, Joseph, 'Jim Crow goes abroad', *The Nation*, 5 December 1942, p. 610.

Kaiser, Susan, Lesley Rabine, Carol Hall and Karyl Ketchum, 'Beyond binaries: respecting the improvisation in African-American style', in *Black Style*, ed. Carol Tulloch (London: V&A Publications, 2004), pp. 48–67.

Kay, Jackie, *Trumpet* (London: Picador, 1998).

Kay, Jackie, 'Silence is golden', *Time Out*, 3 February 2002, p. 105.

Kay, Jackie, 'Souls of the sea', *The Guardian*, 28 April 2007, p. 13.

Kay, Jackie, interview, *The Poetry Archive*, http://www.poetryarchive.org/poetry archive/singleInterview.do?interviewId=6580 [accessed 12 March 2008].

Kean, Hilda, 'Personal and public histories: issues in the presentation of the past', in *The Ashgate Research Companion to Heritage and Identity*, ed. Brian Graham and Peter Howard (Aldershot: Ashgate, 2008).

Keizer, Arlene R., *Black Subjects in the Contemporary Narrative of Slavery* (Ithaca, NY: Cornell University Press, 2004).

Kreamer, Christine Mullen, 'Shared heritage, contested terrain: cultural negotiation and Ghana's Cape Coast Castle exhibition "Crossroads of People, Crossroads of Trade"', in *Museum Frictions: Public Cultures/Global Transformations*, ed. Ivan Karp et al. (Durham, NC: Duke University Press, 2006), pp. 435–468.

LaCapra, Dominick, *History in Transit: Experience, Identity, Critical Theory* (Ithaca, NY: Cornell University Press, 2004).

Lambo, Roger, 'Achtung! The black prince: West Africans in the Royal Air Force, 1939–46', in *Africans in Britain*, ed. David Killingray (London: Frank Cass, 1993), pp. 145–163.

Lenz, Gunter H., 'Black poetry and black music: history and tradition: Michael Harper and John Coltrane', in *History and Tradition in Afro-American Culture*, ed. Gunter H. Lenz (Frankfurt: Campus, 1984), pp. 277–326.

Levine, Lawrence W., *Black Culture and Black Consciousness* (Oxford: Oxford University Press, 1977).

Levy, Andrea, *Small Island* (London: Headline, 2004).

Lewis, Peter, *A People's War* (London: Thames Methuen, 1986).

Lhamon, W. T., *Raising Cain: Blackface Performance from Jim Crow to Hip Hop* (Cambridge, MA: Harvard University Press, 1998).

Linebaugh, Peter and Marcus Rediker, *The Many-Headed Hydra: Sailors, Slaves, Commoners and the Hidden History of the Revolutionary Atlantic* (London: Verso, 2000).

Linenthal, Edward T., 'Epilogue: reflections', in *Slavery and Public History: The Tough Stuff of American History*, ed. J. O. and L. E. Horton (New York, NY: The New Press, 2006), pp. 213–224.

Lorde, Audre, *Sister Outsider* (New York: Thunder's Mouth Press, 1984).

Lovelace, Earl, *The Wine of Astonishment* (London: Heinemann, 1982).

Macdonald, Murdo, 'The uneasiness inherent in culture: a note on Michael Visocchi's memorial to the abolition of the transatlantic slave trade', *International Journal of Scottish Literature* 4 (Spring/Summer 2008), http://www.ijsl.stir.ac.uk/issue4/macdonaldOP.htm [accessed 10 June 2009].

McFeely, William S., *Frederick Douglass* (New York, NY: WW Norton, 1991).

Mack, Tara, 'The US isn't great on race: are you Brits any better?', *Observer Magazine*, 20 February 2000, p. 2.

McKay, George, *Circular Breathing: The Cultural Politics of Jazz in Britain* (Durham, NC: Duke University Press, 2005).

McKay, Nellie Y., 'An interview with Toni Morrison', *Contemporary Literature* 24 (1983), pp. 413–429.

Mackie, James, 'Why be slaves to our past?', letter to *Lancaster Guardian*, 7 January 2005, p. 6.

McMillan, James A., *The Final Victims: Foreign Slave Trade to North America, 1783–1810* (Columbia, SC: University of South Carolina Press, 2004), pp. 104–105.

McPherson, Tara, *Reconstructing Dixie: Race, Gender and Nostalgia in the Imagined South* (Durham, NC: Duke University Press, 2003).

Mann, Gregory, *Native Sons: West African Veterans and France in the Twentieth Century* (Durham, NC: Duke University Press, 2006).

Martin, Courtney J., 'In financial time' in *Financial Times*, exhibition catalogue (London: Hackney Museum, 2007), pp. 2–9.

Mercer, Kobena, 'Back to my routes: a postscript to the 1980s', in *Writing Black Britain 1948–1998: An Interdisciplinary Anthology*, ed. James Proctor (Manchester: Manchester University Press, 2000), pp. 285–293.

Mercer, Kobena, 'Black hair/style politics', in *Black British Culture and Society: A Text Reader*, ed. Kwesi Owusu (London: Routledge, 2000), pp. 111–121.

Mercer, Kobena and Isaac Julien, 'True confessions', in *Black Male: Representations of Masculinity in Contemporary American Art*, ed. Thelma Golden (New York, NY: Whitney Museum of American Art, 1994), pp. 191–200.

Mitchell, W. J. T., *Picture Theory* (Chicago, IL: University of Chicago Press, 1994).

Monson, Ingrid, 'Doubleness and jazz improvisation: irony, parody and ethnomusicology', *Critical Inquiry* 20 (1994), pp. 283–313.

Monson, Ingrid, *Saying Something: Jazz Improvisation and Interaction* (Chicago, IL: University of Chicago Press, 1997).

Morehouse, Maggi M., *Fighting the Jim Crow Army: Black Men and Women Remember WWII* (Lanham, MD: Rowman and Littlefield, 2000).

Morrison, Toni, *Sula* (London: Triad Grafton, 1980).

Morrison, Toni, *The Bluest Eye* (London: Triad Granada, 1981).

Morrison, Toni, 'Rootedness: the ancestor as foundation', in *Black Women Writers 1950–1980*, ed. Mari Evans (London: Pluto, 1985), pp. 339–345.

Morrison, Toni, 'A bench by the road', *The World* 3.1 (1989), pp. 4–5 & 37–41.

Morrison, Toni, *Jazz* (London: Chatto and Windus, 1992).

Morrison, Toni, *Playing in the Dark: Whiteness and the Literary Imagination* (Cambridge, MA: Harvard University Press, 1992).

Mullen, Bill V., *Popular Fronts: Chicago and African-American Cultural Politics, 1935–46* (Champaign, IL: University of Illinois Press, 1999).

Nash, Gary B., 'For whom will the Liberty Bell toll? From controversy to cooperation', in *Slavery and Public History: The Tough Stuff of American History*, ed. J. O. and L. E. Horton (New York, NY: The New Press, 2006), pp. 75–102.

Nielsen, Aldon L., *Writing Between the Lines: Race and Intertextuality* (Athens, GA: University of Georgia Press, 1994).

Night Waves feature on Ellen Gallagher, BBC Radio 3, broadcast 23 March 2009.

Nora, Pierre, 'Between memory and history: les lieux de mémoire', in *History and Memory in African American Culture*, ed. Geneviève Fabre and Robert O'Meally (Oxford: Oxford University Press, 1994), pp. 284–300.

Oguibe, Olu, 'Slavery and the diaspora imagination', in *Facing up to the Past: Perspectives on the Commemoration of Slavery from Africa, the Americas and Europe*, ed. Gert Oostindie (Kingston, Jamaica: Ian Randle Publishers, 2001), pp. 95–101.

Oldfield, John R., *'Chords of Freedom': Commemoration, Ritual and British Transatlantic Slavery* (Manchester: Manchester University Press, 2007).

Oliver, Paul, 'Taking the measure of the blues', in *Cross the River Blues: African American Music in Europe*, ed. Neil Wynn (Jackson, MI: University Press of Mississippi, 2008).

Oostindie, Gert, ed., *Facing up to the Past: Perspectives on the Commemoration of Slavery from Africa, the Americas and Europe* (Kingston, Jamaica: Ian Randle Publishers, 2001).

Ostendorf, Berndt, *Black Literature in White America* (Totowa, NJ: Barnes and Noble, 1982).

Osur, Alan M., *Blacks in the Army Air Forces During World War II* (Washington, DC: Office of Air Forces' History, 1977).

Palmer, Annette, 'The politics of race and war: black American soldiers in the Carribean theater during the Second World War', *Military Affairs* 47 (April 1983), 59–62.

Palmer, Roy, *A Touch of the Times: Songs of Social Change* (Harmondsworth: Penguin, 1974).

Parliament and the British Slave Trade, www.parliament.uk/slavetrade [accessed 15 November 2007].

Peretti, Burton W., *The Creation of Jazz: Music, Race and Culture in Urbanizing America* (Urbana, IL: University of Illinois Press, 1992).

Phillips, Caryl, *Crossing the River* (London: Picador, 1994).

Phillips, Caryl, *The Atlantic Sound* (London: Faber, 2000).

Postlethwayt, Malachy, 'The national and private advantages of the African trade considered' (1746), in *The British Atlantic Slave Trade*, vol. 2, ed. Kenneth Morgan (London: Pickering and Chatto, 2003), pp. 195–328.

Potter, Lou, William Miles and Nina Rosenblaum, *Liberators: Fighting on Two Fronts in World War II* (New York, NY: Harcourt Brace Jovanovich, 1992).

Price, Richard, 'Monuments and silent screamings: a view from Martinique', in *Facing up to the Past: Perspectives on the Commemoration of Slavery from Africa, the Americas and Europe*, ed. Gert Oostinde (Kingston, Jamaica: Ian Randle, 2001), pp. 58–62.

Priestly, Brian, *Mingus: A Critical Biography* (London: Quartet, 1982).

Rampersad, Arnold, ed., *The Collected Poems of Langston Hughes* (New York, NY: Vintage, 1995).

Rampersad, Arnold, *The Life of Langston Hughes, Volume 2: 1941–1967, I Dream a World* (Oxford: Oxford University Press, 2002).

Ramsey, James, 'Notebook', in *The Slave Trade Debate: Contemporary Writings For and Against*, ed. John Pinfold (Oxford: The Bodleian Library, 2007), pp. 9–172.

Rawlinson, Abraham, 'The Lancaster slave trade' (1792), in A. and J. Rawlinson, *Letter Book* (Lancaster: unpublished manuscript).

Rediker, Marcus, 'The red Atlantic; or, "a terrible blast swept over the heaving sea"', in *Sea Changes: Historicizing the Ocean*, ed. Bernhard Klein and Gesa Mackenthun (London: Routledge, 2004), pp. 111–130.

Rediker, Marcus, *The Slave Ship: A Human History* (London: John Murray, 2007).

Reinhardt, Catherine A., *Claims to Memory: Beyond Slavery and Emancipation in the French Caribbean* (Oxford: Berghahn Books, 2008).

Reynolds, David, *Rich Relation: The American Occupation of Britain 1942–45* (London: Harper Collins, 1996).

Rice, Alan, unpublished interview with Tony Morrison, 29 February 1988, transcript in author's possession.

Rice, Alan, 'Exploring inside the invisible: an interview with Lubaina Himid', *Wasafiri* 40 (Winter 2003), pp. 21–26.

Rice, Alan, *Radical Narratives of the Black Atlantic* (London: Continuum Press, 2003).

Rice, Alan, interview with Godfried Donkor, 'Commemorating abolition' (2005), http://www.uclan.ac.uk/ahss/journalism_media_communication/literature_culture/abolition/godfried_donkor.php [accessed 27 July 2009].

Rice, Alan, interview with Kevin Dalton-Johnson, 'Commemorating abolition' (2005 and 2006), http://www.uclan.ac.uk/abolition [accessed 27 July 2009].

Rice, Alan and Martin Crawford, *Liberating Sojourn: Frederick Douglass and Transatlantic Reform* (Athens, GA: University of Georgia Press, 1999).

Ricoeur, Paul, *Memory, History and Forgetting*, trans. Kathleen Bramley and David Pellauer (Chicago, IL: University of Chicago Press, 2004).

Roach, Joseph, *Cities of the Dead: Circum-Atlantic Performance* (New York, NY: Columbia University Press, 1996).

Roberts, John Storm, *Black Music of Two Worlds*, second ed. (Florence, KY: Wadsworth, 1998).

Robertson, Alan, *Joe Harriott: Fire in His Soul* (Wendover, Bucks: Northway Publications, 2003).

Roushanzamir, Ellie L. and Peggy J. Kreshel, 'Gloria and Anthony visit a plantation: history into heritage at Laura, a Creole plantation', in *Slavery, Contested Heritage and Thanotourism*, ed. G. Dann and A. Seaton (London: Haworth Press, 2001), pp. 169–189.

Rudd, Natalie, 'In the city', in *Fabrications: New Art and Urban Memory in Manchester*, ed. Mark Crinson, Helen Hills and Natalie Rudd (Manchester: Cube Publications, 2002), pp. 4–9.

Ruggles, Jeffrey, *The Unboxing of Henry Brown* (Richmond, VA: Library of Virginia, 2003).

Saffron, Inga, 'Changing skyline: slave memorial could let city stand out, but design risks sending wrong message', *Philadelphia Inquiry*, 14 February 2003, http://www.ushistory.org/presidentshouse/news/inq021403.htm [accessed 18 February 2005].

Sansone, Livio, 'Remembering slavery from nearby: heritage, Brazilian style', in *Facing up to the Past: Perspectives on the Commemoration of Slavery from Africa, the Americas and Europe*, ed. Gert Oostinde (Kingston, Jamaica: Ian Randle, 2001), pp. 83–89.

Saul, Scott, *Freedom Is, Freedom Ain't: Jazz and the Making of the Sixties* (Cambridge, MA: Harvard University Press, 2003).

Schuller, Gunther, *Early Jazz* (Oxford: Oxford University Press, 1968).

Seaton, A. V., 'Sources of slavery – destinations of slavery: the silences and disclosures of slavery heritage in the UK and US', in *Slavery, Contested Heritage and Thanotourism*, ed. G. Dann and A. Seaton (London: Haworth Press, 2001), pp. 107–129.

Senghor, Leopold Sedar, *The Collected Poetry of Leopold Sedar Senghor*, trans. Melvin Dixon (Charlottesville, VA: University of Virginia Press, 1998).

Shakespeare, William, *The Tempest*, Act I, scene ii, *The Comedies of William Shakespeare* (London: Dent, 1916), p. 16.

Shange, Ntozake, *See No Evil: Prefaces, Essays and Accounts, 1976–1983* (San Fransisco, CA: Momo's Press, 1984).

Sherwood, Marika, *After Abolition: Britain and the Slave Trade Since 1807* (London: IB Tauris, 2007).

Sidran, Ben, *Black Talk* (New York, NY: Da Capo, 1981).

Singleton, T., 'The slave trade remembered on the former Gold and Slave

Coasts', in *From Slavery to Emancipation in the Atlantic World*, ed. S. Frey and B. Wood (London: Frank Cass, 1999), pp. 150–169.

Sissay, Lemn, *Gilt of Cain* (2007), http://www.cityoflondon.gov.uk/NR/rdonlyres/94CC1E18-C97F-4475-B082-C9E92316E5CE/0/MC_cain.pdf [accessed 27 July, 2009].

Small, Christopher, *Music of the Common Tongue* (London: John Calder, 1987).

Smallwood, Stephanie E., *Saltwater Slavery: A Middle Passage from Africa to the American Diaspora* (Cambridge, MA: Harvard University Press, 2007).

Smartt, Dorothea, '*Lancaster Keys*' (Lancaster: Slave Trade Arts Memorial Project, 2003).

Smartt, Dorothea, *Ship-Shape* (Leeds: Peepal Tree Press, 2008).

Smith, Graham, *When Jim Crow Met John Bull: Black American Soldiers in WWII Britain* (London: IB Tauris, 1987).

Smith, J. T., *Vagabondiana or, Anecdotes of Mendicant Wanderers Through the Streets of London; With Portraits of the Most Remarkable* (London: Chatto and Windus, 1874).

Snead, James A., 'On repetition in black culture', *Black American Literature Forum* 15 (1981), pp. 146–154.

Solomon, Abraham, *Mrs Rosa Samuel and her Three Daughters*, pencil sketch (Manchester: Whitworth Art Gallery, 1845).

Spillers, Hortense, 'Mama's Baby, Papa's Maybe: an American grammar', in *Within the Circle: An Anthology of African American Literary Criticism from the Harlem Renaissance to the Present*, ed. Angelyn Mitchell (Durham, NC: Duke University Press, 1994), pp. 454–481.

St Clair, William, *The Grand Slave Emporium: Cape Coast Castle and the British Slave Trade* (London: Profile Books, 2006).

Stearns, Marshall, *The Story of Jazz* (Oxford: Oxford University Press, 1956).

Stepto, Robert B. and Michael S. Harper, 'Study and experience: an interview with Ralph Ellison', in *Chant of Saints*, ed. Michael S. Harper and Robert B. Stepto (Chicago, IL: University of Illinois Press, 1979), pp. 451–469.

Stewart, Susan, *On Longing: Narratives of the Miniature, the Gigantic, the Souvenir, the Collection* (Durham, NC: Duke University Press, 1993).

Stothard, Thomas, *Voyage of the Sable Venus* (engraving) in Bryan Edwards, *History Civil and Commercial of the British Colonies of the West Indies* (London: John Stockdale, 1793–1801).

Stuart, Andrea, 'Performing writes', *The Independent*, 8 August 2000, p. 8.

SuAndi, 'Untitled Poem' (n.p., 2006).

Sulter, Maud, 'Without tides, no maps', in *Revenge: A Masque in Five Tableaux* by Lubaina Himid (Rochdale: Rochdale Art Gallery, 1992).

Sweeney, Fionnghuala, *Frederick Douglass and the Atlantic World* (Liverpool: Liverpool University Press, 2007).

T., J., 'Samboo's Grave', *Lonsdale Magazine and Kendal Repository* 3.29, 31 May 1822, pp. 188–192.

Tate, Claudia, ed., *Black Women Writers at Work* (New York, NY: Continuum, 1983).

Tate, Greg, 'Are you free or are you a mystery?', in *Coral Cities*, by Ellen Gallagher, exhibition catalogue (London: Tate Publishing, 2007), pp. 16–29.

Tawadros, Gilane, 'The Sphinx contemplating Napoleon: black women artists in Britain', in *New Feminist Art Criticism*, ed. Katy Deepwell (Manchester: Manchester University Press, 1995) pp. 25–30.

Taylor, Alan, 'Two-way traffic', *Scotland on Sunday*, 30 May 1993, p. 2.

Taylor, Art, *Notes and Tones* (London: Quartet, 1986).

Thompson, Edward P., *The Making of the English Working Class* (Harmondsworth: Penguin, 1963).

Trevor, Tom, 'Maria Thereza Alves', in *Port City: On Mobility and Exchange*, ed. Tom Trevor et al. (Bristol: Arnolfini, 2007), pp. 66–75.

Turner, J. M. W., *St Agatha's Abbey, Easby, Yorkshire, from the River Swale* (Manchester: Whitworth Art Gallery, 1798–1799).

Turner, J. M. W., *Upnor Castle, Kent*, (Manchester: Whitworth Art Gallery, 1832–1833).

Tyler-Mcgraw, M., 'Southern comfort levels: race, heritage tourism and the Civil War in Richmond', in *Slavery and Public History: The Tough Stuff of American History*, ed. J. O. and L. E. Horton (New York, NY: The New Press, 2006), pp. 151–168.

Verdelle, A. J., 'The truth of the picnic: writing about American slavery', *Representing Slavery: A Roundtable Discussion, Common-Place* 1.4 (July 2001), http://www.common-place.org/vol-01/no-04/slavery/verdelle.shtml [accessed 10 February 2006].

Visocchi, Michael, 'Memorial notes, personal email correspondence, 25 June 2009.

Vlach, John M., 'The last great taboo subject: exhibiting slavery at the Library of Congress', in *Slavery and Public History: The Tough Stuff of American History*, ed. J. O. and L. E. Horton (New York, NY: The New Press, 2006), pp. 57–74.

von Eschen, Penny M., *Race Against Empire: Black Americans and Anticolonialism, 1937–1957* (Ithaca, NY: Cornell University Press, 1997).

Walker, Alice, *In Search of Our Mothers' Gardens* (London: Women's Press, 1984).

Wallace, Michele, *Invisibility Blues* (London: Verso, 1990).

Walvin, James, 'Public history and abolition: a review of *"Chords of Freedom"'*, *Patterns of Prejudice* 41.3–4 (July/September 2007), pp. 398–399.

Weiss, John, 'Notes on Althea McNish', personal email correspondence, 17 May 2007.

Werrell, Ken, 'The Mutiny at Bamber Bridge', *After the Battle* 22 (1978), pp. 1–11.

White, Graham and Shane White, *Stylin': African American Expressive Culture from Its Beginnings to the Zoot Suit* (Ithaca, NY: Cornell University Press, 1999).

White, Shane and Graham White, *The Sounds of Slavery: Discovering African American History through Songs, Sermons and Speech* (Boston, MA: Beacon Press, 2005).

Whitehead, Anne, *Memory* (London: Routledge, 2009).

Williams, W., 'Boll Weevil', in *Deep River of Song: Virginia and the Piedmont Minstrelsy, Work Songs, and Blues*, The Alan Lomax Collection, CD (Cambridge, MA: Rounder Records, 2000).

Wilmot, Alan, 'Making a difference – experiences of a black British serviceman', oral memoir on 'WW2: People's War', BBC, http://www.bbc.co.uk/ww2peopleswar/stories/96/a1921196.shtml [accessed 14 July 2008].

Wilson, Sue, 'Jazz messenger: an interview with Toni Morrison', *The List* 177 (June 1992), p. 12.

Winter, Jay, *Remembering War: The Great War Between History and Memory in the Twentieth Century* (New Haven, CT: Yale University Press, 2006).

Wood, Marcus, *Blind Memory: Visual Representations of Slavery in England and America 1780–1865* (Manchester: Manchester University Press, 2000).

Wood, Marcus, 'Packaging liberty and marketing the gift of freedom: 1807 and the legacy of Clarkson's chest', in *The British Slave Trade: Abolition, Parliament and People*, ed. Stephen Farrell, Melanie Unwin and James Walvin (Edinburgh: Edinburgh University Press, 2007), pp. 203–223.

Wyke, Terry, *Public Sculpture of Greater Manchester* (Liverpool: Liverpool University Press, 2004).

Young, Al, Larry Kart and Michael S. Harper, 'Jazz and letters: a colloquy', *Tri-Quarterly* 68 (1987), pp. 118–159.

Young, Hershini Bhana, *Haunting Capital: Memory, Text and the Black Diasporic Body* (Lebanon, NH: Dartmouth College Press, 2006).

Young, James E., *At Memory's Edge: After Images of the Holocaust in Contemporary Art and Architecture* (New Haven, CT: Yale University Press, 2000).

Young, James E., 'Daniel Libeskind's Jewish Museum in Berlin: the uncanny arts of memorial architecture', in *Visual Culture and the Holocaust*, ed. Barbie Zelizer (London: Athlone, 2001), pp. 179–197.

Young, Robert, *Colonial Desire: Hybridity in Theory and Practice* (London: Routledge, 1995).

Younge, Gary, 'Congo boys of Cardiff', *The Guardian*, 1 June 2002, p. 16.

Index